Emigrat. o

Going to
Australia

Explore if Australia offers the bright new frontiers that you wish for yourself and your family

Chee Min Ng

Australia
2013

Published in 2013 by CMN & Associates
www.goingtoaustralia.net

Cataloguing in publications data available from the National Library of Australia

Emigrating – Going to Australia
ISBN: 9780992303501 (pbk)

Printed in Malaysia by Percetakan Lai Sdn. Bhd.

Preface

"What is life like in Australia?" "How can I migrate to Australia?"

I am often asked these questions and many more by visitors to Australia or during my trips overseas. This has motivated me to write this book. I started writing this book a couple of years ago after living in Australia for almost a quarter of a century.

According to international studies, one in seven adults want to leave their country. It is hardly surprising that there is so much interest on migration in general and Australia in particular.

Australia as a modern 21st Century society ranks highly in human development, standards of living and outlook.

Australia is one of the few developed countries with an active and supportive immigration program. Seven million people have migrated to Australia since 1945. Today, more than ever, it is a popular migration destination. Since the 1980's, net immigration has overtaken natural increase to become the main contributor to Australia's population growth. Forty-six percent of its population were either born overseas or have a parent who was born overseas.

Migration is a major life event and requires comprehensive research and assessment prior to any final decision. This book brings together all the essential information about Australia for intending migrants and others who want to know more of what the largest island continent has to offer. It includes chapters on various migration programs, contains 135 tables and factsheets of useful information and a chapter for self-assessing eligibility for migration.

As the saying goes - *We can't change our past but we can plan for our future.*

Let's explore if Australia offers the bright new frontiers that you wish for yourself and your family.

Chee Min Ng
September 2013
Australia

Contents

Fact Sheets

1 Why Do People Migrate?

If you are pondering, you are not alone.

Migrants Are Everywhere

Migrants are 3 % of world population

Of the world's total population of seven billion, 3% or 214 million live outside their countries of birth, while 740 million moved elsewhere within their countries. This gives a total of almost a billion people who are on the move.[1]

To put this in perspective, the 214 million international migrants would constitute the fifth largest country in the world in numbers.

Very large migrant populations abound

In several countries, a very high percentage of the population are migrants. Qatar, in the Middle East, has the highest proportion of 87%, Luxemburg leads in the OECD with a migrant population of 32%, and 41% of Singapore's population are immigrants, which is the highest proportion among Asian countries.[2]

A whole new world of migrant workers

The Middle East has a migrant work force of some 15 million people, spread out in Saudi Arabia, Kuwait, Bahrain, Oman,

---

[1] United Nations Department of Economic and Social Affairs *Human Development Report 2009*

[2] The World Bank *Migration and Remittance Fact Book* (Nov 2010)

Qatar and United Arab Emirates. Of this number, 75% come from India, Bangladesh and Pakistan.[3]

Mexico, Philippines and Turkey are also leading labour-sending countries. Eleven million Mexicans work in USA, Canada, United Kingdom, Germany, Spain and other European countries. Seven million Filipinos are guest workers, mainly in Singapore, Malaysia, Hong Kong, Taiwan, Saudi Arabia, Bahrain, Kuwait, and United Arab Emirates. Turkish migrant workers, numbering 3.5 million, are mostly in Europe, with more than half of them in Germany.

Refugee migrants awaiting resettlement

At the end of 2010, there were 27 million internally displaced persons and 15 million international refugees. Of the latter, more than 7 million have been living in exile for longer than five years, and some for more than 30 years.[4]

The majority of refugees will never be resettled in their lifetime. At the current annual intake and resettlement by third countries, it will take over a century to resettle them.

Permanent Migration

Adult population who wish to migrate

A survey conducted between 2008 and 2010 in 146 countries found that 14% of the adult population worldwide, that is, 630

---

[3] See (1)
[4] See (1)

million adults, wish to migrate abroad permanently if they had the chance.[5]

Adding the hopeful 630 million adults to the 214 million people already living outside their countries of origin gives a total of 844 million people, or almost one person in seven worldwide, who desire a future away from their homeland. To put it in perspective, the total of migrant and would-be migrant population far exceeds the population of any one country except China and India.

Rich Chinese also looking abroad

A survey reported in 2010 that 520,000 or almost 60% of China's wealthiest people want to emigrate.[6] Another survey in 2010 of 18 major Chinese cities found that 46% of the respondents were thinking of emigrating and another 14% had either emigrated or filed immigration papers. One half of the respondents attributed better education opportunities abroad as the reason for their desire to migrate. About a third of them have invested money abroad as a step towards emigration.[7]

New Zealand attracts Singaporeans

Even as Singapore continues to be a desired migration destination for many people, some of its citizens are thinking of leaving. A recent pilot project of the New Zealand Immigration aimed at enticing Singaporeans to New Zealand received interest at a rate of more than 1,000 registrations a week. Within three weeks, 3,565 potential immigrants had registered their interest.[8]

---

[5] OECD (2012), *Connecting with Emigrants: A Global Profile of Diasporas*
[6] China Merchant Bank Bain & Co 2011 *Private Wealth Report*
[7] Bank of China and Hurun Research Institute *Private Banking White Paper* (Oct 2011)
[8] New Zealand Herald, *Singapore envies Kiwi Lifestyle* (Feb 2010)

Revolving doors for some countries

Some countries are seeing the phenomenon of incoming migrants happening concurrently with an expanding emigrant diaspora of its own citizens. Among them are Malaysia and New Zealand.

Malaysia is home to two million registered foreign workers and also increasing numbers of unregistered migrant workers who are mainly unskilled. At the same time, a large and growing number of its citizens either work in another country or are emigrating permanently. A World Bank report conservatively estimated that, at the end of 2010, one million Malaysians were working overseas with almost 60% of them in Singapore.[9]

Even as New Zealand has been successfully attracting migrants to the *Land of the Long White Cloud*, the country has also been losing a significant proportion of its citizens to neighbouring Australia in particular. The Australian 2011 population census counted almost half-a-million New Zealand-born in Australia.[10] This number does not include non-native New Zealand citizens who immigrated to Australia after acquiring New Zealand citizenship.

'Push', 'Pull' and Other Stimuli

Migrating - whether internal or external, temporary or permanent, forced or voluntary - is not a new social phenomenon. Economic, social, political and environmental factors, singly or collectively, have always been the causes or impetuses of human migration. The main historical events are recounted below.

---

[9] The World Bank, *Malaysia Economic Monitor* (April 2011)
[10] Australia Bureau of Statistics (cat. no. 3412.0), 2009

Migration in the 18th and 19th centuries

Far-reaching events in the 18th and 19th centuries propelled the trans- continental mass movement of people:

- Rise of European mercantile powers
  For almost two hundred years from 1750, Western Europe was the primary source of world migration - sending 70 million people or a third of its population growth overseas. European mercantile powers - Britain, Netherlands, Spain and France, promoted large-scale settlements of their nationals abroad in the process of colonial expansion.

- Trans-Atlantic slave trade
  The forced deportation of slaves, known infamously as the *Transatlantic Slave Trade*, started in the 16th century and was carried on for almost three and a half centuries, sending more than 10 million enslaved Africans to the Americas. European slave traders from Britain, Portugal, Spain, France, Holland and the Americas established outposts in Africa to seize and ship slave labour to toil in coffee, tobacco, cocoa, cotton and sugar plantations, gold and silver mines and the construction industry, or as household labourers.

- Asian indenture labour
  Upon the cessation of the Trans-Atlantic slave trade, *Coolie or* Asian indentured labour, mostly from China, India and Japan, became the second wave of the labour force for the plantations, mines and railways in the Americas and the British Empire.

- Discovery of gold
  The discovery of precious metals, especially gold, was another stimulus for the mass migration of labour. In the 19th century,

the discovery of gold led to feverish migration to the United States, Canada, Australia, South Africa and Brazil.

Seismic political events of the 20th century

In the last century, political upheavals and convulsions were the triggers that launched feverish waves of migration:

- Russian Revolution of 1917
  About 1.5 million Russians fled the country during and after the Russian Revolution of 1917.

- End of World War II
  The end of World War II marked the beginning of a migration era that lasted more than two decades in Europe. Labour was needed to fuel and sustain the booming post-war economies in Europe, North America and Australia. Turks transplanted themselves to work in Germany and North Africans to France and Belgium. A million Britons landed in Australia including those so-called 'Ten Pound Poms'.

- Founding of People's Republic of China
  The founding of the People's Republic of China in 1949 saw the exodus of more than two million Chinese to Taiwan and Hong Kong.

- Partitioning of India and founding of Pakistan
  The partitioning of British India in 1947 caused the movement of 18 million Hindus and Muslims between the two countries.

- Establishment of the Israeli State
  Israel's declaration of independence in 1948 saw the exodus of 700,000 Palestinians in the following two years and the arrival

of more than a million Jews in Israel over the next two decades.

- Partitioning of Germany after World War II
  More than 2.7 million East Germans left for West Germany from 1949 until the Berlin Wall was erected in 1961.

- End of America's war in Vietnam
  The exodus of refugees from Vietnam, Laos and Cambodia lasted two decades after America's withdrawal from Vietnam in 1975. More than a million were eventually resettled, mostly in the United States, Australia, Canada, France and the United Kingdom.

- The Balkan Wars
  The outbreak of war (known as the Balkan Wars 1991–1995) that followed the break-up of the Yugoslav Federation and the resulting mass population movement of more than 2.5 million refugees completely changed the demographics of the former Yugoslav republics, now divided as Serbia, Bosnia Herzegovina and Croatia.

- China's opening-up and reforms
  China's economic reforms that began in the late 1970's have increased internal population movement and the more liberal emigration policies of the 1980's facilitated external migration. Export of labour followed, initially at the request of foreign countries but subsequently as manpower for infrastructure and agricultural projects of Chinese investments overseas.

For the past two decades, China has been an important source of permanent migrants and overseas students for countries such as Australia, Canada, New Zealand and the United States.

Europe too has its share of increased Chinese immigrants. Italy's Chinese residents doubled while Spain registered a six-fold increase in the last decade of the 20th century. Today, an estimated three-quarter million Chinese are in Africa. Russia's Far East and Japan are increasingly popular destinations for Chinese migrants.

- Disintegration of the Soviet Union
  The breaking-up of the Soviet Union in 1991 was followed by mass emigration within the newly formed Commonwealth of Independent States (CIS).   Russia received 3.7 million migrants and became a net migration recipient from all the other states of the CIS and the Baltics, except for Belarus. Many returned to their ethnic homelands but at the same time, fifteen percents or more of the populations of Armenia, Albania, Georgia, Kazakhstan and Tajikistan migrated permanently. Between 1990 and 1994, 1.6 million people left, mostly for the United States, Germany, Greece and Israel.[11]

- Return of Hong Kong to China
  The return of Hong Kong to China in 1997 triggered a decade-long migration wave from Hong Kong to the economically advanced countries, mainly to Canada, the United Kingdom, Australia, New Zealand, the United States and Singapore.

---

[11] D.L. Poston, M. Micklin, *Handbook of Population*, Springer New York 2006

Migration Is Here to Stay

Trans-national labour supply

Some countries, e.g. Philippines and Indonesia, encourage the migration of labour abroad. This has resulted in many of their citizens residing overseas mainly as guest workers.

The Philippines started a regulated temporary labour migration program as part of its economic and social development policy more than four decades ago, which looks set to continue for the foreseeable future. Besides relieving the pressure on domestic employment, the program has been generating huge foreign remittances. Today, overseas remittance is the second largest foreign exchange earner and accounts for 9% of the country's GDP.

At the end of 2010, there were 9.4 million Filipinos overseas including 6 million Filipinos temporarily working overseas in more than 200 countries and 347,000 working as merchant seamen in ships plying international waters. Another 3 million Filipinos reside permanently outside the Philippines, mainly in the United States (1.2 million), Canada (0.3 million), and 0.1 million each in Japan and Australia.[12]

Indonesia is increasingly a major labour-supplying country with an estimated 6 million of its citizens working overseas in 2011. The top destination countries include Malaysia (2.5million), Saudi Arabia (1.5million), and more than 100,000 in both Hong Kong, Taiwan and Singapore.

---

[12] Commission on Filipinos Overseas *Stock Estimate of Overseas Filipinos 2010*

Popular destinations remain open

In the first decade of the 21st century, the United States, Canada, Australia and New Zealand continued their migration programs aimed at enticing preferred migrants.

After abolishing their major immigration restrictions about half a century earlier, these countries recorded unprecedented increases in migration from non-European countries especially from Asia.

- The United States of America
  The United States has long been a migration destination from the colonial period till the present day. The Immigration and Nationality Act of 1965, that effectively removed ethnic immigration quotas during periods of increased economic activity, has brought about an almost four-fold increase in overseas-born residents, from 10 million in 1970 to 38 million in 2007. For the first decade of the 21st century, 14 million immigrants entered the United States.

- Canada
  In 1962, Canada abandoned its *White Canada* immigration policy and has since become home to a million migrants from non-English speaking countries. Together with the United States, Australia and New Zealand, Canada continues to be a preferred migration destination for many.

- Australia
  Australia has been an immigrant nation since 1788. Australia embarked on a massive immigration effort after World War I to increase its population. After World War II, Arthur Calwell, the first Minister for Immigration, promoted mass migration with the slogan *Populate or Perish*. During the period 1945 to

1965, Australia embarked on a post-war reconstruction and immigration expansion program.

In 1972, Australia dismantled the infamous *White Australia* immigration policy. This policy change has greatly affected Australian demographics, allowing non-European immigrants especially those from Asia to arrive in significant numbers. In the late 1970s, Australia opened its doors to Vietnamese refugees. By 2011, one million people, or five per cent of Australia's population, were people born in Asia. Forty-four percent of its population were either born overseas or have a parent who was born overseas and twenty percent of the population speak a language other than English.[13]

As an aftermath to the global financial crisis, many in the crisis-hit countries like Ireland and Greece have begun to look at migrating to Australia. "Every week, a thousand mothers and fathers watch their children pack up their lives, put their degrees in beside their dollars and their bitter disappointment and head for Sydney, Brisbane and Vancouver".[14] In 2011, 2,500 Greeks relocated to Australia, and officials in Athens told the *Guardian* that a further 40,000 have 'expressed interest' in relocating.[15] The Australian Broadcasting Corporation in a broadcast titled *Greek Exodus* reported that the Australian embassy in Athens had recorded an increase in immigration enquiries.[16]

- New Zealand
  After ending its 'White New Zealand' immigration policy, New Zealand received a substantial increase in migrants from

---

[13] Australian Bureau of Statistics *2011 Population Census*
[14] AFP, Dublin *Emigration returns to stalk crisis hit Ireland* (Feb 25 2011)
[15] The Guardians, *Fleeing Greeks bank on new Australian gold rush* (Dec 21, 2011)
[16] Australian Broadcasting Corporation, *Greek Exodus*, (Nov 10, 2011)

non-European backgrounds, especially from Asia. In 2006, 879,000 people comprising 23% of New Zealand's population were people born overseas.[17] However, many New Zealanders have chosen to go over the Tasman Sea to live in Australia. In 2011, there were more than 483,000 New Zealand-born living in Australia.

Down to You to Decide

Individual circumstances

While there might be 'pull' and 'push' factors, it is the individual who has to decide and initiate the move. The decisive reality is as the famous saying by Lao-tzu goes: *A journey of a thousand miles begins with a single step.*

Although individual circumstances do differ, the main motivation for a person to migrate is always the vision of a better future for oneself and one's family.

Changes in personal or family circumstances could be the trigger for a person to re-examine and re-focus his or her life and choose the migration path for a fresh start in a new land.

Personal stories of new Australians

Every migrant has a story to tell. The following are the real-life stories of some of the many who have migrated to Australia in the last two decades. The outcomes of their decision and journeys are told in Chapter 2 *Turning Dreams to Reality*.

---

[17] Statistics New Zealand, 2007c Table 7

- The T family
  T and his wife were both graduates from the University of Malaya. In the early 1980's, the T family migrated to Australia from Malaysia. T cited his concern for his children's future and opportunities for their education as the two main reasons for their decision to emigrate. He estimated, at that time, that the cost for his four children's education in Australia would be RM 2million. T was doubtful that he would be able to put aside the necessary funds.

- The W family
  W and his wife were professionals and graduates from Rangoon University. Political events in Burma pushed W and his family to migrate to Melbourne in the early 1980s.

- The L family
  L worked in Kuala Lumpur before he and his wife moved to Singapore. During a holiday trip to Australia, they realised what a great country it is to raise their family and that his children would have far better opportunities. They migrated to Australia in 1988.

- The O'Brien family
  In 1997, O'Brien decided to move to Australia from South Africa. According to O'Brien, escalating crime and his vision of the country's future convinced him to leave South Africa. He decided on Melbourne as it reminded him of Johannesburg in South Africa.

- O and his wife
  O and his wife were working at the University Hospital in Kuala Lumpur in 1969. They decided that they wanted to start their family in Australia as the country seems to have a lot to

offer. They realised their dream only years later when health professionals came on the skill migration list.

- The young men and women from China
  The S brothers, J, Q and G were in their 20s and found the opportunity to leave China when the country relaxed its policy on studying overseas. By the late 1980's, Australian private colleges were actively promoting their short English language courses in China. They raised enough money and embarked on their journey to Australia.

You are not alone

If you are thinking of migrating, you are not alone. Millions have left and millions like you are mulling over it.

However, migrating is a life-changing choice that should warrant serious research to arrive at an informed decision. It is important that you know clearly what you are seeking. It will be helpful, and indeed necessary, to identify your own 'pull' and/or 'push' factors. Knowing your aims and desires, and armed with sound basic research, you can proceed to the exciting task of discovering more of the country that best fits your personal aspirations.

Our life is not a rehearsal. We can't change the past but we can plan for the future.

2 Turning Dreams to Reality

Possibility to reality!

Australia, as an immigrant nation, has many migrant success stories.

The success stories of earlier migrants are in exhibits in museums or documented in research and other publications. A number of museums in Australia are dedicated migration museums - *Migration Heritage Centre* (Sydney), *Immigration Museum* (Melbourne) and *Migration Museum* (Adelaide). Museums in the other capital cities have permanent exhibits and displays on Australian migration history and the migrant success stories.

Each wave of migration generates its own migrant success stories. Many of the large corporations are results of the enterprising ingenuity of post-World War II migrants.

The ending of the 'White Australia' immigration policy in the 1970s brings another set of success stories – this time from migrants of non-European backgrounds. The *Ethnic Business Award* entries for the last 24 years are inspiring migrant success stories.

In the professions, the migrant contribution goes beyond their adopted home.

With so many success stories and positive settlement outcomes, it is not surprising that Australia continues to be a popular migration destination.

Business Success Stories

The annual entries for many business awards, e.g. *Australian Business Awards, Ethnic Business Awards, Telstra Business Awards*, include many migrant business success stories. The *Ethnic Business Awards* is now in its 25th year and is Australia's longest running business awards. The awards "celebrate diversity and multiculturalism and the achievements of migrants who come to Australia with a suitcase full of dreams".[18]

Annually, the *Business Review Weekly* (BRW) publishes the 'Rich 200', 'Young List', 'Top 1000 companies' and 'Fast Starters'. Many of the listed entries are migrants or companies started by migrants.

Some of the well-documented business success stories are listed in the following pages.

Sidney Myer – Russia

In 1899, Simcha Baeski joined his brother, who arrived three years earlier, in Melbourne to work with a relative. A few months later, adopting the family name of Myer, the brothers moved to Bendigo to start a drapery shop. Sidney Myer began peddling goods in country Victoria.

In 1911, Sidney Myer bought Wright & Neil, a drapery store in Bourke Street, Melbourne. This marked the beginning of the Myer's retail empire.

Sidney Myer was ahead of his time with employee benefits - offered 73,000 'staff partnership' shares of £1 each on easy terms;

---

[18] http://www.ethnicbusinessawards.com

shares for executives based on merit, paid vacation, sick fund and even a free hospital within the store.

Sidney Myer's civic leadership and philanthropy during his lifetime were legendary. When he died in 1934, he bequeathed one-tenth of his estate to be held in trust for charitable, philanthropic and education needs. The Myer Foundation has continued the legacy since.

Vittorio and Giuseppina De Bortoli – Italy

In 1924, Vittorio De Bortolli arrived in Melbourne with "little but his clothes, a few shillings, boundless optimism and a new capacity for hard work".[19] He took a train to Griffith where he worked on farm and winery. Three years later, he bought a 55-acre mixed 'fruit salad' farm in Bilbul near Griffith. His fiancée Giuseppina was working in France saving to join him in Australia. Giuseppina and Vittorio married in 1929. Later the wine-making business expanded and became the main business.

The second and third generations expanded the business further and today De Bortoli is one of Australia's leading wine producers and exporters.

Bing Lee – China

In 1929, Bing Lee came to Australia leaving his family behind and started trading in Chinese handicraft. The family was reunited after the end of World War II. He then bought a fruit shop in Fairfield and ran it with his eldest son. Bing Lee later bought a

---

[19] Vittorio De Bortoli: The Early Days http://www.debortoli.com.au/about-us/history/the-early-days.html

small electrical shop - the beginning of present-day Bing Lee retail electrical empire with close to 40 outlets.

Cees and Johanna Tesselaar – The Netherlands[20]

In 1939 – just weeks before the outbreak of World War II, the couple left Holland on their wedding day aboard the *Strahallan* heading for Australia. They brought little but their farming expertise and a firm belief in hard work and the land of opportunity. In 1945, they planted Tulips and Gladioli in their small newly purchased six-hectare farm in Silvan in the Dandenong Ranges outside Melbourne. They also helped other Dutch immigrants establish their own nursery businesses.

Today, Padua Bulb Nurseries is Australia's largest family-owned floricultural operation. Flowers grown by some 140 growers are also marketed through the Tesselaar network of companies. in Victoria, New South Wales, Queensland and Western Australia.

The annual Tesselaar Tulip Festival, held in October at the Silvan farm, is a major event. Visitors to the farm see blooming tulips and other flowers and members of the Tesselaar family and extended family dressed in traditional Dutch costume and clogs.

Dick Dusseldorp AO - The Netherlands

In 1950, Dick Dusseldorp visited Australia for business opportunities for Bredero's - a large Dutch building company. He secured the joint venture contract for his employer and returned to Sydney a year later with his family and some workers to build 200 prefabricated worker houses for the Snowy Hydro-Electric scheme. The Australian operation was in the name of Civil and

---

[20] http://www.tesselaar.net.au/public/about_tesselaar

Civic. In 1958, he formed Lend Lease with Civil and Civic as the largest shareholder. Later, he created the world's first listed property trust. In the 1960s, Lend Lease acquired Civil and Civic from Bredero's.

When "Duss" (as he was known to his workers) retired in the 1980s, Lend Lease has long been an Australian blue chip and highly regarded for its employee benefits. It introduced staff superannuation entitlement two decades before it became an industry practice in Australia.

Franco Belgiorno-Nettis AC – Italy

In 1951, Franco was sent by his company in Italy to Australia to construct power lines. In 1956, Franco and his colleague Carlo Salteri established Transfiled Pty Limited. In less than 10 years, the company became Australia's most successful company handling projects that ranged from transmission towers to hydro-electricity stations, bridges to oil platforms. In 1989, the company was awarded a $6b contract to build 10 ANZAC class frigates for the Australia and New Zealand governments. In 1989, the two founders stood down as joint managing directors of Transfield Holdings (as the company was then named) in favour of their eldest sons.

Frank Lowry – Czechoslovakia

Frank Lowry arrived in Sydney in 1952. His work ethic impressed John Saunders, another former refugee who was running a milk bar then. The two later partnered and established a delicatessen in Blacktown. Their business flourished. The partners began to dabble in property and named their property venture Westfield

Investments Pty Ltd. In 1958, they sold the delicatessen business to concentrate on the property business.

In 1960, Westfield was listed on the Sydney Exchange. In 1977, Westfield entered the property market in the United States and twenty years later into the New Zealand property market. In 2011, Westfield announced that it has entered the Italy property market by taking a half share in a joint venture to develop a 60-acre site next to Milan's airport.

Today, the Westfield Group has interests in and operates one of the world's largest shopping centre portfolios with 104 shopping centres (housing 23,000 retail outlets and assets under management of $63b) in Australia, New Zealand, the United States, the United Kingdom and Brazil.

Investors who invested in Westfield when it first listed in 1960 and remained as shareholders by the end of the last century would find their initial $1,000 investment worth around $109m.[21]

Maha Sinnathamby – Malaysia

Maha came to Australia to study civil engineering in 1962. He worked for several organisations before establishing his property business in Perth in 1976. He moved to Queensland in the 1980s and continued his involvement in the property business. In the early 1990s, Maha secured a large land-parcel in Ipwich with his business partner. Today, Maha's Springfield Land Corporation is developing the 2,860-hectaer land-parcel into Greater Springfield – Australia's first privately-built city and the country's largest planned community. Maha is ranked 45th in the 2013 BRW "Rich 200" with an estimated wealth of $845m.

---

[21] Westfield Annual Report 2000

Tony and Maureen Wheeler – United Kingdom

The couple arrived in 1972 in Sydney after a 6-month overland trip from Europe with 27 cents between them. In 1973, they started Lonely Planet Publications and published *Across Asia on the Cheap*.

In 2007, the Wheelers sold 75% of their shares in Lonely Planet for £88m. Lonely Planet, by then, has become the world's largest independent guidebook publisher. In 2011, they disposed the remaining shareholding for £42m.

Sam Chong – Malaysia

Chong arrived in 1973 in Sydney from Malaysia for post-graduate engineering study. After graduating, Chong worked for several companies and settled in Queensland's Bowen Basin. In 2011, Chong came on to the "Rich 200" list published by the *Business Review Weekly* (BRW). In 2013, BRW estimated Chong's fortune at $800m. Chong is a substantial shareholder in Jellinbah Resources.

Tetsuya Wakuda – Japan

Tetsuya arrived in Sydney from Japan in 1982. After working for a year as a kitchen hand, he worked for Sydney chef Tony Bilson. He discovered his love for cooking. In 1983, Tetsuya partnered with the headwaiter and started *Ultimo*. Six years later, he opened his own restaurant Tetsuya's. The restaurant was popular with daily waiting list. It went on to win many awards and received high ratings. In 2000, Tetsuya's was relocated to Kent Street, Sydney. Tetsuya's has continued to receive awards and high ratings by international magazines.

David and Vicky Teoh – Malaysia

David and his wife migrated to Australia in 1986. In 1992, David founded Total Peripherals Group (TPG) selling computer hardware, e.g. pcs, printers and services for network. Their customers included federal and state governments. By 2005, the company has become an internet service provider. In 2008, TPG was listed on the Australian Securities Exchange by a reverse takeover of SP Telemedia.

TPG Telecom is now the 4th largest Australian ISP and ICT firm, with over 500,000 ADSL2+ subscribers, 192,000 mobile subscribers, 36,000 internet telephone subscribers and more than 23,000 PSTN telephony subscribers. In 2013, BRW 'Rich 200' estimated the couple's wealth at $1.06b.

The Professions and Others

In the professions and in services, there is no shortage of migrant success stories. One mustn't forget many ordinary people are behind these successful stories.

Dr Victor Chang AC – Hong Kong[22]

The late Victor Yam Him Chang came to Australia in 1953 to complete his secondary education in Sydney. In 1962, he graduated with a MBBS from Sydney University. In 1972, he returned from the United States after obtaining a Fellowship in Surgery and joined the cardiothoracic team at St Vincent's Hospital.

---

[22] http://www.victorchang.edu.au/

Victor Chang is credited with establishing the National Heart Transplant Program at St Vincent's Hospital. The Program has performed more than 1200 successful heart, heart-lung, and single lung transplants at St Vincent's hospital since 1984.

He founded the Australasian-China Medical Education and Scientific Research Foundation sponsoring doctors, nurses and students to work in Australia, enabling them to return to improve the quality of patient care in their own countries. He also sponsored many teams from St. Vincent's to China, Singapore and Indonesia where they shared their medical, surgical, nursing, hospital administration and audio-visual skills and knowledge.

In 1986, he was awarded a Companion of the Order of Australia by the Governor-General. The University of New South Wales conferred Victor the highest degree of M.D. Honoris Causa for "scholarly achievement and humanitarian endeavour".

Fred Hollows – New Zealand

Fred moved to Sydney to become Professor of Ophthalmology at the University of New South Wales in 1965. For the next seven years, Fred chaired the ophthalmology division overseeing the teaching departments at the University of New South Wales as well as the Prince of Wales and Prince Henry hospitals.

The late Fred Hollows has been credited with many achievements both in Australia and overseas. In the late 1970s he headed the National Trachoma and Eye Health Program (NTEHP) in Australia. During the NTEHP, more than 465 communities were visited, about 100,000 people were screened, 27,000 people were treated for trachoma and 1,000 surgeries were performed.

Five months before his death in 1992, Fred together with his wife and supporters established the Fred Hollows Foundation to continue the sight saving work. The Fred Hollows Foundation has now helped restore sight to over one million people in the developing world.

Fred received numerous awards. He was named as Australian of the Year in 1990.

Professor Fiona Wood AM – United Kingdom

Fiona Wood and her West Australia-born surgeon husband and their two children arrived in Perth in 1987.

In 1993, Fiona Wood together with scientist Marie Stoner set up a skin culture facility. In 1999, they set up The McComb Foundation with the aim of advancing tissue engineering technology technologies. They moved from growing skin sheets to spraying skin cells; earning a global reputation as pioneers in their field. In 2000, Clinical Cell Culture Pty Ltd C3 was established to distribute the spray on skin technology.

Fiona came to the media spotlight in 2002 when she led the team to work on burn victims of the Bali bombing. The spray on skin technology was used in treating the burn survivors. She has received many awards including Member of the Order of Australia and Australian of the Year for 2005.

Jimmy Pham – Vietnam

Jimmy Pham migrated to Sydney as a young child with his mother and siblings. In 1996, aged 24, he returned to Vietnam on a temporary assignment as a tour operator. He later started KOTO – "Know One Teach One" a social enterprise training disadvantaged kids. For more than a decade, the two centres in Hanoi and Saigon have trained over 400 students with another 200 under training. Many graduates of KOTO work at the KOTO restaurants and other businesses of KOTO or in the hospitality industry. [23]

In 2013, Jimmy was awarded a Member in the General Division of the Order of Australia.

Some Ordinary People

They were mentioned in Chapter 1 *Why People Migrate*. The following section completes their stories.

G

G came to Australia from Fuzhou, China to study English in the late 1980s. G was allowed to stay in Australia after the political event in China.

G married a Malaysian-born lawyer and later worked at her husband's law practice. The sole practice flourished as G's language skill has been very useful to service the increasingly large Chinese-speaking clientele. They have two girls. The eldest is studying law at university.

J

After her secondary education in Canton, J came to Australia in 1988 to attend an English course at a private college. J was issued with temporary visa and later a permanent resident visa.

---

[23] hhtp://www. http://www.koto.com.au/

With the help of relatives in the food business, she started a Chinese restaurant. She later married the cook and had two children. J later sponsored his brothers to migrate to Australia.

Her brother, after a short stay at the restaurant, started his own in a nearby suburb. The parents migrated years later under the family migration stream.

J is very happy with the opportunities, the uncomplicated business bureaucracy and the high quality lifestyle available in Australia. She has since sold her successful business after running it for over 20 years.

O'Brien

In 1997, O'Brien decided to move to Australia from South Africa. According to him, escalating crimes and other reasons prompted him to leave South Africa. He decided on Melbourne for it reminded him of Johannesburg where he came from.

When a senior role was available in the Australian affiliate, he and his family were relocated with the usual relocation benefits.

O'Brien later moved to Sydney to work for a large Australian financial services group overseeing the international division.

O and his wife

O and his wife were working at the University Hospital in Kuala Lumpur in 1969. They decided that they wanted to start their family in Australia as the country has a lot to offer.

Years later they realised their dream when health professionals came on the skill migration list. Q continued his specialist practice in Australia. Today, they are proud grandparents. Two of their children are medical specialists and one qualified as a lawyer. Their daughter-in-law and son-in-law are also medical specialists.

Q

Like many of his compatriots from China at that time, Q came to Melbourne from Shanghai to study English in the late 1980s. Later, Q and his wife were allowed to stay.

Q started a Chinese newspaper with advertisement income as its main source of revenue. The paper was given away free. With a growing Chinese population, the business prospered. While the newspaper is still being given away free on weekends, the mid-week edition is a paid edition with substantial news and other contents.

Five years after Q started the paper, he and his family moved to a new house on a large allotment. His parents soon joined them in Melbourne.

S brothers

S came to Australia to attend an English language course. S started working part-time at a factory. The following year, his brother aged 21 joined him.

In the late 1980s, the S brothers together with the 37,000 Chinese citizens were issued with temporary visas and allowed to stay in Australia. They were later granted permanent residency.

The S brothers have now lived in Australia for over 20 years. Both are married with children and own successful businesses.

T

After graduating from the university in the early 1970s, T and his wife both found employment in Kuala Lumpur and settled in Petaling Jaya. T later ran a successful business while his wife worked with the government.

In the early 1980s, they migrated to Sydney. T cited his concern for his children's education opportunity and future motivated them to emigrate.

In Australia, they started a small business but sold it 25 years later. They are now grandparents, happily retired after selling the business. All four children are professionals.

W

The political event in Burma prompted W and his family to migrate to Melbourne in the early 1980s.

After working at a number of jobs, W decided to run a milk bar (corner grocery shop) with his wife assisting him after work and during weekends. W later sold the business and worked for a motor manufacturer till retirement.

Their three children excelled in schools and later graduated with excellent results from universities. The eldest went on to win a scholarship for a post-graduate program. Later, with a group of business colleagues, she started a successful regional medical enterprise and later listed the company.

In their retirement, W and his wife make frequent overseas trips on holiday. They are glad that they made the decision to come to Australia three decades ago.

3 Australia Fair!

Home is where you find it

What is enviable about Australia – is it the great outdoors, natural resources, beautiful cities, educating the young, civil liberties, the rule of law, the playing fields of enterprise and opportunity, social caring, greenness and healthiness, diversity of cuisine and culture, public services and amenities, awareness of the environment, and modernity?

What has Australia to Offer?

Australians may justifiably claim they are a modern 21st Century society in human development, standards of living and outlook. Many studies have rated Australia very commendably in *human development* as well as in *standards of living*.

High human development

The *UNDP Human Development Index* ranks Australia *second in the world*. Table 3.1 compares it with some of its migration sources.

Table 3.1 UNDP Human Development Index 2012

	Australia	Malaysia	China	South Africa	India
World ranking	2	64	101	121	138
Life expectancy (years)	82	74.5	73.7	53.4	65.8
Schooling (mean yrs)	12	9.5	7.5	8.5	4.4
Income (US$ per capita PPP)	34,340	13,676	7,945	9,594	3,285
Inequality (adj. HDI value)	0.864	n.a.	0.543	n.a.	0.392
Multidimensional poverty index	n.a.	n.a.	0.056	0.057	0.283
Gender inequality index	0.115	0.256	0.213	0.462	0.610
Non-income HDI value	0.978	0.791	0.728	0.608	0.575
Phone subscriber/100 persons	139.7	135.3	86.2	109.2	64.3
Income index	0.862	0.726	0.646	0.674	0.515

Good quality of life

The OECD *Your Better Life Index* profiles countries across eleven measures of human well-being. It showed that Australia ranks in total score higher than all the other English speaking countries.

Table 3.2 OECD Better Life Index 2012

Index	Australia	Canada	New Zealand	United States	United Kingdom
Housing	7.5	7.7	6.2	7.7	6.1
Income	4.5	5.8	3.3	10.0	5.5
Jobs	7.6	7.6	7.2	7.4	7.7
Community	8.3	8.4	8.0	6.8	8.8
Education	7.6	7.5	7.5	6.9	5.9
Environment	8.7	8.4	8.7	7.9	9.5
Civic Engagement	9.4	6.0	7.3	5.8	7.0
Health	9.3	9.2	9.3	8.4	8.3
Life Satisfaction	8.1	8.8	8.2	7.5	6.9
Safety	9.5	9.7	9.4	8.9	9.5
Work-Life Balance	6.5	7.5	7.2	6.7	7.2
Total	87.0	86.6	82.3	84.0	82.4

Nature's bounty

Australia has an abundance of valuable *natural resources* that has been and will continue to be a pillar of its economy. Its physical size, surrounded by the vast ocean on all sides, and its geographical latitudes endow it with sparkling beaches, *climates* that vary from the tropical monsoonal North to snowfalls in the mountains of Victoria, New South Wales and Tasmania, vast farmlands and vineyards, and *natural wonders* such as the *Great Barrier Reef*.

Sustained conservation efforts have preserved its unique flora and fauna, forested parks and heritage sites. Its *great outdoors* give the *holiday-maker* a choice of adventure or relaxation or an educational sojourn. Unsurprisingly, Australia has always been a great *travel destination* for local and international tourists.

Green environment

Australia is one of the "greenest" and healthiest places on earth and Australians are among the most passionate people over the *care of the environment*. There is strict prohibition or quarantine to prevent the entry of anything not already found in Australia that may be disease-prone or environmentally harmful.

Most liveable cities

Australia's major cities (*Sydney, Melbourne, Brisbane, Canberra, Adelaide and Perth*) rank among the world's most liveable cities, with *Melbourne* and *Sydney* inevitably in the top three or top ten in surveys and studies.

The cities have good *infrastructural facilities*. They are clean, green and safe. The urbanisation growth is planned and controlled, and residents are served by adequate public transport and efficient services. The streets are safe and general civility and order in public places is very good.

The overall averages for urban and suburban *housing types* are 76% detached houses, 10% semi-detached, terrace or townhouse, and 13% apartment, flat or condominium.

Economic opportunities

Inclusive access to housing, education, healthcare, employment and business, among others, impacts on an individual's or a family's economic prospects. *Non-discrimination* as to gender, age, colour, creed and sexual orientation is embedded in Australia's laws and public policies, and is testimony of its advances as a progressive modern society.

For a large majority of people, education is the only route to a better life. Australia's childcare, schools, training institutes, universities and its overall *education system* are among the top in the world for their quality and affordability. Permanent residents are charged the same tuition fees as citizens. However, citizens are allowed to defer their university fees until they have graduated and are earning above the threshold income of $51,309 (2013-14 tax year) per annum.

Australia's *unemployment rate* (below 5.5% in 2012) is among the lowest of the OECD's 34 countries. It was the only one among the developed nations to have successfully weathered the worldwide financial crisis that had begun in 2008.

Australia's *business environment* is one positively supported by its legal and ethics structures, transparent public policies and regulations and a skilled and literate workforce. For new migrants, the choice of employment, self-employment or running a small business is widened by the varied lifestyles in Australian society.

Society's care

Australia's federal and state governments play a very large role in ensuring that quality healthcare is both accessible and affordable. Its public healthcare system may be fairly described as excellent in its reach and quality.

Australia has a "catch-all" social security system that is structured to ensure the well-being of families, dependents and retirees.

Reliable law enforcement

Law enforcement by the police and other authorities is competent, impartial and reliable. The ordinary person can feel very safe from street crimes, break-ins and organised criminal threats.

Democratic governance

The democratic *rule of law* prevails firmly in Australia, both in legislation and practice. Judicial independence, civil liberties and freedom of the press are safeguarded by law as well as by public opinion. There is a high degree of transparency and accountability in governance. The public service sector is responsive, reliable and generally highly competent.

Embracing Multiculturalism

Australia is a nation of immigrants. Since the 1980's, net immigration has overtaken natural increase to become the main contributor to its population growth. The 2011 census shows that thirty percent are born overseas and forty-six percent of the population have one or both parents who are migrants.

Australia is one of the very few countries that continue to have an active and supportive immigration policy. Today, more than ever, it is a popular migration destination.

Multicultural immigration

Ever since dismantling its *White Australia Policy* four decades ago, Australia has embraced multiculturalism in no uncertain terms in immigration policies and migrant intake. Since the turn of the last century, annual migrant intake from Asia has exceeded that from the United Kingdom; and in the last few years, the latter has been matched by the annual intakes from China as well as India as the main migration source countries to Australia.

In 2011, Chris Bowen, Australia's Immigration Minister, declared that Australia's multicultural experience "has worked" and "had strengthened Australian society". He stressed that, "We are not a guest-worker society. Rather, people who share respect for our democratic beliefs, laws and rights are welcome to join us as full partners with equal rights", and that Australian multiculturalism is "built differently to other models around the world".

Community tolerance

The vast majority of the community shares the official multicultural outlook. On the broader scale of tolerance towards minority groups, Australians have shown a high degree of *live and let live*. It ranked *second* among all English-speaking countries and also *among all OCED countries* in a 2011 report.

Table 3.3 Community Tolerance towards Minority Groups

Country	Community Tolerance Index	OECD Country Ranking
Canada	84.4	1
Australia	84.1	2
New Zealand	81.5	3
United States	76.5	9
United Kingdom	70.6	13

Source: OECD Society at a Glance 2011 - Social Indicators

Advance Australia Fair

The verses in the Australian national anthem *Advance Australia Fair* on page 36 sum up appropriately on what Australia has to offer.

Factsheet

Please refer to Factsheet 4.1 on page 43 of Chapter 4 *About Australia* for summary data on Australia.

Australian National Anthem
Advance Australia Fair

Australians let us all rejoice,
For we are young and free;
We've golden soil and wealth for toll;
Our home is girt by sea;
Our land abound in nature's gifts
Of beauty rich and rare;
In history's page, let every stage
Advance Australia Fair.

In joyful strains then let us sing,
Advance Australia Fair.

Beneath our radiant Southern Cross
We'll toll with hearts and hands;
To make this Commonwealth of ours
Renowned of all the lands;
For those who've cross the seas
We've boundless plains to share;
With courage let us all combine
To Advance Australia Fair.

In joyful strains then let us sing,
Advance Australia Fair.

4 About Australia

A bright new frontier

Geography

Australia is a vast island continent, including numerous small islands and a portion of the Antarctic. Its mainland coastline is 35,900 km and its total land area is 7.69 million sq. km. It is 95% the size of the United States excluding Alaska and 77% the size of Canada. It has a population of 23.0 million as at December 2012.

About 52% of land or 4 million sq. km is used for farming, livestock or crops while the rest of the mainland is arid but holds rich deposits of minerals. Forests, including plantations, cover about 19% of the continent.

Australia is the world's lowest lying continent, having an average elevation of only 330 meters. Overall, it is not mountainous and its tallest peak, *Mount Kosciuszko*, stands at 2,228 meters.

In land area Australia is the world's *sixth largest country*, being 1.2 times larger than all of Western Europe, 95% the size of the USA minus Alaska, 79% of China and 77% of Canada. However, its population of 23.0 million in 2012 is only a mere 5.5% of Western Europe's 420 million, 7.4% of the United States' 312 million, 1.7% of China's 1.35 billion and only 65% of Canada's 35 million.

Administratively, Australia comprises the five mainland states of Western Australia, South Australia, Queensland, New South Wales and Victoria, the mainland's Northern Territory and Australian Capital Territory (ACT) and the island state of Tasmania.

Table 4.1 below gives the basic geographical data for the six states and the two main territories.

Table 4.1 Basic geographical data in 2012 – national and states

	Pop 2012 ('000)	Land Area ('000 sq km)	Pop Density (per sq km)	Urban Pop (%)	Capital City
Australia*	22,906	7,693	2.80	85	Canberra
NSW	7,349	801	8.64	86	Sydney
Victoria	5,680	227	23.59	89	Melbourne
Queensland	4,611	1,731	2.50	83	Brisbane
W Australia	2,473	2,530	0.88	87	Perth
S Australia	1,662	984	1.62	84	Adelaide
Tasmania	512	68	7.28	71	Hobart
ACT	380	3	119.00	100	Canberra
N Territory	237	1,349	0.16	62	Darwin

* Includes Jervis Bay Territory, Christmas Island and the Cocos (Keeling) Islands. Population increased from 21.5m in 2011.

Climate

Climatic conditions in Australia vary widely, with tropical, sub-tropical and temperate or oceanic climates along most parts of the continental edge, and desert or semi-arid grassland in the interior.

The range of climates gives Australia a wide variety of fruits, vegetation and creatures, some of which are ecologically unique/native to Australia, such as the kangaroo, wallaby, wombat, koala, emu, platypus and kookaburra.

Political System

Australia is a multi-party electoral democracy, with separation of power into executive, legislative and judicial branches. At federal level, parliament consists of a 76-member *Senate* (Upper House) and a 150-member *House of Representatives* (Lower House), which are elected for a three-year term although elections may be called before the term completes. A Lower House member is elected to represent a single electoral division. Voting in elections is compulsory for all citizens aged 18 and above.

At federal level, the head of state is a titular Governor-General. The federal *prime minister* is the head of government for the nation and is chosen by the Lower House members of the ruling party. Australia is a member state of the British Commonwealth.

For practical purposes, Australia is usually taken to consist of the *six states* (Western Australia, South Australia, Queensland, New South Wales, Victoria and Tasmania) and the *two main territories* (Northern Territory and Australian Capital Territory). Each has its own Governor, parliament, and *Premier* or *Chief Minister*. Elected local councils are the third and lowest tier of government, serving under the jurisdiction of the state or territory government.

The highest court is the High Court of Australia, which is also the final court of appeal and headed by the Chief Justice of Australia. The six states and two territories each has a supreme court, from which appeal can be made to the High Court of Australia.

The main political parties at national level are the *Liberal Party of Australia*, its permanent coalition partner the *National Party of Australia*, the *Australian Labour Party* (ALP) and the *Australian Greens* party. Non-party candidates may also stand for election.

Economy

Australia's GDP *per capita* reached US$67,000 in 2012, ranking it the *top among the countries listed* in Table 4.2. Allowing for cost of living disparities, it ranked substantially better off than most countries other than Singapore, Hong Kong, United States and Canada.

Table 4.2 GDP (US$'000) Per Capita and Government Debt as % of GDP 2012

Country	GDP Per Capita (Current prices)	GDP Per Capita (PPP)	Government Debt as % of GDP	
			Net Debt	Gross Debt
Australia	67.0	42.6	12	27
Canada	52.2	43.6	34	87
China	6.0	9.1	23	n.a.
Hong Kong	36.6	51.4	32	n.a.
India	1.5	3.8	67	n.a.
Indonesia	3.6	4.9	24	n.a.
Ireland	45.9	41.9	102	117
Malaysia	10.3	16.9	n.a.	55
New Zealand	38.2	29.7	26	38
Pakistan	1.3	2.9	59	62
Philippines	2.6	4.4	n.a.	42
Singapore	51.1	60.4	n.a.	111
South Africa	7.5	11.3	36	42
South Korea	23.1	32.2	n.a.	34
Sri Lanka	2.8	6.1	n.a.	n.a.
Taiwan	20.3	38.7	n.a.	41
United Kingdom	38.5	36.9	83	90
United States	49.9	49.9	88	106
Vietnam	1.5	3.5	49	52

Source: International Monetary Fund

Australia's government gross debt as a percentage of GDP is the lowest among the countries listed in Table 4.2.

Australia's economy expanded by over 20% over the five years 2008 to 2012, producing a GDP of *$1.52 trillion* in 2012; year-on-year GDP growth averaged 4.0%. External trade in goods and services totalling $316 billion in 2012 remains the main driver of the economy, with the ratio of exports to GDP ranging between 19% and 23% in this period. Australian imports of trade and services amounted to $311 billion in 2012.

The principal sectors of Australia's economy are mining, tourism, education, agriculture and other services.

Major exports are minerals (iron ore, coal, gold), crude petroleum, natural gas, education, tourism, dairy produce, meat and wool. Major imports are crude and refined petroleum, medicaments, passenger motor vehicles, telecommunication equipment and various services.

The main export destinations are China, Japan, South Korea and the United States, while the main import sources are China, the United States, Japan, Singapore and Germany. Since late 2007, China has become Australia's largest trading partner in both exports and imports. In recent decade, India has emerged as a promising export destination for Australia. In 2012, Australia's export to India amounted to $14 billion and Australia ranked 14th as India's principal import source.

Demographics

Australia's population reached 22.9 million as at December 2012. This is an increase of 1.4 million from the 2011 population census.

Table 4.3 shows the demographics based on the 2011 census. Seventy percent of the population were Australian-born. For overseas-born population, the most common countries of birth were England (4.2%), New Zealand (2.2%), China excluding Hong Kong and Macau SARs and Taiwan (1.5%), India (1.4%) and Italy (0.9%).

Table 4.3 Australia's demographics

Population	21.5 million					
Gender	Male		49.8%	Female		50.2%
Age	Median	0 - 14 yr	15 - 29 yr	30 - 44 yr	45 – 59 yr	≥ 60 yr
	37	19%	21%	21%	19%	20%
Residence	Urban		85%	Rural and Remote		15%
Languages spoken at home	Only English		77%	Two or more		20%
Birth Origin	Individual	Born in Australia			70%	
		Born overseas			30%	
	Parent	Both born overseas			34%	
		Only one born overseas			12%	

Source: ABS 2011 Population Census

Fact Sheet 4.1

Fact Sheet 4.1 overleaf gives the summary data on geography, government, economy, taxation, employment, income, mortgage, rent, housing (type/ownership), motor vehicle ownership, education, healthcare, planned migrant intake.

Fact Sheet 4.1: About Australia

Geography

Land area	7.7 million sq. km.			
Population *	21.5 million	Median age		37
	Aged 50 and over		26%	
National capital	Canberra			
States/Territories	Australian Capital Territory, New South Wales, Northern Territory, Queensland, South Australia, Tasmania, Victoria, Western Australia			
State capitals	Sydney, Melbourne, Brisbane, Adelaide, Perth, Darwin, Hobart			
Climate	Climate varies because of geographical size; tropical north, sub-tropical, dry interior, temperate south; 80% of Australia has <600mm of rainfall annually; snow falls in winter in parts of New South Wales, Victoria, Australian Capital Territory and Tasmania			

Cultural diversity *	Ancestry (Top 5)				
	Australian	English	Irish	Scottish	Italian
	25%	26%	7%	. 5%	3%
	Born overseas				30%
	One or both parents born overseas				46%
	Only English spoken at home				77%
	2 or more languages spoken at home				20%

Government

- Independent parliamentary democracy
- Compulsory voting for citizens over the age of 18
- A written constitution
- 3 tiers of governments – federal, state and local
- Federal Parliament consists of House of Representatives (150 members of parliament) and Senate (76 senators)
- Federal government is responsible for foreign relations, trade, defence and immigration
- State and territory governments are responsible for other matters
- Federal and state government work cooperatively in education, transport, health and law enforcement.
- Council of Australian Governments (COAG) is the forum to initiate, develop and implement national policy reforms.

Economy *(2012 data)*

Gross domestic product (GDP)	Total	Per capita
	$1,486b	$68,916
Investment	Foreign investment in Australia	Australian investment abroad
	$2,115b	$1,234b
Major industries	Mining, tourism, education, agriculture, services	
Exports	$312b	Imports	$286b
Major trading partners	China, Japan, USA, India, Republic of Korea, Singapore, Germany	
Major exports	Iron ore and concentrates, coal, gold, crude petroleum, natural gas, education, travel	
Major imports	Crude and refined petroleum, passenger motor vehicles, medicaments, telecommunication equipment and parts, services	
Major export destinations	China, Japan, Republic of Korea, India, United States	
Major import sources	China, United States, Japan, Singapore, Germany	
Australian stock exchange	Listed entities	Market capitalisation
	2,184	$1.3 trillion

Taxation *(2013-14 tax year))*

Personal income tax rate	Income	Tax Rate Residents	Tax Rate Non-Residents
	$0 - $18,200	Nil	32.5%
	$18,201 - $37,000	19%	
	$37,001 - $80,000	32.5%	
	$80,001 - $180,000	37%	37%
	>$180,000	45%	45%
Goods and services tax	At 10% on most goods and services consumed in Australia. Basic food items, health care, child-care, rent, and education are excluded.		
Medicare levy	At 1.5% on personal taxable income		
Company tax	At 30% on all earned income		
Fringe benefits tax	At 46.5% of the gross-up taxable value of certain non-cash benefits that are provided to their employees.		
Tax on superannuation	At 15% on contribution, realised capital gains and investment income.		

Employment *

Employment in the state	Total labour force	10.6 million
	Full-time	60%
	Part-time	29%
	Away from work	6%
	Unemployed	5%
Occupations	Professionals	21%
	Clerical/administrative	15%
	Managers	13%
	Technicians/trades	14%
	Community/personal services	10%
	Sales	10%
	Labourers	10%
	Machine operators/drivers	7%
National minimum wage	$16.37 per hour or $622.06 per 38-hour week and at least 24% casual loading for casual employees covered by the national minimum wage	

Family income, mortgage, rent *

Median weekly family income	Couple with children	Couple with children
	$2,310	$2,081
Median monthly mortgage repayments		$1,800
Median weekly rent		$285

Housing and motor vehicle ownership *

House type	Detached	76%
	Semi-detached, terrace, townhouse	10%
	Flat, unit, apartment	13%
	Other	1%
Home ownership	No mortgage	33%
	With mortgage	33%
	Rented	30%
Number of motor vehicles/household	1	36%
	2	36%
	3	18%

Education

Schooling		Schools	Students
	Total number	9,468	3.5million
	As % of total	%	%
	Government schools	71	66
	Catholic schools	18	20
	Independent schools	11	14
TAFE	60 state-run TAFE (Technical and Further Education) colleges and over 300 private providers.		
Universities	39 universities, some with branch campuses within and outside Australia		

Healthcare

Life expectancy	Male		Female	
	79		84	
Hospitals	752 public hospitals, 588 private hospitals			
Medical practitioner/100,000	Major cities	Inner regional areas	Outer regional areas	
	392	224	206	
Nurses /100,000	Major cities		Very remote areas	
	997		1,240	
Private health insurance	46% of population with private health insurance cover			

Planned migrant intake 2014

Total	203,750			
Skilled migration	General skills	Business skills	Distinguished talents	
	121,090	7,260	200	
Family migration	Partner	Parent	Child	Other
	47,525	8,925	3,850	585
Other	Humanitarian		Special eligibility	
	13,750		565	

Note: Humanitarian number is based on 2013 Planning level.

* *ABS 2011 Census of Population and Housing*

5 States and Cities

Where the koala and wallaby play

Australia is usually taken to consist of *six states* and *two territories* – the mainland states of New South Wales, Victoria, Queensland, Western Australia and South Australia (in which live 90% of the country's population), the mainland Australian Capital Territory (ACT) and Northern Territory, and the island state of Tasmania. Excluded are six small island territories, the anomalous mainland territory of Jervis Bay and Australian Antarctic Territory, as they are hardly inhabited and economically insignificant.

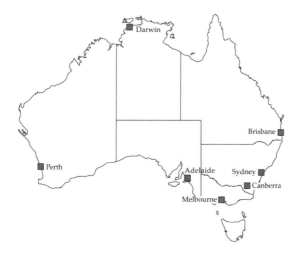

Four states –New South Wales, Victoria, Queensland and Western Australia – account for 90% of national gross domestic product. They are also the location for 95% of the headquarters of the top 500 listed companies, 95% of all banks and 90% of international tertiary students.

New South Wales

Key Facts

Land area: 800,642 sq km
Location: East coast
Climate: Mild temperate
Population: 7.3 million (6.9 million 2011 census)
Population density: 9/sq. km.
Capital: Sydney
Economy:
  31% of country's GDP
  AA credit rating (S&P)
  6% unemployment

web: http://www.visitnsw.com/

New South Wales's land area is only 10.4% of Australia's total size but it is 3.3 times the size of the United Kingdom. It is Australia's most populous state (31% of Australia's population, 11.4% of the UK's) and also the largest in GDP (31% of national GDP).

New South Wales hosts the head offices of:
- 40% of Australia's top 500 companies
- 75% of the banks (local and foreign)
- 63% of companies in financial services
- 53% of companies in machinery and equipment manufacture
- 88% of companies in motion pictures, radio and television

Sydney, the state capital, has a population of 4.6 million or 63% of the state's population.

Fact Sheet 5.1 on page 58 provides further information on the state.

Victoria

Key Facts

Land area: 227,416 sq km
Location: South east coast
Climate: Mild temperate
Population: 5.6 million (5.3 million *2011 census)*
Capital: Melbourne
Economy:
  22% of country's GDP
  AAA credit rating (S&P)
  5% unemployment
web::http://www.visitvictoria.com

Victoria's land area is 3% of Australia's total size (bigger only than the island of Tasmania) but 93% as large as the United Kingdom. It is Australia's second most populous state (24% of Australia's population, 8.8% of the UK's) and also the second largest in GDP (22% of national GDP).

The head offices of 28% of Australia's top 500 companies and two of the three automotive plants in Australia are located in Victoria. Thirty one percent of international tertiary students in Australia study in Victoria. Other large industries include food processing, textiles, clothing and footwear, paper, paper products, oil refining, petrochemicals, aluminium smelting, aircraft production, ICT (45% of Australia's total) and tourism.

Metropolitan Melbourne, the state capital, has a population of 4.2 million or 75% of the state's population.

Fact Sheet 5.2 on page 61 provides further information on the state.

Queensland

Key Facts

Land area: 1,730,648 sq km
Location: North east coast
Climate: Mild temperate
Population: 4.6 million (4.3 million *2011 census*)
Capital: Brisbane
Economy:
  19% of country's GDP
  AA+ credit rating (S&P)
  6% unemployment

web: http://www.tq.com.au

Queensland is Australia's third most populous state (19% of total population) and also third largest in GDP (19% of national GDP).

Mining is a major industry in the state. Queensland is among the world's leading producers of lead, silver and zinc. It is Australia's largest copper, lead, silver and zinc producer, the second largest bauxite producer and the third largest gold producer.

The state attracts large numbers of interstate and overseas visitors to its many holiday destinations including world heritage sites, hundreds of islands, beaches, and the scores of theme parks in the Gold Coast (which is known as Australia's 'theme park capital').

Brisbane, the state capital, is home to 2.1 million or almost 50% of the state's population.

Fact Sheet 5.3 on page 64 provides further information on the state.

Western Australia

Key Facts

Land area: 2,529,875 sq km
Location: Western part
Climate: Sub-tropical in the north to mild temperate south
Population: 2.4 million (2.2 million *2011 census*)
Capital: Perth
Economy:
  16% of country's GDP
  AAA credit rating (S&P)
  5% unemployment

web: http://www.western australia.com/

Western Australian is the largest state in land area, being nearly a third of Australia's total size and 10.4 times the United Kingdom. However, it is only the fourth largest in both population (9.6% of Australia's population, merely 3.5% of the UK's) and GDP (16% of national GDP but 80% of Malaysia's GDP).

In recent years, a surge in mining and construction activity has led to robust growth in the economy, employment and population. It registered a population increase of 3.5% in 2012 – the highest of all the states and territories. It is estimated that an additional 500,000 workers are needed in the coming decade.

Metropolitan Perth, the state capital, is home to 1.7 million or 77% of the state's population.

Fact Sheet 5.4 on page 67 provides further information on the state.

South Australia

Key Facts

Land area: 983,482 sq km
Location: South central
Climate: Mediterranean south, semi-arid north
Population: 1.7 million (1.6 million *2011 census*)
Capital: Adelaide
Economy:
  6% of country's GDP
  AA credit rating (S&P)
  6% unemployment

web:http://www.south australia.com/

South Australia is the fourth largest state in land area and fifth largest in both population and GDP. It shares borders with all the other four mainland states and the Northern Territory. It is four times the size of the United Kingdom but has a population of just 1.6 million (2.5% of the UK's population).

Manufacturing and agriculture are the main economic sectors but healthcare and social assistance are now the largest employers. Major parts of Australia's defence industry as well as the Holden car plant are located here. About half of all Australian wines are produced in South Australia.

Adelaide, the state capital, has a population of 1.2 million or 75% of the state's population.

Fact Sheet 5.5 on page 70 provides further information on the state.

Australian Capital Territory

Key Facts

Land area: 2,358 sq km
Location: South east bordered by state of New South Wales around
Climate: 4 distinct seasons, hot summer and cold frosty winter
Population: 0.376 million (0.357 million *2011 census*)
Capital: Canberra
Economy:
  2% of country's GDP
  AAA credit rating (S&P)
  4% unemployment

web: http://www.tourismact.gov.au/

Australian Capital Territory (ACT) is a purposely-created territory to locate Canberra as the nation's capital. In land area, it is 3.3 times the size of Singapore.

In addition to Canberra, the Australian Capital Territory includes some agricultural land, the Namadgi National Park and the small townships of Williamsdale, Naas, Uriarra, Tharwa and Hall.

The public sector is the employer for 50% of the workforce. The University of Canberra and Australian National University are located in Canberra, which also has branch campuses for the University of New South Wales (incorporating the Australian Defence Force Academy), the Australian Catholic University and Charles Sturt University.

Fact Sheet 5.6 on page 73 provides further information on the ACT.

Tasmania

Key Facts

Land area: 68,401 sq km
Location: South east
Climate: Temperate maritime
Population: 0.512 million (0.495 million
2011 *census*)
Capital: Hobart
Economy:
  2% of country's GDP
  AA+ credit rating (S&P)
  6% unemployment

web: http://www.discovertasmania.com.au/

Tasmania is a large island (plus many smaller islands) located at the south-eastern corner of the Australian mainland. Although it is the smallest state in land area, Tasmania is 28% the size of the United Kingdom, about 1.9 times the size of Taiwan, 1.6 times the Netherlands and 96 times the size of Singapore.

Sixty percent of the population live in the capital Hobart (212,000) and Launceston (106,000).

Tasmania offers holidaymakers many nature-based attractions with opportunities for a range of outdoor and adventure activities. Visitors to Tasmania will marvel at the variety of quality food produce – from cheeses, fruits, herbs, premium beef, cool climate wines and beers to marine produce including Atlantic salmon, abalone, scallops, octopus and rock lobster.

Fact Sheet 5.7 on page 75 provides further information on the state.

Northern Territory

Darwin

Key Facts

Land area: 1,349,129 sq km
Location: Central north
Climate: Tropical
Population: 0.237 million (0.236 million *2011 census*)
Capital: Darwin
Economy:
  1% of country's GDP
  Aa1 credit rating (Moody)
  5% unemployment

web: http://www.territorydoscovery.com/

Northern Territory is Australia's third largest state in land area (after Western Australia and Queensland) but the most sparsely populated. It is 5.5 times the size of the United Kingdom but its population of 230,000 is only 3.7% of the UK's.

About half of the state's population live in Darwin and the rest inhabit areas centred in towns along the Stuart Highway.

The major employers are the public sector, mining and tourism. A significant armed forces presence also contributes to its economy.

Northern Territory has many natural attractions including the iconic world heritage sites Uluru and Kakadu.

Fact Sheet 5.8 on page 78 provides further information on the state.

Capital Cities

All the eight capital cities, except Canberra, lie on the coast. All, except Darwin, are riverine cities, each with a large river running through it. The ocean and river add greatly to the cities' charm, offering cruises, boating, water sports, riverside cafes, waterfront homes and breath-taking scenery. Fourteen million people, or 60% of Australia's population, live in the largest five capital cities.

Table 5.1 Australian Capital Cities

Capital City	Population (000)	% of Total*	Land area (sq km)	City River
Sydney	4,600	20	1,530	Parramatta River
Melbourne	4,200	18	1,812	Yarra River
Brisbane	2,100	9	1,127	Brisbane River
Perth	1,730	8	963	Swan River
Adelaide	1,230	6	644	River Torrens
Canberra	370	2	221	Molonglo River
Hobart	220	1	68	River Derwent
Darwin	120	0.5	124	-

* % of Australia's total population

Given Australia's expanse, the capital cities lie over vast distances from one another, although this is overcome by both air and road transport, and in some cases, rail or sea transport.

Table 5.2 Road Distances between Australia's Capital Cities

	Canberra	Sydney	Melbourne	Brisbane	Perth	Adelaide	Darwin
Canberra	-	292	656	1,246	3,741	1,198	4,003
Sydney	292	-	881	966	3,972	1,417	4,301
Melbourne	656	881	-	1,676	3,456	733	3,189
Brisbane	1,246	966	1,676	-	4,363	2,055	3,406
Perth	3,741	3,972	3,456	4,363	-	2,700	4,032
Adelaide	1,198	1,417	733	2,055	2,700	-	3,026
Darwin	4,003	4,301	3,189	3,406	4,032	3,026	-

Table 5.3 Flying Times (hours) between Australia's Capital Cities

	Canberra	Sydney	Melbourne	Brisbane	Perth	Adelaide	Darwin	Hobart
Canberra	-	0.8	1.2	1.8	4.6	1.8	6.7	4.3
Sydney	0.8	-	1.6	1.5	4.9	2.1	4.5	1.9
Melbourne	1.2	1.6	-	1.5	4.0	1.3	5.6	1.2
Brisbane	1.8	1.5	1.5	-	5.2	2.7	4.0	4.2
Perth	4.6	4.9	4.0	5.2	-	2.9	3.6	7.0
Adelaide	1.8	2.1	1.3	2.7	2,9	-	3.6	4.5
Darwin	6.7	4.5	5.6	4.0	3.6	3.6	-	10.0
Hobart	4.3	1.9	1.2	4.2	7.0	4.5	10.0	-

Detailed information on the capital cities is given in Factsheet 5.9 through to Factsheet 5.16 on pages 81 to 88.

Fact Sheet 5.1 – New South Wales

Geography			
Land area	800,642 sq. km. (3.3 times the size of United Kingdom)		
Population *	6.9 million	Median age	38
Capital	Sydney		
Other urban centres	Newcastle, Central Coast, Wollongong, Maitland, Tweed Heads, Wagga Wagga, Albury, Port Macquarie, Orange		
Climate	Mild temperate climate - sunny springs, warm to hot summers, mild autumns, cool to cold winters. Climate varies across the state: coastal area - temperate climate, slightly humid during the summer; south - hot summer and cool winter; north - hot and wet summer and cooler and drier winter; Snowy Mountains - snow and frost during winter		

Cultural diversity *	Ancestry (Top 5)				
	Australian	English	Irish	Scottish	Chinese
	25%	24%	7%	6%	4%
	Born overseas				23%
	One or both parents born overseas				48%
	Only English spoken at home				73%
	2 or more languages spoken at home				25%

Economy		
Gross state product (GSP)	Total ($ billion)	As % of Australia's GDP
	446	31
Exports/imports	$59b / $106b	
Major trading partners	China, Japan, USA, Germany, Republic of Korea, Taiwan, Singapore,	
Major exports	Coal, copper ores and concentrates, aluminium, refined petroleum, medicaments, wheat, cotton, uncoated flat rolled iron and steel, beef, wool and other animal hair, travel, legal and professional services	
Major imports	Medicaments, telecom equipment and parts, crude petroleum, computers, passenger vehicles, refined petroleum, office machines, monitors projectors and televisions, goods vehicles, medical instruments, travel, freight transport and passenger fares	

Employment *		
Labour force	Total labour force	3.3 million
	Full-time	60%
	Part-time	28%
	Away from work	6%
	Unemployed	6%
Occupations	Professionals	23%

	Clerical/administrative	15%
	Managers	13%
	Technicians/trades	13%
	Community/personal services	10%
	Sales	9%
	Labourers	9%
	Machine operators/drivers	6%

Family income/Mortgage repayment/Rent *

Median weekly family income (couple with 2 incomes)	Family with children	$2,370
	Family with no children	$2,120
Median monthly mortgage repayments		$1,993
Median weekly rent		$300

Housing/Motor vehicles *

House type	Detached	69%
	Semi-detached, terrace, townhouse	11%
	Flat, unit, apartment	19%
	Other	1%
Home ownership	No mortgage	33%
	With mortgage	33%
	Rented	30%
Number of motor vehicles/house	1	38%
	2	34%
	3 or more	15%

Education

Schooling	Compulsory schooling for students aged between 6 and 17. All students must complete Year 10. In 2010, of the 2.2 million school students, 68% attended state schools, 22% Catholic schools and 10% independent (private) schools.
TAFE colleges	10 state-run TAFE institutes with metropolitan and regional campuses.
Universities	12 universities

Health

Hospitals	226 public hospitals and 177 private hospitals

Transport

Public transport	New South Wales has an established network of roads, rail and sea freight corridors. Rail Corporation New South Wales operates City Rail providing service to greater Sydney region and Country Link with services to over 365 destinations in New South Wales, the Australian Capital Territory, Queensland and Victoria.
Major airports	Airports in Sydney, Albury, Armidale, Ballina (Byron), Coffs

	Harbour, Dubbo, Lord Howe Island, Moree, Newcastle, Tamworth, Port Macquarie, Wagga Wagga

Tourism

Major tourism regions	Sydney, Blue Mountains, Southern Highlands, Central Coast & Hawkesbury, Hunter Valley and Coast, Holiday Coast, Tropical North Coast, New England, Central West, South Coast, Snowy Mountains, Riverina, Murray, Outback, Lord Howe Island
Islands	103 islands Major islands - Broughton Island, Lord Howe Island, Montague Island, Sydney Harbour Islands
Surfing	Kingscliff, Cabarita Beach, Brunswick Heads, Byron Bay - The Pass, Lennox Head Beach, Ballina, Iluka, Yamba, Park Beach – Coffs, Jetty Beach – Coffs, Sawtell, South West Rocks, Port Macquarie, Shoal Bay, Nobbys Beach, Newcastle Beach, Dixon Park, Merewether, Swansea, Wamberal, Terrigal, Avoca, Palm Beach, Avalon, Newport, Mona Vale, Narrabeen, South Narrabeen, Dee Why, Manly - Nth Steyne, Sydney Harbour, North Bondi, Bondi, Maroubra, Wanda – Cronulla, Cronulla, Thirroul, Shoalhaven, Sussex Inlet, Moruya, Narooma, Bermagui, Meri
World Heritage listed properties	Cultural - Old Government House and Domain, Hyde Park Barracks, Old Great North Road, Cockatoo Island Convict Site, Sydney Opera House Natural - Greater Blue Mountains Area, Lord Howe Island Group Mixed - Willandra Lakes Region
Major festivals/events	Sydney Festival, Apia International, Sydney Chinese New Year Festival, Australian Open of Surfing, Surfest, Tamworth Country Music Festival, Sydney Gay and Lesbian Mardi Gras Parade, Yonex Australia Open, Sydney Royal Easter Show, Sydney Cup Week, Australian Celtic Festival, Fashion Week Australia, Sydney Writers' Festival, Half Marathon, Sydney Film Festival, Australian Surf Festival, City2Surf, Bathurst 1000, Sydney 500, A Taste of Manly, Australian Masters Alpine Ski Races, Sydney Sleaze Ball, Sydney-Hobart, Stonehaven Cup, Carols in the Domain, New Year's Eve celebrations with fireworks
Museums/art galleries	Australian Museum, Power House Museum, Australian National Maritime Museum, Museum of Contemporary Art, Art Gallery of New South Wales

* ABS: *2011 census*

Fact Sheet 5.2 - Victoria

Geography	
Land area	227,000 sq. km. (6 times the size of Taiwan)
Population *	5.3 million	Median age	37
Capital	Melbourne
Other major urban centres	Geelong, Ballarat, Bendigo, Latrobe Valley, Shepparton, Mildura, Wodonga, Warrnambool
Climate	Mild temperate climate - sunny springs, warm to hot summers, mild autumns, cool to cold winters. Climate varies across the state

Cultural diversity *	Ancestry (Top 5)				
	Australian	English	Irish	Scottish	Italian
	23%	24%	8%	6%	5%
	Born overseas				31%
	One or both parents born overseas				50%
	Only English spoken at home				72%
	2 or more languages spoken at home				26%

Economy		
Gross state product (GSP)	Total ($ billion)	As % of Australia's GDP
	323	22
Exports/imports	$32b / $71b	
Major trading partners	China, USA, Japan, Germany, Thailand, New Zealand and Saudi Arabia.	
Major exports	Wool and other animal hairs, passenger motor vehicles, aluminium, milk, cream whey and yoghurt, wheat, beef, cheese and curd, refined petroleum, edible products and preparations, education	
Major imports	Passenger vehicles, crude petroleum, refined petroleum, vehicle parts and accessories, goods vehicles, medicaments, prams, toys, games and sporting goods, telecom equipment and parts, computers, furniture, mattresses and cushions, personal travel, freight transport and passenger fares	

Employment *		
Employment in the state	Total labour force	2.7 million
	Full-time	59%
	Part-time	30%
	Away from work	5%
	Unemployed	5%
Occupations	Professionals	22%
	Clerical/administrative	14%
	Managers	13%
	Technicians/trades	14%

	Community/personal services	9%
	Sales	10%
	Labourers	9%
	Machine operators/drivers	6%

Family income/Mortgage repayment/Rent *

Median weekly family income (couple with 2 income)	Couple with children	$2,310
	Couple without children	$2,081
Median monthly mortgage repayments		$1,800
Median weekly rent		$277

Housing/Motor vehicles *

	Detached	77%
House type	Semi-detached, terrace, townhouse	9%
	Flat, unit, apartment	13%
	Other	1%
	No mortgage	34%
Home ownership	With mortgage	36%
	Rented	27%
	1	35%
Number of motor vehicles/house	2	37%
	3 or more	17%

Education

Schooling	In Victoria, children of compulsory school age (aged 6 to 17 years) are required by law to enroll in a school registered in Victoria or be registered for home schooling. All children of compulsory school age who are home schooled must be registered with the Victorian Registration and Qualifications Authority (VRQA)
TAFE colleges	18 state-run TAFE colleges and many private providers.
Universities	10 universities, many with branch campuses within the state and outside Australia

Health

Hospitals	151 public hospitals and 166 private hospitals

Transport

Public transport	Train, tram and bus network in Melbourne. Regional public transport network includes buses and trains which serve around and between towns and for travel to Melbourne. Train services operate between Melbourne and key centres including Albury / Wodonga, Bairnsdale, Ballarat, Bendigo, Echuca, Geelong, Sale, Seymour, Shepparton, Swan Hill, Traralgon and Warrnambool. V/Line operates coach services connected to the rail network and serve regional Victoria where trains do not operate.
Major airports	Melbourne, Avalon, Essendon, Mildura, Mount Hotham

Tourism	
Major tourism regions	Melbourne, Yarra and Dandenong Ranges, Mornington Peninsula, Phillip Island, Spa and Garden Country, Werribee and Bellarine, South West Coast, Goldfields, Grampians and Central West, Mallee Country, Goulburn and Murray, High Country, East Gippsland
Islands	184 islands Major islands - French Island, Gabo Island, Kanowna Island, Lady Julia Percy Island, Norman Island, Phillip Island, Shellback Island
World Heritage listed property	Royal Exhibition Building and Carlton Gardens
Beach	Mornington Peninsula
Major festivals and events	Australian Tennis Open, Australian Grand Prix, Phillip Island Superbike World Championship, Moomba Waterfest, Melbourne Grand National, Royal Melbourne Show, Australian Motorcycle Grand Prix, Melbourne International Arts Festival, Melbourne Cup, New Year's Eve celebrations with fireworks
Museums/art galleries	Melbourne Museum, Immigration Museum, Scienceworks Museum, National Sports Museum, National Gallery of Victoria, Australian Centre for Contemporary Art

* ABS: *2011 census*

Fact Sheet 5.3 - Queensland

Geography			
Land area	1.73m sq. km. (5.8 times the size of the Philippines)		
Population *	4.3 million	Median age	36
Capital	Brisbane		
Other major urban centres	Gold Coast, Townsville, Thuringowa, Cairns, Toowoomba, Rockhampton, Mackay, Bundaberg,		
Climate *	Mild temperate climate - sunny springs, warm to hot summers, mild autumns, cool to cold winters. Climate varies across the state		

Cultural diversity *	Ancestry (Top 5)				
	Australian	English	Irish	Scottish	German
	27%	28%	8%	7%	5%
	Born overseas				26%
	One or both parents born overseas				39%
	Only English spoken at home				85%
	2 or more languages spoken at home				12%

Economy		
Gross state product (GSP)	Total (billion)	As % of Australia's GDP
	281	19
Exports/imports	$60b / $44b	
Major trading partners	Japan, China, India, Republic of Korea, USA, Papua New Guinea, Singapore	
Major exports	Coal, beef, copper, cotton, aluminium, lead ores and concentrates, zinc ores and concentrates, copper ores and concentrates, meat, wheat, travel	
Major imports	Crude and refined petroleum, passenger vehicles, goods vehicles, civil engineering equipment and parts, gold, rubber tyres treads and tubes, copper, furniture and mattresses and cushions, mechanical handling equipment and parts, travel and freight transport	

Employment *		
Employment in the state	Total labour force	2.2 million
	Full-time	60%
	Part-time	28%
	Away from work	6%
	Unemployed	6%
Occupations	Professionals	19%
	Clerical/administrative	15%
	Managers	12%

	Technicians/trades	15%
	Community/personal services	10%
	Sales	10%
	Labourers	11%
	Machine operators/drivers	7%

Family income/Mortgage Repayment/rent *

Median weekly family income (couple with 2 income)	Couple with children	$2,256
	Couple without children	$2,011
Median monthly mortgage repayments		$1,850
Median weekly rent		$300

Housing/Motor vehicles *

House type	Detached	79%
	Semi-detached, terrace, townhouse	8%
	Flat, unit, apartment	12%
	Other	1%
Home ownership	No mortgage	29%
	With mortgage	35%
	Rented	33%
Number of motor vehicles/house	1	35%
	2	37%
	3 or more	17%

Education

Schooling	Compulsory for all children aged between 6 and 15. Students are legally required to attend school until 16 years old.
TAFE colleges	13 state-run TAFE colleges
Universities	10 universities

Health

Hospitals	170 public hospitals and 106 private hospitals

Transport

Public transport	QR Citytrain provides commuter rail services throughout greater Brisbane and between Brisbane and the Sunshine Coast and the Gold Coast regions. QR Traveltrain services provide long-distance and tourist passenger services along the Queensland coastline between Brisbane and Cairns, and throughout regional Queensland.
Air access/major airports	Brisbane, Airlie Beach, Barcaldine, Biloela (Thangoo), Bundaberg, Cairns, Charlesville, Cloncurry, Emerald, Fraser Coast (Harvey Bay), Gladstone, Gold Coast, Hamilton Island, Hayman Island, Hervey Bay, Horn Island, Longreach, Mackay, Mount Isa, Moranbah,Proserpine, Rockhampton, Roma, Sunshine Coast, Townsville, Weipa, Whitsunday

Tourism	
Major tourism regions	Brisbane, Brisbane Hinterland, Brisbane Islands, Gold Coast and Hinterland, Darling Downs, Sunshine Coast, Fraser Island and Coast, Great Barrier Reef, Capricorn, Cairns and The Tropics, The Mid-Tropics, Cape York, Gulf Savannah, Outback
Islands	1,955 islands. Major island - Badu Island, Curtis Island, Fraser Island, Great Palm Island, Hinchinbrook Island, Horn Island, Magnetic Island, Mornington Island, Moreton Island, North and South Stradbroke Islands, Thursday Island, Torres Strait Islands, The Whitsunday Islands,
World Heritage listed properties	Australian Fossil Mammal Sites – Riversleigh, Fraser Island, Gondwana Rainforests, Great Barrier Reef, Wet Tropics of Queensland
Beaches	Four Mile Beach, Mission Beach, Surfers Paradise Beach, Whitehaven Beach, Whitsundays
Snorkelling	Cairns, Coral Sea, Elliot Island, Heron Island, Lizard Island, Port Douglas, Whitsunday Islands, *Yongala* wreck
Surfing	Alma Bay, Rainbow Beach, Noosa Bar, Noosa, Sunshine Beach, Peregian, Coolum, Marcoola, Maroochydore, Alex Headland, Mooloolaba, Kawana – Buddina, Kings Bulcock Beach, Seaway Spit, Main Beach, Narrowneck, Artificial Reef, Surfers Paradise, Northcliffe, Miami, Burleigh Heads, Palm Beach, Currumbin, Kirra, Rainbow Bay, Snapper, Duranbah
Major festivals and events	Brisbane Cup, Gold Coast Marathon, Royal Queensland Show, Mount Isa Rodeo and Festival, Gold Coast 600, Carnival of Flowers, Birdsville Races, New Year's Eve celebrations with fireworks
Museums/art galleries	Queensland Museum, Museum of Tropical Queensland, Queensland Art Gallery

* ABS: *2011 census*

Fact Sheet 5.4 – Western Australia

Geography				
Land area	2,5 million sq. km. (10 times the size of U.K.)			
Population *	2.2 million	Median age		36
Capital	Perth			
Other major urban centres	Rockingham, Mandurah, Bunbury, Kalgoorlie, Geraldton, Albany			
Climate	Mild temperate climate - sunny springs, warm to hot summers, mild autumns, cool to cold winters. Climate varies across the state			

Cultural diversity *	Ancestry (Top 5)				
	Australian	English	Irish	Scottish	Italian
	25%	29%	6%	6%	4%
	Born overseas				37%
	One or both parents born overseas				56%
	Only English spoken at home				79%
	2 or more languages spoken at home				17%

Economy		
Gross state product (GSP)	Total ($ billion)	As % of Australia's GDP
	236	16
Exports/imports	$125b / $39b	
Major trading partners	China, Japan, Republic of Korea, India, United Kingdom, Singapore, United Arab Emirates	
Major exports	Iron ore and concentrates, gold, crude petroleum, natural gas, wheat, copper ores and concentrates, precious metal ores, nickel ores and concentrates, gold coins and legal tender coins, liquefied propane and butane, travel	
Major imports	Gold, crude petroleum, refined petroleum, ships and boats, passenger vehicles, civil engineering equipment and parts, goods vehicles, silver and platinum, iron, steel and aluminium structures, specialised machinery and parts, travel, freight, architectural and other technical services	

Employment *		
Employment in the state	Total labour force	1.1 million
	Full-time	61%
	Part-time	28%
	Away from work	6%
	Unemployed	5%
Occupations	Professionals	20%
	Clerical/administrative	14%
	Managers	12%
	Technicians/trades	17%

	Community/personal services	10%
	Sales	9%
	Labourers	10%
	Machine operators/drivers	8%

Family income/Mortgage repayment/Rent *

Median weekly family income (couple with 2 income)	Couple with children	$2,497
	Couple without children	$2,257
Median monthly mortgage repayments		$1,950
Median weekly rent		$300

Housing/Motor vehicles *

House type	Detached	80%
	Semi-detached, terrace, townhouse	11%
	Flat, unit, apartment	9%
	Other	1%
Home ownership	No mortgage	30%
	With mortgage	38%
	Rented	29%
Number of motor vehicles/house	1	33%
	2	39%
	3 or more	20%

Education

Schooling	Compulsory schooling for all children aged between six and 15. Students are legally required to attend school until they are 16 years old.
TAFE colleges	9 state-run TAFE colleges.
Universities	5 universities

Health

Hospitals	94 public hospitals and 58 private hospitals

Transport

Public transport	Transwa operates regional rail and coach services to more than 275 locations in the State. Train services are available for travel to Northam, Toodyay, Kalgoorlie, and Bunbury. Coach services operate from Kalbarri, Meekatharra, Esperance and Augusta. In Perth, public transport consists of train, bus and ferry. There is less reliance on rail service and higher car use.
Air access/major airports	Perth, Albany, Broome, Busselton, Exmouth (Learmouth), Geraldton, Kalgoorlie, Karratha, Kununurra, Newman, Paraburdoo, Port Hedland

Tourism	
Major tourism regions	Perth, Rottnest island, Darling and Swan, South-West, Heartlands, Great Southern, Esperance and Nullarbor, Goldfields, Outback Coast and Mid-West, Pilbara, Kimberley
Islands	3,747 islands Major islands - Barrow Island, Dirk Hartog Island, Houtman Abrolhos Islands, Monte Bello Islands, Recherche Archipelago, Rottnest island,
World Heritage listed property	Fremantle Prison
Beaches	Cable Beach, Cottesloe Beach, Margaret River
Snorkelling	Ningaloo Reef, Rottnest Island
Surfing	Margaret River, Smiths – Yallingup) Ningaloo Reef, Denmark, Esperance, LancelinLancelin/Yanchep, Geraldton, Rottnest Island, Kalbarri,Mandurah, Perth
Major festivals and events	Perth Cup, Perth Festival, Western Australia Turf Club Derby, New Year's Eve celebrations with fireworks.
Museums/art galleries	Western Australian Museum, Western Australian Maritime Museum, The Art Gallery of Western Australia

* ABS: *2011 census*

Fact Sheet 5.5 – South Australia

Geography				
Land area	983,482 sq. km. (3 times the size of Malaysia)			
Population *	1.6 million	Median age		39
Capital	Adelaide			
Other major urban centres	Mount Gambier, Whyalla, Gawler			
Climate	Mild temperate climate - sunny springs, warm to hot summers, mild autumns, mild to cool winters. Weather varies across the state			
Cultural diversity *	Ancestry (Top 5)				
	Australian	English	Irish	Scottish	German
	27%	29%	6%	6%	6%
	Born overseas				27%
	One or both parents born overseas				43%
	Only English spoken at home				81%
	2 or more languages spoken at home				16%

Economy		
Gross state product (GSP)	Total ($ billion)	As % of Australia's GDP
	91	6
Exports/imports	$14b / $9b	
Major trading partners	China, USA, Japan, Malaysia, Singapore, India, Republic of Korea	
Major exports	Wheat, copper, alcoholic beverages, iron ores and concentrates, copper ores and concentrates, lead, meat, passenger vehicles, vegetables, oil-seeds & oleaginous fruits, travel	
Major imports	Refined petroleum, passenger vehicles, lead ore and concentrates, goods vehicles, electronic integrated circuits, fertilisers, alcoholic beverages, furniture, mattresses and cushions, rubber tyres, treads and tubes, personal travel and freight transport	

Employment *		
Employment in the state	Total labour force	784,000
	Full-time	57%
	Part-time	31%
	Away from work	6%
	Unemployed	6%
Occupations	Professionals	20%
	Clerical/administrative	14%
	Managers	13%
	Technicians/trades	14%

	Community/personal services	10%
	Sales	10%
	Labourers	11%
	Machine operators/drivers	6%

Family income/Mortgage repayment/Rent *

Median weekly family income (couple with 2 income)	Couple with children	$2,130
	Couple without children	$1,906
Median monthly mortgage repayments		$1,500
Median weekly rent		$220

Housing/Motor vehicles *

House type	Detached	80%
	Semi-detached, terrace, townhouse	11%
	Flat, unit, apartment	9%
	Other	1%
Home ownership	No mortgage	33%
	With mortgage	35%
	Rented	28%
Number of motor vehicles/house	1	37%
	2	36%
	3 or more	16%

Education

Schooling	Compulsory schooling for all children aged between six and 15. Students are legally required to attend school until they are 16 years old.
TAFE colleges	TAFE SA with campuses in Adelaide CBD and suburbs and in rural and regional South Australia
Universities	Flinders University, University of Adelaide, University of South Australia

Health

Hospitals	80 public hospitals and 59 private hospitals

Transport

Public transport	Train, tram and buses for Adelaide. Bus and coach operators travelling to country areas of South Australia and interstate Interstate train service: <ul><li>The Overland travels between Adelaide and Melbourne in both directions. The journey covers 828 km. and operates three times a week.</li><li>The Ghan travels twice a week between Adelaide, Alice Springs and Darwin. The journey covers 2,979 km. and travels over two nights.</li><li>The Indian Pacific travels twice a week between</li></ul>

	Sydney, Adelaide and Perth. The journey covers 4,352 km. and takes three nights in either direction.
Air access/major airports	Adelaide, Port Lincoln

Tourism	
Major tourism regions	Adelaide, Fleurieu Peninsula, Kangaroo Island, Adelaide Hills, Barossa Valley, Mid-North, York Peninsula, Murray, Limestone Coast, Finders Ranges and Outback, Eyre Peninsula and Nullarbor
Islands	346 islands Major islands - Hindmarsh Island, Kangaroo Island, Thistle Island
Beaches	Fleurieu Peninsula
Surfing	Chiton Rocks, Seaford, Glenelg, York Peninsula, Kangaroo Island, Robe, Beachport, Port Lincoln *Victoria* - Woolamai, St Kilda Lighthouse, Ocean Grove, 13th Beach, Jan Juc – Winki, Lorne, Bells Beach, Torquay, Point Lonsdale, Thirteenth Beach, Point Addis, Boobs, Cape Conran, Raffs, Suck Rock
Major festivals and events	Port Lincoln Tunarama Festival, Adelaide Festival of Arts, Clipsal 500, South Australia Week Vintage Festival, Barossa Valley Balloon Regatta, Adelaide Cup, Royal Adelaide Show, New Year's Eve celebrations with fireworks
Museums/art galleries	South Australian Museum, Migration Museum, South Australian Maritime Museum, Art Gallery of South Australia

* ABS: *2011 census*

Fact Sheet 5.6 – Australian Capital Territory
ABS: 2011 census

Geography

Land area	2,358 sq. km. (3 times the size of Singapore)				
Population *	357,000		Median age		34
Capital	Canberra				
Climate	Mild temperate climate - sunny springs, warm to hot summers, mild autumns, cool to cold winters.				
Cultural diversity *	Ancestry (Top 5)				
	Australian	English	Irish	Scottish	German
	27%	24%	9%	7%	3%
	Born overseas				39%
	One or both parents born overseas				47%
	Only English spoken at home				78%
	2 or more languages spoken at home				21%

Economy

Gross state product (GSP	Total ($ billion)	As % of Australia's GDP
	32	2
Exports/imports	$1.2b / $1.5b	
Major trading partners	United Arab Emirates, Austria, Papua New Guinea, Samoa, India, United Kingdom, China	
Major exports	Gold coin and legal tender coins, optical instruments, government services, travel	
Major imports	Gold, artworks, antiques, silver and platinum, electronic and integrated circuits, Gold coin and legal tender coins, optical instruments, measuring and analysing instruments, specialised equipment and parts, prams, toys and sporting goods, office machines, government services, travel	

Employment *

	Total labour force	203,000
Employment in the state	Full-time	65%
	Part-time	25%
	Away from work	6%
	Unemployed	4%
Occupations	Professionals	30%
	Clerical/administrative	19%
	Managers	16%
	Technicians/trades	10%
	Community/personal services	9%
	Sales	7%
	Labourers	5%
	Machine operators/drivers	2%

Family income/Mortgage repayment/Rent *		
Median weekly family income (couple with 2 income)	Couple with children	$3,060
	Couple without children	$2,662
Median monthly mortgage repayments		$2,167
Median weekly rent		$380

Housing/Motor vehicles *		
House type	Detached	73%
	Semi-detached, terrace, townhouse	15%
	Flat, unit, apartment	12%
	Other	0.2%
Home ownership	No mortgage	28%
	With mortgage	39%
	Rented	31%
Number of motor vehicles/house	1	37%
	2	39%
	3 or more	16%

Education	
Schooling	Compulsory schooling for all children aged between six and 15. Students are legally required to attend school until they are 16 years old.
TAFE colleges	Canberra Institute of Technology
Universities	Australian National University, University of Canberra, Australian Defence Force Academy

Health	
Hospitals	3 public hospitals and 15 private hospitals

Transport	
Public transport	Road transport is the main transport link. The interstate rail link is provided by the CountryLink operation of the NSW Government-owned Rail Corporation. The service runs from Sydney's Central Station to the Canberra Railway Station
Major airport	Canberra

Tourism	
Major tourism regions	Canberra, Snowy Mountains, Capital Country
Islands	7 major island groups - Ashmore and Cartier Islands, Christmas Island, Cocos (Keeling) Islands, Coral Sea Islands, Heard Island, Norfolk Island
Major festivals and events	Summernats, Canberra National Multicultural Festival, Floriade, New Year's Eve celebrations with fireworks
Museums/art galleries	National Museum of Australia, National Gallery of Australia Canberra Museum and Gallery, The National Science and Technology Centre (Questacon),

Fact Sheet 5.7 – Tasmania

Geography					
Land area	68,401 sq. km. (1.5 times the size of Netherlands)				
Population *	495,000		Median age		40
Capital	Hobart				
Other urban centres	Launceston, Devonport, Burnie				
Climate	Temperate maritime climate - sunny springs, warm to hot summers, mild autumns, cool to cold winters. Climate varies across the state.				
Cultural diversity *	Ancestry (Top 5)				
	Australian	English	Irish	Scottish	German
	34%	34%	8%	7%	3%
	Born overseas				26%
	One or both parents born overseas				24%
	Only English spoken at home				92%
	2 or more languages spoken at home				6%

Economy		
Gross state product (GSP)	Total ($ billion)	As % of Australia's GDP
	24	2
Exports/imports	$3.5b / $1.5b	
Major exports	Zinc, aluminium, iron ores, copper ores, wood chips and particles, tin ores and concentrates, beef, goods vehicle, dairy products, education and travel	
Major imports	Iron, steel and aluminium structures, refined petroleum, animal feeds, rubber tyres, coke, cocoa and passenger vehicles	
Major trading partners	China, United States, Taiwan, Indonesia, Japan, Malaysia, Singapore, Republic of Korea	

Employment *		
Employment in the state	Total labour force	232,000
	Full-time	55%
	Part-time	33%
	Away from work	6%
	Unemployed	6%
Occupations	Professionals	19%
	Clerical/administrative	14%
	Managers	12%
	Technicians/trades	15%
	Community/personal services	11%
	Sales	10%
	Labourers	11%

	Machine operators/drivers	7%
Family income/Mortgage repayment/Rent *		
Median weekly family income (couple with 2 income)	Couple with children	$1,999
	Couple without children	$1,771
Median monthly mortgage repayments		$1,300
Median weekly rent		$200
Housing/Motor vehicles *		
House type	Detached	86%
	Semi-detached, terrace, townhouse	5%
	Flat, unit, apartment	8%
	Other	1%
Home ownership	No mortgage	36%
	With mortgage	34%
	Rented	26%
Number of motor vehicles/house	1	36%
	2	36%
	3 or more	18%
Education		
Schooling	Compulsory schooling for all children aged between 6 and 15 years old. Students are legally required to attend school until they are 16 years old.	
TAFE colleges	The Institute of TAFE Tasmania	
Universities	University of Tasmania	
Health		
Hospitals	23 public hospitals and 8 private hospitals	
Transport		
Public transport	Metro Tasmania, owned by the Tasmanian State Government, operates the public passenger bus services in the major urban areas of Hobart, Launceston and Burnie. An extensive road network serves the decentralised population and also for freight movement. Tasmanian Rail Network operates for freight-only commercial purpose. Spirit of Tasmania's Melbourne-Devonport ferry service operates daily service linking Tasmania to the mainland.	
Major airports	Major airports at Hobart, Devonport, Launceston	
Tourism		
Major tourism regions	Hobart, East Coast, South-East, South West Wilderness, North-West, Midlands and the North, Bass Straits Islands	

Islands	1,000 islands Major islands - Bruny Island, Flinders Island, King Island, Macquarie island, Maria Island, Schouten Island
World Heritage listed properties	Cascades Female Factory, Port Arthur Historic Site, Coal Mines Historic Site, Tasmanian Wilderness
Beach	Wineglass Bay
Surfing	Shipstern Bluff, Park and Clifton Beaches, Eaglehawk Neck, the east coast from Orford to Bicheno, Bruny Island's Cloudy Bay, South Cape Bay, Tam O'Shanter, Mersey Mouth, Marrawah
Major festivals and events	Hobart Summer Festival, Targa Tasmania, Launceston Cup, Royal Hobart Agricultural Show, New Year's Eve celebrations with fireworks
Museums/art galleries	Tasmanian Museum and Art Gallery, (MONA) Museum of Old and New Art

* ABS: *2011 census*

Fact Sheet 5.8 – Northern Territory

Geography			
Land area	1.35 million sq. km. (10% larger than South Africa)		
Population *	236,000	Median age	31
Capital	Darwin		
Other major urban centres	Alice Springs, Palmerston		
Climate	Tropical climate with two seasons. Warm and sunny during the dry season and tropical cyclones and monsoon rains during the wet season.		

Cultural diversity *	Ancestry (Top 5)				
	Australian	English	Irish	Scottish	Aboriginal
	24%	19%	6%	5%	15%
	Born overseas				25%
	One or both parents born overseas				33%
	Only English spoken at home				63%
	2 or more languages spoken at home				24%

Economy		
Gross state product (GSP)	Total ($ billion)	As % of Australia's GDP
	18	1
Exports/imports	$6b / $4b	
Major trading partners	Japan, China, Singapore, Kuwait, Indonesia, Republic of Korea, Oman, International water (Timor Gap)	
Major exports	Natural gas, manganese ores and concentrates, zinc ores and concentrates, live animals, pearls and gems, iron ore and concentrates, refined petroleum, aluminium ore and concentrates, hides and skin, government services, travel	
Major imports	Natural gas, refined petroleum, pearls and gems, passenger vehicles, goods vehicles, trailers, semi-trailers and containers, civil engineering equipment and parts, specialised machinery and parts, measuring and analysing instruments	

Employment *		
Employment in the state	Total labour force	104,000
	Full-time	67%
	Part-time	20%
	Away from work	8%
	Unemployed	5%
Occupations	Professionals	20%
	Clerical/administrative	15%
	Managers	12%
	Technicians/trades	15%

	Community/personal services	13%
	Sales	7%
	Labourers	10%
	Machine operators/drivers	6%

Family income/Mortgage repayment/Rent *

Median weekly family income (couple with 2 income)	Couple with children	$2,475
	Couple without children	$2,300
Median monthly mortgage repayments		$2,058
Median weekly rent		$225

Housing/Motor vehicles *

House type	Detached	68%
	Semi-detached, terrace, townhouse	11%
	Flat, unit, apartment	17%
	Other	4%
Home ownership	No mortgage	16%
	With mortgage	31%
	Rented	49%
Number of motor vehicles/house	1	33%
	2	34%
	3 or more	17%

Education

Schooling	Compulsory schooling for all children aged between six and 15. Students are legally required to attend school until they are 16 years old.
TAFE	None
Universities	One

Health

Hospitals	5 public hospitals and 2 private hospitals

Transport

Public transport	The Territory faces challenges because of its vast area, low population density and the impact of the wet season. Three national highways provide the only sealed road links between the Territory and the rest of Australia. The Territory is linked to Queensland by the Barkly Highway, South Australia by the Stuart Highway and to Western Australia by the Victoria Highway. The railway provides mainly freight services between Adelaide and Darwin and between the mine sites and the Port of Darwin. The passenger service – the Ghan does a twice-weekly return trip between Adelaide and Darwin during the peak season. Darwin and Alice Springs have an excellent public transport

	system. Students, seniors and pension card- holders enjoy free bus travel.
Air access/major airports	Darwin, Alice Springs, Ayers Rock, Broome, Gove (Nhunbury)

Tourism	
Major tourism regions	Darwin, Lichfield, Kakadu, Katherine, Alice Spring, Uluru/Ayers Rock, Kings Canyon, Arnhem Land, Tenant Creek, Australia's North
Islands	887 islands Major islands - Groote Eylandt, Melville Island, The Tiwi Islands, Wessel Islands,
World Heritage listed properties	Kakadu National Park, Kakadu National Park
Surfing	Shattered Strand, Maria Island, Nightcliff Beach, Vashon Head, Smith Point, Cape Cockburn, Gningarg Point, Town Beach, Little Bondi, Turtle Beach, Point Alexander
Major festivals and events	Darwin Beercan Regatta, Camel Cup, Royal Darwin Show, Australasian Safari, Henley-on-Todd Regatta, Jabiru Wind Festival, New Year's Eve celebrations with fireworks.
Museums/art galleries	Museum and Art Gallery of the Northern Territory

* ABS: *2011 census*

Fact Sheet 5.9 – Sydney – Capital of NSW

Geography											
Land area		1,530 sq km		Population			4.39 million				

Temperature												
°c	J	F	M	A	M	J	J	A	S	O	N	D
Max	30	29	27	26	23	20	19	21	23	26	27	29
Min	16	17	15	12	9	7	6	7	9	11	14	15

Public Transport

For those working in the city public transport is the main means of transport. Almost 75 percent of commutes to the CBD are by public transport. According to the New South Wales Bureau of Transport, every weekday the population of Sydney's CBD grows from its 50,000 residents to around half a million people. The city has extensive rail, bus and ferry networks. The monorail runs in a circular route around the CBD.

Major Events

Archibald Prize, City to Surf, Crave Sydney International Food Festival, New Year's Eve, Royal Easter Show, Rugby League Grand Final, Sydney Comedy Festival, Sydney Festival, Sydney Film Festival, Sydney Mardi Gras, Sydney to Hobart Yacht Race, Vivid Sydney

City Attractions

Art Gallery of NSW, Australian Centre for Photography, Balmoral, Bare Island, Bondi Beach, Brett Whiteley Studio, Chinese Garden of Friendship, Circular Quay, Elizabeth Farm, Featherdale Wildlife Park, Government House, Hambledon Cottage, Hyde Park, Kings Cross, Manly, Martin Place, The Mint, Nutcote, Observatory Park, Ocean-world Manly, Parliament of NSW, Pitt Street Mall, Royal Australian Navy Heritage Centre, Royal Botanic Garden, Q Station, Queen Victoria Building, Sydney Aquarium, Sydney Fish Market, Sydney Harbour Bridge, Sydney Olympic Park, Sydney Opera House, State Theatre, Sydney Tower, Taronga Zoo, Vaucluse House, Watsons Bay, Wild Life Sydney, Army Museum, Australian Museum, Australian National Maritime Museum, Hyde Park Barracks Museum, Justice and Police Museum, La Perouse Museum, Museum of Contemporary Art, Museum of Sydney, Powerhouse Museum, The Rocks Discovery Museum, The Star, Susannah Place Museum, Sydney Tramway Museum,

Day Trips

Blue Mountain, Central Coast and Hawkesbury, Hunter Valley, Ku-ring-gai Chase, Southern coast, Southern Highlands

Fact Sheet 5.10 – Melbourne – Capital of Victoria

Geography											
Land area		1,812 sq km		Population				3.99 million			
Temperature											
°c	J	F	M	A	M	J	J	A	S	O	N	D
Max	31	30	29	24	20	18	16	18	20	23	27	28
Min	12	11	10	9	6	3	4	4	6	7	8	10

Public Transport

Melbourne has a good network of train, tram and buses. Melbourne tram 250km network is the longest tram network in the world.

Major Events

AFL Grand Final, Australian Open, Australian Grand Prix, Boxing Day Test Cricket, L'Oréal Melbourne Fashion Festival, Melbourne Cup, Melbourne Festival, Melbourne Food and Wine Festival, Melbourne Fringe Festival, Melbourne International Arts Festival, Melbourne International Comedy Festival, Melbourne International Film Festival, Melbourne International Flower and Garden Show, Melbourne International Jazz Festival, Melbourne Marathon, Melbourne Music Week, Melbourne Spring Fashion Week, Melbourne Writers Festival, Moomba, New Year's Eve, Royal Melbourne Show, Visions Australia's Carols by Candlelight

City Attractions

ANZ Banking Museum, Arts Centre Melbourne, Australian Centre for the Moving Image, Block Arcade, China Town, Chinese Museum, Crown Entertainment Complex, Degreaves Street, Docklands, Ethihad Stadium, Eureka Tower, Federation Square, Flagstaff Gardens, Government House, Ian Potter Centre: NGV Victoria, Immigration Museum, Kings Domain, Koorie Heritage Trust, Lygon Street, Melbourne Cricket Ground, Melbourne Aquarium, Melbourne Central, Melbourne Exhibition Centre, Melbourne Park, Old Melbourne Gaol, Melbourne Zoo, NGV International, Parliament of Victoria, QV Melbourne, Queen Victoria Market, Rippon Lea, Royal Arcade, Royal Botanic Gardens, Shrine of Remembrance, Sidney Myer Music Bowl, Southgate, St Kilda, State Library of Victoria

Day Trips

Bellarine Peninsula, The Dandenongs, Geelong, Queenscliff, Mornington Peninsula, Mount Macedon and Hanging Rock, Philip Island, Sovereign Hill, Spa Country, Yarra Valley and Healesville

Fact Sheet 5.11 – Brisbane – Capital of Queensland

Geography											
Land area		1,127 sq km			Population			2.07million			
Temperature											
°c	J	F	M	A	M	J	J	A	S	O	N	D
Max	30	31	29	27	25	23	22	24	26	27	28	30
Min	20	20	18	14	11	9	6	7	11	15	16	18

Public Transport

Public transport networks include trains, buses and ferries.

Major Events

Brisbane Comedy Festival, Brisbane Festival, Brisbane International Film Festival, Ekka (Royal Queensland Show, Queensland Winter Racing Carnival, Woodford Folk Festival

City Attractions

Alma Park Zoo, ANZAC Square, Brisbane Botanic gardens-Mount Coot-tha, Brisbane City Hall, City Botanic Gardens, Chinatown, Clem Jones Promenade, Conrad Treasury Casino, Deanery, Kangaroo Point, Miegunyah House Museum, ZMount Coot-tha Lookout, Museum of Brisbane, New Farm Park, Northern Beaches, Old Government House, Parliament House, Old Windmill, Queensland Art Gallery, Queensland Museum South Bank, Queensland Performing Arts Centre, Queensland Police Museum and Victoria Barrack Museum, Queen Street Mall, Roma Street Parkland, Queensland State Library, XXXX Brewery,

Day Trips

Bribie Island, Daisy Hill Street Forest, Gold Coast and its hinterland, Moreton Island, Mount Glorious, North Stradbroke Island and Toowoomba

Fact Sheet 5.12 – Perth – Capital of W Australia

Geography											
Land area		963 sq km			Population			1.73 million			
Temperature											
°c	J	F	M	A	M	J	J	A	S	O	N	D
Max	34	35	32	28	24	20	20	20	22	25	30	32
Min	17	17	15	12	9	6	4	6	8	10	12	14

Public Transport

Public transport consists of train and bus network. However, there is higher car use and less reliance on rail service.

Major Events

Blessings of the Fleet, Freemantle Festival, Fremantle Street Arts Festival, Freo's West Coast Blues 'n Roots Festival, St Patrick Parade and Concert

City Attractions

Adventure World, Aquarium of Western Australia, Art Gallery of Western Australia, Burswood Entertainment Complex, Claremont Museum, Hay Street Mall, Hillary Boat Harbour, Kings Park and Botanic Garden, Lake Monger, Murray Street Mall, Forrest Place, Northbridge, Parliament House, Perth Institute of Contemporary Arts, Perth Mint, Perth Zoo, Point Heathcote Reserve, Point Walter Reserve, Queens Gardens, Scitech Discovery Centre, Stirling Gardens, Subiaco, Supreme Court Gardens, Tranby House, Western Australian Museum, Wireless Hill Park

Day Trips

Darling Range, Rottnest Island Swan Valley, Yanchep National Park, Freemantle

Fact Sheet 5.13 – Adelaide – Capital of S Australia

Geography											
Land area		644 sq km			Population			1.22 million			

Temperature

°c	J	F	M	A	M	J	J	A	S	O	N	D
Max	34	33	31	26	21	18	17	20	21	24	31	29
Min	14	15	13	10	9	6	6	7	8	9	12	13

Public Transport

Public transport in Adelaide includes tram service (from Glenelg to the city), train network and guided bus service (Adelaide O-Bahn).

Major Events

Adelaide Festival of the Arts, Adelaide Fringe, Carnevale Adelaide, Clipsal 500 Adelaide, Credit Union Christmas Pageant, Feast Festival, Glendi Festival, Santos Tour Down Under, Schutzenfest, Tasting Australia, WOMADelaide.

City Attractions

Adelaide Central Market, Adelaide Zoo, Art Gallery of South Australia, Botanic Gardens of Adelaide, Carrick Hill, Haigh's Chocolates, Hindley Street, Historic Adelaide Gaol, Glenelg, JamFactory, National Wine Centre of Australia, Parliament House and Government House, Rundle Mall, South Australian Brewing Company, South Australian Maritime Museum, Penfolds MaGill Estate, South Australian Museum, State Library of South Australia.

Day Trips

Adelaide Hills, Barossa Valley, Clare Valley, Fleurieu Peninsula, Murraylands.

Fact Sheet 5.14 – Canberra – National Capital

Geography											
Land area		221 sq km			Population			367,000			

Temperature

°c	J	F	M	A	M	J	J	A	S	O	N	D
Max	32	32	30	25	18	16	13	17	20	24	29	30
Min	10	10	8	4	-3	-3	-3	-1	1	4	4	8

Public Transport

Buses and taxis are the only available public transport in Canberra.

Major Events

Fireside Festival, Floriade, National Autumn Balloon Spectacular, National Multicultural Festival, Summernats Car Festival, Wine, Roses and All That Jazz

City Attractions

Australian Institute of Sport, Australian National Botanic Gardens, Australian War Memorial, The Bird Walk, Black Mountain Tower, Blundell's Cottage, Calthorpes House, Canberra Reptile Museum, CSIRO Discovery, High Court of Australia, Mount Ainslie Lookout, Museum of Australian Democracy, National Archives of Australia, National Capital Exhibition, Ginninderra Village, National Dinosaur Museum, National Film and Sound Archive, National Gallery of Australia, National Museum of Australia, National Portrait Gallery, National Zoo and Aquarium, Parliament House, Questacon – The National Science and Technology Centre, Royal Australian Mint, Tuggeranong Homestead, Lake Tuggeranong

Day Trips

Canberra wine district, historic towns (Braidwood, Bungendore, Captains Flat, Goulburn, Yass, Young), Lanyon Homestead, Namadgi National Park, Tidbilla Nature Reserve

Fact Sheet 5.15 – Hobart – Capital of Tasmania

Geography											
Land area		68 sq km			Population			212,000			

Temperature

°c	J	F	M	A	M	J	J	A	S	O	N	D
Max	25	25	23	20	17	14	14	16	17	20	21	24
Min	10	10	8	7	5	3	2	3	4	6	7	9

Public Transport

Metro Tasmania, owned by the Tasmanian State Government, operates the public passenger bus services in the major urban areas of Hobart, Launceston and Burnie.

Major Events

Australian Wooden Boat Festival, Clarence Jazz Festival, The Fall Festival, Festival of Voices, Hobart Cup Day, MONA FOMA, Royal Hobart Regatta, Royal Hobart Show, Spring Community Festival, Sydney to Hobart and Melbourne to Hobart Yacht Races, Targa Tasmania, Taste of Tasmania, Ten Days on the Island.

City Attractions

Battery Point, Cascade Brewery, Cascade Female Factory Historic Site, Government House, Maritime Museum of Tasmania, Military Museum of Tasmania, MONA (Museum of Old and New Art), Mount Nelson Signal Station, Parliament House, Royal Tasmania Botanical Gardens, Salamanca Place, Sandy Bay Beach, Storm Bay Beaches, Tasmania Museum and Art Gallery, Tasmania Transport Museum, West Point Casino.

Day Trips

Derwent Valley, D'Entrecasteaux Channel, Richmond, Tasman Peninsula

Fact Sheet 5.16 – Darwin – Capital of Northern Territory

Geography											
Land area		124 sq km			Population			120,000			
Temperature											
°c	J	F	M	A	M	J	J	A	S	O	N	D
Max	33	33	34	34	33	32	33	33	34	35	34	34
Min	24	24	23	23	20	16	16	18	21	23	24	24

Public Transport

A network of buses serves Darwin and its suburbs and the satellite town of Palmerston.

Major Events

Darwin Beer Can Regatta, Darwin Cup Carnival, Festival of Darwin, Royal Darwin Show, Sky City Triple Crown V8 Supercars Championship, Telstra National Aboriginal and Torres Straits Islander Art Awards.

City Attractions

Aquascene, Australian Aviation Heritage Centre, Casuarina Coastal reserve, Charles Darwin National park, Crocodylus Park, Cullen Bay Marina, Deckchair Cinema, Fannie Bay Gaol Museum, George Brown Darwin Botanic Gardens, Government House, Holmes Jungle Nature Park, Leanyer Recreation Park, Mindil Beach Sunset Markets, Museum and Art Gallery of the Northern Territory, Parliament House, Skycity Darwin, Stokes Hill Wharf.

Day Trips

Litchfield National park, Territory Wildlife Park and Berring Springs Nature Park, Tiwi Islands.

6 Living in Australia

No worry mate!

Australians have enjoyed a very high *quality of life* and *standard of living* for many decades. International studies consistently rank Australia among the top in both respects.

Australian cities and towns are generally clean, well maintained and unpolluted, and most of Australia's capital cities receive high rankings as the world's most liveable cities.

Australia is an excellent place for family. Much of the way most Australians live their day-to-day life centres on family.

The average earning of the working person in Australia is 20% higher than the OECD average. This, together with a wide range of state-aided services for family, education and health, enables Australians to afford an enviable living standard.

Local government in Australia, which is the tier of government that is closest to the community, has evolved through decades of significant reforms. It has a good record in the delivery and maintenance of social and community services.

For new migrants settling in, adapting to Australian society is not difficult, for it would be rare that they would not, soon enough, meet some familiar Australian faces who are compatriots from the country they had left. Generally, Australians are friendly, helpful and civic-minded, and the state provides various services, such as language classes, to help new arrivals to settle in as quickly and smoothly as possible.

Standard of Living

Incomes

Australia's average household income of US$29,000 is 25% more than the OECD average of US$23,000 according to the 2012 OECD *Better Life Index*. The research recognised that "while money may not buy happiness, it is an important means to achieving higher living standards and thus greater well-being."

A national minimum wage system and the National Employment Standards (NES) serve as a framework and safety net for a living wage for the ordinary worker. The minimum wage is $16.37 *per hour* or $622.06 per 38-hour week. Casual employees covered by the national minimum wage receive a minimum loading of 24%, bringing their hourly wage to not less than $20.30. Employees are entitled to 4 weeks paid annual leave under NES.

The median starting annual salary for bachelor degree graduates aged below 25 ranges from $40,000 to $80,000, varying with the field of study (see Fact Sheet 6.1 on page 105).

The Australian Taxation Office reported that for tax-year 2010-11, 12.6 million individual taxpayers declared income of $662 billion and paid $133.1 billion in tax. The average taxable income was $51,342. Fact Sheet 6.2 on page 105 lists the average taxable income for 32 widely-held occupations.

Access to housing

The 2011 Population and Housing Census shows that 66% of Australians own their own homes and 76% of home units are detached houses.

Most housing properties are freehold. Sale and purchase is by private sale through a real estate agent or auction. For renting, a bond equal to one month's rent and one month's rent in advance is usually required. The bond is returned at the end of the tenancy, minus any repairs or other costs.

Table 6.1 gives median house prices and weekly rents in 2013 as an indication of prices and rentals in the 8 major capital cities

Table 6.1 Median House Prices and Median Rents, Jun 2013

	Median Price ($000)		Rent/week ($)	
	House	Unit	House	Unit
Sydney	690	492	500	470
Melbourne	553	412	360	360
Brisbane	440	347	390	360
Perth	584	387	490	425
Adelaide	435	280	340	280
Canberra	576	410	480	410
Hobart	318	252	310	250
Darwin	641	426	690	520
AUSTRALIA	564	427	-	-

Australian Property Monitor Rental Report, House Price Report Jun 2013

Normally, a buyer can get a loan of 80% of the property value and a maximum repayment period of up to 30 years. Depending on the lender's requirements, a buyer with mortgage insurance may be able to borrow up to 95% of the purchase price. As at July 2013, housing loan interest ranges from 5.25% to 6.75%. Stamp duty ranges from 4% to 6.75%.

The *annual* costs of home ownership include building insurance premium of around $1,000 depending on replacement value, etc, and council rates of $1,500. Operating costs, which also apply to renting, include $4,000 for utilities (gas, electricity and water) and $1,000 for phone and internet expense.

Access to education

Australia has an all-inclusive education system that is aimed at providing education opportunity for all. There are also schools or classes catering to the gifted or talented, and children with special needs or disabilities. Distance education programs are available to students living in remote and isolated areas and those unable to attend school physically.

Schooling runs for 13 years commencing with a preparatory or kindergarten year and then Years 1-12 of school. It is compulsory for children between 6 and 15 years of age.

Government schools are free for children of citizens and residents. However, schools do request parents for voluntary contribution of between $100 to $400 for primary and $300 to $800 for secondary students per annum. Participation in school camps, excursions and other activities is charged separately.

Almost 60% of Australia's working age residents have a post-school education. Fifty percent of school leavers choose vocational education and training. It has many advantages, including lower costs compared to undergraduate studies, acquiring specific skills for industry and good employment prospects

For undergraduate studies, citizens and permanent residents are charged a "student contribution" in lieu of fees. Depending on the course of study, the contribution is 2013 is $5,868, $8,363 or $9,792 for 2013. Citizens may defer their payment by participating in the Higher Education Loan Program (HELP) and repay the interest-free loan when they are working and when their annual income is above the threshold level (at $51,309 for 2013-14). University entry is on merit, i.e. scores achieved in secondary school examinations.

Chapter 8 *Education System* covers this topic in more detail.

Access to healthcare

Australian life expectancy, at 84 years for females and 79 years for male, ranks third in the world. The contributing factors include lifestyle, environmental care, food safety, socioeconomic factors, occupational health, and, very critically, a workable public health system with accessibility based on need and not the ability to pay.

All Australian citizens and permanent residents (unless specially excluded) have access to country-wide free or low-cost medical, optometric and public hospital care as shown in Table 6.2 below.

Table 6.2 Medicare Benefits

Public hospital services	Free in-patient, out-patient and emergency, as public patient
	75% of Medicare schedule fees for services by doctor, as private patient
Consulting fees (partly or fully free)	General practitioners, specialists, some surgical procedures by dentists, Cleft Lips and Palate scheme,, Allied health services as part of Chronic Disease Management, surgical and therapeutic procedures of doctors
Cost of medicine (part subsidised	Medicines covered by Pharmaceutical Scheme

About half of the population supplement their public health cover with private health insurance. Private health insurance premiums vary between insurers and coverage, e.g. whether only hospital cover, or including cover for extras (physiotherapy, optical, dental, podiatry, osteopathy, chiropractic, acupuncture), or combined cover. Annual premium ranges from $800 to $2,800 for single, $2,500 to $4,500 for couples and $2,500 to $4,500 for family.

Chapter 10 *Healthcare System* covers healthcare in greater detail.

Access to childcare

Childcare in Australia includes both *formal* care (before and after school care, long day care and occasional care) and *informal* care (care by relatives, friends, neighbours, nannies or babysitters). The *formal* childcare industry is strictly regulated and operators are subjected to audit and quality accreditation rules.

About half of all children aged below 12 attend *formal* childcare provided by not-for-profit community service providers and an increasing number of private providers (this has also contributed greatly to freeing parents to join the labour force). The usual cost of formal childcare per child is about $90 per day for the majority of children (with no special needs) after government subsidy.

Playgroups are regular gatherings for parents and caregivers to bring babies or toddlers to meet other children and develop their social skills. Playgroups are generally free or incur a small fee.
Most children attend kindergarten one to two years before they begin primary schooling. There is a range of kindergarten options, commonly for 15 hours a week. Fees vary from free or low cost to charges of $10,000 a year. Kindergarten operators receive funding from the government.

Access to transport

Intra-city public transport

In the capital cities, transport networks are well developed and maintained. In Sydney and Melbourne, where 90% of residents working in the city live away from the inner city, trains and buses (plus trams in Melbourne) are the main forms of public transport. Perth and Canberra are the two cities that rely much less on mass public transport.

Public transport fares vary among cities and towns. For example, in Melbourne, the annual public transport fare (full fare) costs $1,397.50 for zone 1 (CBD and inner city suburbs) and $2,158 for zones 1 & 2 (outer suburbs of metropolitan Melbourne). The Student Pass costs $489 for a year's travel. Seniors age ≥60 pay $3.80 a day on weekdays and $3.50 on public holidays (but travel for free on weekends) for unlimited travel within metropolitan Melbourne. Children aged 3 years and under travel for free on Victorian public transport. Concession fares apply to pensioners and other social security recipients.

Taxi fares also vary among the capital cities. A 10km travel will cost $25 in Sydney, Brisbane and Canberra and $20 in Melbourne, Adelaide and Darwin.

Private car ownership

Australia has the second highest level of car ownership in the world. The 2011 census shows that 72% of the households have at least one car and 17% of the households have three cars or more.

Car ownership is very affordable. For example, one can drive away a Mitsubishi Mirage ES for $12,990 or a Hyundai i20 for $13,990, not counting cash-back offers during promotion periods. For a fresh graduate teacher earning an *after-tax* annual wage of $47,000, this would amount to just 3 months' after-tax income for a Mitsubishi Mirage ES or 3.3 months' after-tax income for the Hyundai i20. Fact Sheet 6.3 on page 106 lists the 10 most popular cars and the 10 best-selling SUVs in 2012.

Throughout the country, fuel price per litre at the pump is around $1.40 for petrol, $1.45 for diesel and $0.75 for LPG, but subject to the price of crude and the A$/$US exchange rate. For travelling 2,000 kilometres a month at 7 litres per 100 kilometres, the petrol cost would be $196 a month.

Car insurance premium varies according to the car model, driver experience, claim history and location of residence. For example, the annual premium for comprehensive cover of a Toyota Corolla valued at $23,000 would be around $700.

Annual car registration fee varies among the states. For example, in Victoria, it is $712.10 from 1 July 2013.

Intra-state and inter-state rail services

Intra-state rail transport providers include V/Line (regional trains and buses in Victoria), Country LinkRailCorp (New South Wales), TravelTrain/South-East-Queensland (Queensland) and Transwa (trains and buses in Western Australia).

Inter-state rail transport providers include Indian Pacific (Sydney-Adelaide-Perth), The Ghan (Adelaide-Alice Springs-Darwin), The Overland (Melbourne-Adelaide) and CountryLink (Brisbane-Canberra-Sydney-Melbourne).

Air transport

Besides the airports in the capital cities, there are more than 300 other paved airports in Australia. Qantas operates flights to 58 domestic destinations and Virgin Australia flies to 38 domestic destinations. Several regional airlines cater to regional and remote locations.

Food quality and cost

Australia has an immense assortment of home-grown foods and ingredients that cater to its diverse ethnic communities as well as export markets. It produces top quality beef, mutton, chicken and pork, making it the second largest exporter of beef and the third largest exporter of dairy products in the world. A wide variety of temperate and tropical fruits and vegetables are home-grown. Marine produce from its fishing zones (the third biggest in the world) and commercial marine farms have graced dining tables at home and abroad. Australian fine wine is renowned in more than 100 countries around the world.

The great diversity of Australian food produce is exceeded by its acknowledged reputation for their quality and safety, assured through uncompromising safety regulations on food production, preparation and handling.

The prices of many locally-produced foods *at the supermarket* or *market* are very affordable relative to incomes. Affordable prices enable Australian residents to enjoy a varied and healthy diet of a very high standard.

Fact Sheet 6.4 on pages 107 to 108 gives an indicative price guide for the widely consumed meats, fruits, vegetables and other items. The prices shown are for Australian produce only and exclude imported items. Note that as the given prices are as at June 2013 (winter), some of the non-winter fruits and vegetables are priced much higher than when they are in season.

Example of a household budget

Table 6.3 shows a family budget based on the information below:

Michael Tan and Angelina are new migrants. They live with their two children, age 9 and 6, in Ferntree Gully in outer Melbourne. Michael age 38 works as a middle level executive while Angelina age 36 works as a clerical officer.

Both children are in school care before and after school hours. The family entertain friends mostly at home and spend their holidays exploring Melbourne and country Victoria.

Table 6.3 Michael and Angelina Tan – Annual Household Budget

		Michael	Angelina
INCOME	Gross wages	$62,000	$42,000
	After tax wages	51,280	37,466
	Household income after tax		$88,746
EXPENSES			
House	Mortgage repayment ($300,000 loan for 25 years)		23,481
	House insurance		1,000
	Council rates		1,200
Education	Fees, books, uniforms, shoes, excursions etc. for two children		4,000
Schoolcare	Before-and-after-school care		4,000
Food and groceries	Food, groceries, toiletries, etc. at $300/week		15,600
Health insurance	Private hospital cover		3,224
Car (one)	Registration fee		712
	Insurance		600
	Servicing		400
	Petrol		2,400
Public transport	Stephen's Zone 1+2 train ticket		2,158
Clothing	Clothes, shoes, other apparel		4,000
Recreation, socialising	Holidays		3,000
	Dining out/takeaway		3,000
	Shows		600
	Gifts		1,200
Total expenses and mortgage repayments			70,575
Surplus available for saving			18,171

Lifestyle, Variety and Choice

Australia has built a socio-economic and work-life environment as well as the facilities that allow a flexible degree of choice between a relatively relaxed lifestyle and a more work-orientated or faster-paced lifestyle if one so prefers.

Time for leisure or family

Australian society places a high value on leisure time and, even more so, on time for the family. This is reflected in public policies that regulate or influence working life.

Under the National Employment Standards (NES), a full-time employee is entitled to:

- A workweek of a maximum 38 hours not including reasonable additional hours.
- Four weeks of paid-leave annually
- Paid-day off on public holidays

There are around 11 public holidays in a year, with the actual number varying with the state or territory.

Certain flexible working arrangements are not unusual in the Australian workplace. These include flexible working hours, work from home, job-share and the '9 days fortnight' option. The latter is a common practice in the public sector; under this arrangement, the employee works extra time each day and takes a shorter lunch break to clock the same total hours required for the normal 10-day fortnight. Working from home for part of the week is a popular arrangement with information technology companies.

Many working parents take advantage of flexible working hours to tailor their work hours to fit with school-hours (generally 9am to 3:30pm) or choose to work part-time. Weekends are work-free except for certain public and retail services.

Shopping

As with large modern cities elsewhere, Australia's capital cities abound with a variety of shopping malls, retail precincts, discount centres, factory outlets and farmer markets.

On weekdays, most shops open from 9.00am to 5.30pm but many operate extended hours until 8.00pm or 9.00pm on Thursdays and Fridays. Most retail outlets are open on the weekend and many supermarkets, fast-food stores and petrol stations are open 24/7.

Dining and merry-making

All the capital cities have inner-city areas that are lively scenes for cafés, bars, sophisticated drinking spots and restaurants. Dining in Melbourne reflects its vibrant cosmopolitan mix – Chinatown for Chinese and Asian cuisines, Carlton for Italian, Fitzroy for Spanish, Brunswick for Lebanese, and Richmond for Vietnamese. The 500,000 square-metre Crown Entertainment Complex has one of the largest casinos in the Southern Hemisphere. It has fantastic restaurants and other entertainment facilities.

Some restaurants allow 'BYO' (bring your own) wine. Australian wine is renowned and inexpensive. There are about 60 wine growing regions in the country, with many of them within short driving distances from the capital cities or regional centres. In addition to cellar-door wine tasting and sales, many vineyards also offer casual and formal dining facilities with breathtaking picturesque views.

The diversity of cultures among Australia's population offers to the resident or visitor cuisines from all corners of the world. Creative or exotic culinary influences are regularly introduced by popular cooking and lifestyle television series such as *Food Lovers' Guide to Australia, The Cook and the Chef, Food Safari, Master Chefs, Luke Nguyen's Memories of Vietnam, Island Feast with Peter Kuruvita* and *Poh's Kitchen*. Sydney's Seafood Market, Melbourne's Queen Victoria Market and Adelaide's Central Market with their range of readily available high quality fresh food and ingredients would delight the foodie who enjoys cosmopolitan cooking for dining at home with friends.

Sports and outdoor activities

Australia has the natural assets - rugged terrain (in some areas), national parks, state parks, a long coastline, lakes and rivers – that offer incredible choices for *personal outdoor activity*, such as biking, hiking walking, jogging, picnicking, camping, fishing, canoeing, rafting, sailing, surfing, swimming, snorkelling, mountain-biking, four-wheel driving, rock-climbing, abseiling, skiing and more. It is not surprising to find that, according to *ABS Survey of Sports and Physical Recreation 2011-12*, 65% of Australians aged 15 and older engage in physical activity for recreation, exercise or sports.

The popular *spectator sports* are Australian-rules football, rugby, cricket, soccer, basketball and hockey. Motorsports events include, among many, Formula 1 Australian Grand Prix, Superbike World Championship, Australasian Safari and Australian Motorcycle Grand Prix

For many, *horse racing* is a popular weekend outing. Australian Spring Racing Carnival is a three-month-long world-class festival, with lots of horse racing and social events. It culminates with the Melbourne Cup as literally "the race that stops a nation".

Other leisure activities

For every Australian living in the inner city or the suburbs, *parks and gardens* are never far away. Even the large national and state parks are within short driving distances of the capital cities and regional centres. Public parks and gardens are always very well maintained, as they cater for many leisure activities.

Local community facilities such as parks, recreational centres and libraries offer a wide range of activities for people of all ages. The local council plays a major role in the provision and maintenance of these facilities.

Museums and art galleries, despite Australia's short history, have a good range of collections and exhibits that will not disappoint the visitor, including uniquely Australian indigenous art. Many of the museums and galleries hold activities for group or school visits. Some run programs for school children during the holidays.

For patrons of *the performing arts*, there are regular presentations of theatre, concerts, dance and musicals by both international and local artistes and producers.

Holidaying

For holiday makers, there are lots of options – from adventure into Australia's interiors, or a new experience at wakeboarding atop monster waves in the open sea, or relaxing on any one of its

11,000 sun-drenched beaches along 37,000 km of coastline, or quiet seclusion deep inside any of more than 500 national parks, or an eye-opening exploration of your choices of 27 UNESCO World Heritage sites and/or natural wonders.

Despite Australia's vast size, good networks of road, rail, air and sea transport combine to overcome any barriers posed by distance or terrain. Travelling options include car, campervan, bus, train, flying, sailing, cruise-ship, houseboat, bicycling and hiking.

Depending on your itinerary and budget, accommodation ranges from luxury resorts to camping under the stars. In between these extremes are luxury or standard hotels, boutique hotels, motels, serviced apartments, self-serviced apartments, bed and breakfast, country pubs, backpacker hostels and caravan parks.

Safety and Security

Crimes of felony

The ordinary person living in cities, towns and their suburbs can feel very safe from street crimes, break-ins and organised criminal threats. Prevention and law enforcement by the police and other authorities in respect of violent crime is competent and reliable. Table 6.4 shows the incidence of felonies published by Australian Institute of Criminology and the Australian Bureau of Statistics:

Table 6.4 Felonies per 100,000 persons, 2011			
Assault *	766	Murder`	1
Sexual assault	76	Unlawful entry with intent	965
Robbery	60	Motor vehicle theft	245
Kidnap/abduction	3	Other theft	2,155

* 2010 figures as 2011 figures for 3 states were not available

Natural disasters

Australia experiences bushfires, floods, droughts, severe storms such as cyclones and typhoons, minor earthquakes and landslides. New South Wales, Australian Capital Territory, Victoria, South Australia and Western Australia are the most vulnerable to bushfires during the "bushfire season". Severe drought occurs about once in every 18 years and El Niño effects (that may cause extremes of flood and drought) occur every two to seven years. Cyclones and floods affect parts of Northern Territory, Western Australia, New South Wales, Victoria and Queensland.

Australia has long-established and continually-improved risk and emergency management systems and recovery programs to deal with natural disasters. These measures have successfully helped to avoid extensive casualties.

To combat severe drought, it has also established 6 desalination plants as alternative sources of potable water. Two are in Western Australia and one each in New South Wales, Queensland, South Australia and Victoria. The plant in Victoria has not started commercial production as recent rainfall volume precludes the need.

Factsheets

Fact Sheet 6.1 Median Starting Salaries of Bachelor Degree Graduates 2011

	$'000		$'000
Accounting	47.0	Law	51.0
Agricultural Science	45.6	Mathematics	55.0
Architecture and Building	46.0	Medicine	58.5
Art and Design	40.0	Optometry	70.0
Biological Science	47.0	Paramedical Studies	50.0
Computer Science	51.0	Pharmacy	37.0
Dentistry	80.0	Physical Sciences	50.0
Earth Sciences	65.0	Psychology	47.4
Economics, Business	47.0	Social Sciences	43.0
Education	55.0	Social Work	50.0
Engineering	60.0	Veterinary Science	45.0
Humanities	44.0		

Source: Graduate Careers Australia

Fact Sheet 6.2 Annual Taxable Income-Selected Occupations 2010-11

	$'000		$'000
Accountants	86	Mining engineers	157
Accounting clerk	52	Support/ personal care workers	40
Anaesthetists	302	Optometrists	79
Apprentice auto mechanic	36	Other medical practitioners	155
Apprentice electrician	48	Pharmacists	78
Automotive electricians	66	Police	76
Bus and coach drivers	54	Primary school teachers	60
Child carers	39	Graphic/Web Designers,	55
Delivery drivers	39	Registered nurses	56
Early childhood teachers	50	Recycling/rubbish collectors	55
Electrical engineers	98	Secondary school teachers	66
Electronic engineers	85	Solicitors	113
Electricians	78	Surgeons	350
Enrolled mothercraft nurses	43	Train and tram drivers	89
ICT support/ test engineers	72	University lecturer/ tutors	89
Engineering process workers	56	Veterinary nurses	39

Source: Australian Taxation Office 2012 Report

Fact Sheet 6.3 Australia – The 10 Best-Selling Cars and SUVs 2012

Model	Drive-away Price	
	Base Model	Top of the Range
Top 10 cars		
Mazda 3	20,490	32,790
Toyota Corolla	21,490	35,675
Holden Commodore	38,870	53,290
Holden Cruze	20,490	26,990
Hyundai i30	22,990	31,890
Toyota Camry	29,990	45,357
Toyota Yaris	15,990	25,169
Ford Focus	19,990	27,490
Mazda 2	15,990	23,150
Volkswagen Golf	25,157	57,905
Top 10 SUVs		
Holden Captiva	25,990	39,990
Toyota Prado	55,990	75,803
Nissan X-Trail	31,660	38,564
Mazda CX-5	31,396	52,964
Toyota RAV-4	28,490	50,607
Ford Territory	38,490	49,990
Toyota Kluger	39,990	72,123
Nissan Dualis	34,444	42,428
Subaru Forester	34,946	55,034
Hyundai ix35	26,990	40,490

Note: Drive-away price (June 2013) is indicative only

Fact Sheet 6.4 Indicative Price Guide – Food

(Based on normal price, not Weekly special or Daily Value promotions)

Beef – $/kg

Diced – slow cook	9.30	Mince - regular	8.00
Blade roast	9.00	Rib roast	22.00
Corned silverside	6.00	Osso Bucco	11.50
Chuck	8.25	Gravy Beef	9.00
Fillet Steak	40.00	Oyster Blade	11.50
Porterhouse Steak	24.00	Scotch Fillet	28.40
Rib steak bone	23.00	T-bone	18.00
Blade steak boneless	11.50	Rump steak	13.50
Sausages	5.50	Veal mince	13.00
Veal Osso Bucco	13.00	Veal Steak Scallopini	24.00

Chicken - $/kg

Breast skinless	9.50	Drumstick	7.30
Thigh fillets	9.50	Thigh fillets skinless	14.90
Chicken wings	5.40	Sausages	9.25

Lamb - $/kg

Forequarter chops	9.00	Leg chops	18.00
Midloin chops	17.00	Cutlets	25.00
Diced	19.00		

Pork - $/kg

Forequarter chops	10.50	Porkloin cutlets	15.00
Midloin chops	18.00	Diced	17.00
Rashers	11.00	Leg roast	10.50
Porkloin roast boneless	11.00	Shoulder roast	7.00
Loin Medallion Steak	23.00	Scotch Fillet Steak	13.00
Sausages	7.30		

Seafood

Barrumundi Fillets	38.00	Ling Fillets	32.00
Flathead Fillets	44.00	Fresh Black Mussels	9.50
Tasmanian Atlantic Salmon	27.00	Fresh Snapper Crimson Fillets	33.00
Snapper Saddletail Fillets	35.00	Banana Prawns	18.00
King Prawns	27.00		

Fruits: - $/kg

Pink Lady Apples	2.80	Granny Smith Apples	3.90
Avocado (each)	2.50	Banana	2.90
Cherries	13.00	Grapefruits	4.00
Crimson seedless grapes	4.00	Red Globe Grapes	4.00
Green Kiwi Fruits	3.00	Lemon	4.00
Imperial Mandarin	4.00	Water Melon	0.70
Navel Orange	1.33	Red papaya	4.00

Passion Fruit (each)	0.50	Packham Pears	2.28

Vegetables- $/kg

Asparagus (bunch)	3.00	Round beans	6.00
Beetroot	4.00	Broccoli	4.00
Brussel Sprouts (bunch)	8.00	Buk choy baby	2.00
Cabbage Savoy (whole)	5.00	Chinese cabbage (whole)	3.00
Capsicum green	7.00	Capsicum red	10.00
Carrots	2.00	Cauliflower (whole)	2.00
Red chillies	20.00	Celery (bunch)	3.00
Lebanese cucumber	5.00	Choy sum	2.00
Continental cucumber	1.50	Eggplant	6.00
Galingale	10.00	Garlic (Australian)	19.00
Fennel (bunch)	2.00	Ginger	25.00
Leek (bunch)	1.25	Lettuce iceberg (bunch)	2.50
Lettuce butter (bunch)	2.00	Mushrooms cup	11.00
Onions brown	2.00	Onions red	2.40
Potatoes Golden Delight	2.50	Snow peas	13.00
Potatoes Red Delight	1.50	Sweet potatoes	3.00
Pumpkin Kent cut	0.96	Pumpkin Butternut	2.50
Spinach silverbeet (bunch)	2.00	Spring onion	1.80
Gourmet tomatoes	3.90	English spinach (bunch)	3.00
Zucchini	5.00	Roma tomatoes	5.00

Breakfast and other food

Select Mixed Grain Toast (700g)	2.49	Tip Top Original (700g)	4.30
Tip Top Raisin Toast (520g)	4.99	Helgas Traditional (750g)	5.25
Kelloggs Corkflakes (380g)	3.75	Coco Pops (375g box)	5.26
Kelloggs Just Right (460g box)	4.49	Select Finger Biscuits (100g)	2.14
Arnotts Mint Chocolate Biscuits	3.50	Cadbury Chocolate (220g)	4.93
Australian Fresh Juice (2 litres)	6.93	Daily Juice (2 litres0	4.99
Nescafe Blend 43 (150g)	9.23	Bushells Coffee (250g)	5.54
Milo (450g)	6.22	Milo (200g)	3.87
A2 Full Cream Milk (1 litre)	2.99	Woolworth Milk (2 litre)	2.00
Twining Tea Bags (50s)	6.65	Coca Cola (2 ltr bottle)	4.25
Devondale Butter (250g)	2.69	Lurpak Butter (250g)	5.36
Kraft Peanut Butter (375g)	4.83	Kraft Peanut Butter (200g)	3.21
Tableland Margarine (500g)	2.14	MeadowLea (250g)	2.15
Select Free Range Eggs (12)	4.49	Peace Farm Cage Eggs (12)	3.99

7 Working in Australia
A livelihood as good as you wish

Australia's social policies, apart from its economic performance, have greatly affected its employment scene. According to the 2012 OECD Better Life Index, its employment rate was above 73% for persons aged 15 to 64 holding a paid job, compared to the OECD average of 66%; and Australians work 1,693 hours a year, against 1,776 hours for most people in OECD countries.

Close to 30% of the workforce can afford to work part-time, due in part to the National Employment Standards and a minimum wage system that serve as the framework for a living wage and a safety net. Another 6% are "away from work" – including those taking extended unpaid absence from work for family reasons, and still keep the job. Other labour laws ensure safe work environments.

Wage levels are also high – the OECD reported average household net adjustable income of US$29,000 in 2011 for Australia is 25% more than the OECD average; and Australia's 2011 population census showed a median wage of A$30,004 per person. Many occupations including doctors, accountants, and ICT specialists earn higher than in the United Kingdom.

As with other economies, different occupations are in greater or lesser demand, in the short-term as well as the longer term, and skilled migration intake is a principal means of addressing labour shortage. Socially, class distinction by occupational status is given short shrift by a literate and socially aware Australian public.

The Employment Market

Australia had a workforce of 10.7 million in 2011, as reported in the latest Census of Population and Housing. Of this, 59.7% worked fulltime, 28.7% part-time, 5.9% were away from work and 5.6% were not employed.

The workforce is concentrated in the large capital cities, as Australia is highly urbanised. As shown in Table 7.1 below, the proportion of part-time employment is high, averaging 28.7% in the five largest cities as well as nationally. This reflects several factors, such as lifestyle and living-wage levels.

Table 7.1 Employment by Capital Cities and States 2011

City/State	Work Force (000)	Employment Profile (%)			
		Full Time	Part Time	Away From Work	Not Employed
Sydney	2,189	62.1	26.7	5.5	5.7
Melbourne	2,039	60.1	28.8	5.6	5.5
Brisbane	1,073	61.0	27.6	5.5	5.9
Perth	900	60.2	28.9	6.1	4.8
Adelaide	612	56.9	31.6	5.7	5.8
Canberra	202	65.0	25.1	6.3	3.6
Hobart	103	55.1	33.3	5.9	5.7
Darwin	65	69.4	19.6	7.4	3.6
Rest of New South Wales	1,141	56.7	31.0	6.2	6.1
Rest of Victoria	633	56.2	32.2	6.5	5.2
Rest of Queensland	1,093	59.1	28.7	6.0	6.2
Rest of Western Australia	248	62.4	25.6	7.6	4.4
Rest of South Australia	171	56.2	31.6	6.7	5.4
Rest of Tasmania	129	54.0	32.6	6.5	6.8
Rest of Northern Territory	38	62.7	21.0	8.1	8.0
TOTAL Australia	10,658	59.7	28.7	5.9	5.6

Employment by Sector

Public sector

The government – at federal, state and local levels - employed 1.9 million persons in 2011-12, or about 18% of the workforce as shown in Table 7.2.

Table 7.2 Employment (in '000) in Public Sector 2011-12

	Fed	State	Local	Total
New South Wales	55	450	60	565
Victoria	45	330	51	426
Queensland	31	303	40	374
Western Australia	15	113	11	139
South Australia	12	165	23	200
Aust Capital Territory	82	25	0	107
Tasmania	5	39	4	48
Northern Territory	5	25	3	33
TOTAL Australia	250	1,450	192	1,892

Source: Australian Bureau of Statistics

In many regional areas, the public sector is a major employer. In cities like Canberra and Darwin, the public sector is a very significant employer. In education, 64% of the 259,000 school teaching staff in 2012 was employed in government schools.

Private sector

In 2011, there were 2 million private businesses in Australia, of which 96% were small businesses employing less than 20 staff. Sixty-one percent do not employ staff. Skilled technicians, handymen and professionals can generally earn a good income as self-employed one-person businesses with the attendant tax-deductible expenses.

Private businesses, including the self-employed, provide jobs for more than two-thirds of the workforce.

Not-for-profit sector

The Not-for-Profit (NFP) sector is increasingly a significant employer. NPF organisations include those engaged in sports and physical recreation, education and training, community and welfare services, religious groups, charities, trade and industrial associations, employer associations, professional associations and trade unions.

This sector comprises more than 600,000 organisations, of which 10% are considered economically significant. In 2007, the NFP sector contributed $43 billion to Australia's economy and employed 890,000 persons or nearly 9% of the workforce.

Many establishments in this sector work with government to augment the organisation, reach and delivery of a wide range of services, such as in social welfare, education, employment, housing, healthcare, care of the aged, disability care, migrant assistance and settlement, the arts, sports, the environment, and emergency response.

Employment by Industry

The top three industries by employment number are healthcare and social assistance, retail trade, and construction, which together accounted for one-third of total employment; next are manufacturing, professional and technical services, and education and training; and two out of three persons employed worked in these six industries as shown in Table 7.3.

Table 7.3 Employment by Industry 2011

	%		%
Health care/ social assistance	12	Other services	4
Retail trade	11	Wholesale trade	4
Construction	9	Mining	2
Manufacturing	8	Administrative + support	3
Professional, scientific and technical services	8	Agriculture, forestry and fishing	3
Education and training	8	Information/media/telecom.	2
Accommodation and food	7	Arts and recreation	2
Public administration/safety	6	Rental/hiring/real estate	2
Transport/postal/warehousing	5	Electricity/gas/water/waste	1
Financial and insurance	4		
Total			100

Source: ABS Census of Population and Housing Census 2011

Employment by Occupation

Table 7.4 shows employment by occupation.

Table 7.4 Employed Persons Aged ≥15 by Occupation 2011

Occupation	%
Professionals	22
Managers	13
Clerical and administrative workers	15
Technicians and trade workers	14
Sales workers	10
Community/personal service workers	10
Labourers	10
Machinery operators and drivers	6
Total	100

Source: ABS Census of Population and Housing Census 2011

Employment Safety Net

National Employment Standards

The NES regulates maximum work hours, leave entitlement, flexible working arrangements, notice of termination, and redundancy pay. Together with "modern" awards (labour agreements), it serves as the safety net for employees who are covered by the national workplace relations system. Factsheet 7.1 on page 124 covers the NES in greater detail.

Minimum Wage

The national minimum wage applies to employees who are not otherwise covered by award or agreement. The Fair Work Commission annually reviews the minimum wages with any changes to take effect from 1 July of each year. Table 7.5 lists the minimum wage levels for 2013.

Table 7.5 Minimum Wages (per hour) 2013		
Adults	≥21	16.37
Juniors	<16	6.03
	16	7.74
	17	9.46
	18	11.18
	19	13.51
	20	16.00
Apprentices	Year 1	10.49
	Year 2	12.39
	Year 3	15.25
	Year 4	18.11
Trainees	At least the amount from Schedule E – National Training Wage in the Miscellaneous Award 2010	
Employees with disability	There are 2 special national minimum wages for employees with disability.	

The full-time minimum wage from 1 July 2013 for adults is $16.37 per hour, plus an extra 24% for casuals making it $20.30 per hour. Table 7.5 shows the minimum wages for 2013.

Superannuation

From 1 July 2013, employers must contribute a minimum of 9.25% of an employee's salaries and wages up to a 'maximum contribution-base' into a superannuation fund. The rate will increase to 12% by 2019-20.

Employment Incomes

High incomes

Australia's average household net adjustable income of US$29,000 is 25% higher than the OECD average of US$23,000, according to the 2012 OECD *Better Life Index* study. Allowing for cost of living differences, it is still much higher than the OECD average. Even more significantly, median incomes are also high, as seen in the statistics from the 2011 Population Census. Shown in Table 7.6.

Table 7.6 Median Incomes ($) by Capital Cities and States, 2011

	Median Annual Incomes ('000) Persons Aged ≥15		
	Personal	Family	Household
Sydney	32.2	87.5	75.2
Melbourne	30.7	81.9	69.3
Brisbane	32.9	83.9	72.2
Perth	34.8	92.6	75.8
Adelaide	28.8	72.9	57.5
Canberra	47.7	118.4	99.8
Hobart	28.9	70.7	55.4
Darwin	46.6	106.1	93.9

Rest of New South Wales	25.4	63.2	49.9
Rest of Victoria	25.6	62.4	49.1
Rest of Queensland	28.7	69.0	57.5
Rest of Western Australia	33.3	77.7	65.1
Rest of South Australia	24.8	57.5	45.8
Rest of Tasmania	23.8	57.2	45.5
Rest of Northern Territory	24.8	64.9	75.4
AUSTRALIA	30.0	77.0	64.1

Taxable incomes

The Australian Taxation Office reported that for tax-year 2010-11, 12.6 million individual taxpayers declared income of 662 billion and paid 133.1 billion in tax. The top 10 earners in 2011 were surgeons, anaesthetists, internal medicine specialists, financial dealers, judicial and legal professionals, psychiatrists, chief executives, mining engineers and dental practitioners.

Factsheet 7.2 on pages 125 to 128 shows the average taxable incomes for over 200 occupations.

Public sector salaries

The public sector offers very competitive salaries and other employment terms and conditions, including many structured programs for trainees and graduates to gain knowledge, skills and experience. The work-life balance arrangements and initiatives widely adopted in the sector have made working in public service a very attractive option.

Table 7.7 gives an indication of the salary for other jobs in the Victorian public sector. The salary does not include employer's superannuation contribution, generally at 9%.

Table 7.7 Victorian Public Service Annual Salaries Effective 1/1 2013

	Grade	Value Range	Salary Ranges ($) Min	Salary Ranges ($) Max
Victorian Public Service Officer	1	1.1	38,895	41,289
	2	2.1	42,622	48,678
	2	2.2	49,542	54,734
	3	3.1	55,931	61,923
	3	3.2	63120	67,912
	4	4.1	69,242	78,563
Senior Officer	5	5.1	79,894	88,279
	5	5.2	88,280	96,666
	6	6.1	97,996	114,568
	6	6.2	114,569	131,139
Senior Technical Specialist	7	7.1	133,104	149.077
	7	7.2	149,080	165,051
	7	7.3	165,051	181,023

	Grade	Salary Range ($) Min	Salary Range ($) Max
Executive Level	EQ3	141,667	196,752
	EQ2	176,389	281,036
	EQ1	256,334	373,487

Executive Level positions – heads of department and agencies, departmental Deputy Secretaries and Project Directors – are employed on fixed-term contract for up to 5 years. Their total remuneration includes the salary component shown above, superannuation contribution by the state government and performance bonuses.

Employment in the Federal public service is generally open only to citizens. However, for permanent jobs in state and local government, one has to be an Australian citizen or permanent resident.

Table 7.8 gives an indication of salary in Victorian government schools. As education is a state matter, salary scales vary from state to state.

Table 7.8 Annual Salary ('000) in Victorian Government Schools

Job Title	Annual Salary
Graduate Teacher	57-59
Classroom Teacher - Accomplished	62-69
Classroom Teacher - Expert	71-84
Lead Teacher	86-92
Assistant Principal Level 1- Level 2	101-140
Assistant Principal Level 2	122-140
Asst Principal Level 3 – Principal Level 1	101-109
Principal Level 2	122-140
Principal Level 3	147-166

Graduate starting salaries

The median starting annual salaries for bachelor degree graduates *aged below* 25 range from 40,000 to 80,000, varying with the field of study as shown in Table 7.9.

Table 7.9 Median Starting Salaries of Bachelor Degree Graduates 2011

	$'000		$'000
Accounting	47	Law	51
Agricultural Science	45	Mathematics	55
Architecture & Building	46	Medicine	58
Art and Design	40	Optometry	70
Biological Science	47	Paramedical Studies	50
Computer Science	51	Pharmacy	37
Dentistry	80	Physical Sciences	50
Earth Sciences	65	Psychology	47
Economics, Business	47	Social Sciences	43
Education	55	Social Work	50
Engineering	60	Veterinary Science	45
Humanities	44		

Challenges and Prospects

An ageing workforce

Australia's population is ageing and so is its workforce. The median age of the workforce in nine out of the 19 categorised industries is above 40 years, as shown in Table 7.10.

The impact is across industries and has also resulted in skills shortage as people retire, though this is more pronounced in certain sectors than others. Australia has been addressing the shortages by taking in skilled migrants as needed. For example, in the medical profession, trained practitioners from overseas make up 40% of the clinicians in regional Australia.

Table 7.10 Median Age of Workforce by Industry, 2011

Agriculture/ forestry/fishing	47	Rental/hiring/real estate	40
Education and training	44	Professional/technical	39
Transport/postal/warehousing	44	Financial and insurance	38
Health care/ social assistance	43	Construction	37
Public administration/ safety	43	Information/media/telecom	37
Manufacturing	41	Other services	38
Electricity/gas/water/ waste	41	Retail trade	32
Administrative and support	41	Arts/recreation	36
Wholesale trade	41	Accommodation and food	26
Mining	39		39

Skilled migration

Since the 1980s, Australia has been addressing the shortage of skills by developing and reforming migration policies and implementing programs including specific purpose visas aimed at attracting skilled migrants based on occupation, qualification, skills and work experience.

Among the occupations that have been included in the annual lists of the top 10 preferred occupations for immigration are accountant, computer professional, cook, engineer, hairdresser, registered nurse, marketing specialist and medical practitioner.

Immigration programs, in particular those targeting skilled migrants, are expected to continue far into the future in view of Australia's ageing population and its low domestic natural population growth owing to a low fertility rate.

Programs and procedures on migration to Australia are covered in more detail in Chapter 14 *Migration Program,* and Chapter 15 *Skilled Migration.*

Prospects and opportunities

The following are some observations on job prospects in the major industries and sectors:

- Retail trade
  Employment in this sector is still well below its pre-Global Financial Crisis level. Almost 25% of the people employed in retail trade work in supermarkets and grocery stores. In 2012, online shopping in Australia grew by more than 15%, securing 6% of the retail sales revenue. Almost 50% of the online revenue went overseas. It is expected that continued growth of online shopping would adversely impact future employment numbers in this industry.

- Construction
  In recent years, construction has seen a fall in employment. However, there is still a shortage of skills for certain jobs within the industry.

- Manufacturing
  Manufacturing will remain as a significant employer as it has a strong base in Australia, even though employment has been declining at the rate of 1.3% per annum over the last five years. The trend is expected to continue in the near future.

- Professional, scientific and technical services
  Employment in these occupations has been growing at an annual rate of 3.6% over the last five years. Accountants, software application programmers, solicitors, bookkeepers, graphic and web designers and illustrators are among the jobs that are in high demand by employers across the various industries.

- Health care and social assistance
  Employment in this sector has increased by almost 50% over the last decade owing to increasing demand for aged care and childcare. It is expected to continue to be a major employing industry because of the ageing population.

- Education and training
  In recent years, the strong Australian dollar and funding cut by some state governments have adversely impacted the industry, although jobs in education have grown at 2.4% annually over the last five years. Nevertheless, Australia will continue to be a significant education destination for countries in Asia, thus maintaining the importance of this industry both as an employer and an export earner.

- Public administration and safety
  In 2012, employment in this sector fell for the first time in more than a decade mainly resulting from cuts in public sector jobs by the state governments of New South Wales,

Queensland, Western Australia, Victoria and Tasmania. The Australian Congress of Trade Unions (ACTU) in its analysis of state, territory and commonwealth government budgets expects the squeeze on public sector employment to continue and get worse in 2013–14.

- Accommodation and food
Queensland, NSW and Victoria account for 80% of jobs in this industry. Despite growing marginally in employment in the last five years, the industry has struggled from the twin impacts of the Global Financial Crisis and the strong Australian dollar. Travelling overseas became attractive for Australians while GFC-impacted United States and Europe brought fewer travellers.

- Mining
Mining has been and will remain a major export earner for many decades ahead. It will continue to attract substantial foreign direct investments as Australia has an abundance of valuable minerals.

Australia is the world's leading producer of bauxite and iron ore; it is second in alumina, lead and manganese; third in brown coal, gold, nickel, zinc and uranium; fourth in aluminium, black coal and silver; and fifth in tin ore.

The industry directly employs only 2% of the workforce but indirectly another 6% in support industries, including downstream manufacturing, processing and transport. In remote areas, it is one of the few providing employment and business opportunities. While mining activities are centred in the main mining states of Western Australia, Queensland, and New South Wales, it has a flow-on effect on other states.

For mining employees, boom years of high activity mean very much higher income. In 2012, non-managerial adult employees in mining earned average cash wages of $52.50 hourly. This rate is unheard of when compared to $25.20 in the retail industry and $23.90 in the accommodation and food services industries. Thousands of mining workers are deployed weekly over very long distances under the 'fly-in-fly out' or 'drive-in-drive-out' work arrangements.

Employment rates in the mining industry are tied to its cycles of boom and slump. Over the last decade, the sector has almost trebled in employment and further growth is forecast for the next five years.

Fact Sheet 7.1 Ten National Employment Standards

1	Maximum weekly work hours	38 hours + reasonable additional hours
2	Request for flexible working arrangement	By parents or carers of a child under school age, or of a child under 18 with a disability to assist with the care of the child
3	Parental leave and related entitlements	Up to 12 months unpaid leave per employee, plus a right to request an additional 12 months unpaid leave and other forms of maternity, paternity and adoption related leave
4	Annual leave	4 weeks paid annual leave + 1 additional week for certain shift workers
5	Personal/carer's leave and compassionate leave	10 days paid personal/carer's leave, 2 days unpaid carer's leave as required, and 2 days compassionate leave (unpaid for casuals) as necessitated.
6	Community service leave	Unpaid leave for voluntary emergency activities. Leave for jury service, with paid entitlement for up to 10 days.
7	Long service leave	A transitional entitlement for employees as outlined in an applicable pre-modernised award, pending the development of a uniform national long service leave standard
8	Public holidays	A paid day off on a public holiday, except where reasonably requested to work
9	Termination notice and redundancy pay	Up to 5 weeks of termination notice and up to 16 weeks severance pay on redundancy, both based on length of service
10	Provision of a fair work information statement	Must be provided by employers to all new employees, and contains information about the NES, modern awards, agreement-making, the right to freedom of association, termination of employment, individual flexibility arrangements, union rights of entry, transfer of business, and the roles of the Fair Work Commission and the Fair Work Ombudsman

Source: Fairwork OMBUDSMAN Introduction to National Employment Standards

Fact Sheet 7.2 Annual Taxable Income ($'000) By Occupations 2011

Rank	Occupation	$'000 p.a.
	Top 20 Earners	
1	Surgeons	350
2	Anesthetists	303
3	Financial Dealers	270
4	Internal Medicine Specialists	255
5	Judicial and Other Legal Professionals	178
6	Psychiatrists	177
7	Chief Executives and Managing Directors	165
8	Mining Engineers	157
9	Other Medical Practitioners	155
10	Dental Practitioners	141

$131,000 - $140,000 p.a.

Generalist Medical Practitioners, Engineering Managers

$126,000 - $130,000 p.a.

Finance Managers, Consultant - financial investment, Economists

$111,000 – 120,000 p.a.

Other Hospitality, Retail and Service Managers , General Managers Consultant – management, Financial Investment Advisers and Managers, Production Managers, Consultant – engineering

$101,000 - $110,000 p.a.

Chemical and Materials Engineers, Medical Practitioners (other), ICT Managers, Drillers, Miners and Shot Firers, Other Engineering Professionals, Policy and Planning Managers, Corporate Services Managers, Consultant – IT business analyst

$96,000 - $100,000 p.a.

Human Resource Managers, Consultant - construction manager, Civil Engineering Professionals, Electrical Engineers, Other Building and Engineering Technicians, Financial Brokers, Other Natural and Physical Science Professionals, Auditors, Company Secretaries and Corporate Treasurers

$91,000 - $95,000 p.a.

ICT Professionals (other), Manager or director – type not specified (other)

$86,000 - $90,000 p.a.

Consultant – medical, , ICT Business and Systems Analysts, Construction Managers, Practice Managers, Advertising and Sales Managers, Industrial,

Mechanical and Production Engineers, Consultant - urban and regional planner, Other Education Managers, Land Economists and Valuers, Accountants, Telecommunications Engineering Professionals, Software and Applications Programmers, Supply and Distribution Managers

$81,000 - $85,000

Research and Development Managers, Electronics Engineers, Cartographers and Surveyors, Natural and Physical Science Professionals (other),Consultant - real estate representative, Consultant - occupational health and safety, Management and Organisation Analysts, Database and Systems Administrators, and ICT Securit, y Specialists, Artistic Directors, and Media Producers and Presenters, Aircraft Maintenance Engineers

$76,000 - $79,000 p.a.

Electrical Engineering Draftspersons and Technicians, Electricians, Insurance Investigators, Loss Adjusters and Risk Surveyors, Intelligence and Policy Analysts, Structural Steel Construction Workers, Consultant - marketing and public relations, Retail and Wool Buyers, Design, Engineering, Science and Transport Professionals (other), Architectural, Building and Surveying Technicians, Veterinarians

$71,000 - $75,000 p.a.

Consultant – environmental, Other Construction and Mining Labourers, Business and Systems Analysts, and Programmers (other), Commissioned Officers (Management), Medical Imaging Professionals, Other Stationary Plant Operators, Mechanical Engineering Draftspersons and Technicians, Consultant apprentice or trainee - security and correctional services, Consultant - human resources, ICT Support and Test Engineers, Transport Services Managers, Ambulance Officers and Paramedics, Consultant - tax accountant, Nurse Managers, Journalists and Other Writers

$66,000 - $70,000 p.a.

Other Specialist Managers, Civil Engineering Draftspersons and Technicians Contract, Program and Project Administrators, Insurance Agents, Electronic Engineering Draftspersons and Technicians, Other Technicians and Trades Workers (other), Psychologists, Medical Laboratory Scientists, Consultant - sales representative (wholesale), Secondary School Teachers, Automotive Electricians, Insurance, Money Market and Statistical Clerks, Other Information and Organisation Professionals

$61,000 - $65,000 p.a.

Consultant - clinical nurse, Licensed Club Managers, Financial Brokers and Dealers, and Investment Advisers (other), Vocational Education Teachers (Aus),

Multimedia Specialists and Web Developers, Air-conditioning and Refrigeration
Mechanics, Teacher - other school, Toolmakers and Engineering Patternmakers,
Mobile Plant Operators (other), Health and Welfare Services Managers,
Physiotherapists, Nurse Educators and Researchers, Middle School Teachers
(Aus), School Teachers (other), Primary School Teachers, Education Professionals
(other)

$56,000 - $60,000 p.a.

Clay, Concrete, Glass and Stone Processing Machine Operators, Dental
Hygienists, Technicians and Therapists, Other Mobile Plant Operators,
Apprentice or trainee - miner
Building and Engineering Technicians (other), Engineering Production Systems
Workers
Concreters, Actors, Dancers and Other Entertainers, Hotel and Motel Managers,
Other Machine Operators, Conveyancers and Legal Executives, Consultant –
insuranc e (clerical)
Archivists, Curators and Records Managers, Special Education Teachers,
Performing Arts Technicians, Paving and Surfacing Labourers, Office Managers,
Media Professionals (other), Other Miscellaneous Technicians and Trades
Workers, Graphic Pre-press Trades Workers, Other Miscellaneous Clerical and
Administrative Workers,Registered Nurses
Construction and Mining Labourers (other),Metal Engineering Process Workers,
Defence Force Members - Other Ranks

$51,000 - $55,000 p.a.

Consultant, apprentice or trainee - justice and legal services, insurance
investigator, Graphic and Web Designers, and Illustrators, Amusement, Fitness
and Sports Centre Managers, Other Health Diagnostic and Promotion
Professionals, Printing Trades Workers (other), Public servant - administrative
service officer - levels 3-4, Building and Plumbing Labourers, Vehicle Body
Builders and Trimmers, Photographers, Product Quality Controllers, Call or
Contact Centre and Customer Service Managers, Boat Builders and Shipwrights,
Secretaries, Binders, Finishers and Screen Printers, Child Care Centre Managers,
Teachers of English to Speakers of Other Languages, Accounting Clerks,
Machine and Stationary Plant Operators (other), Retail Managers
Other Accommodation and Hospitality Managers, Conference and Event
Organisers, Private Tutors and Teachers, Insurance Agents and Sales
Representatives (other), Architects, Designers, Planners and Surveyors (other),
Office Managers and Program Administrators (other), Other Miscellaneous
Labourers, Retail Supervisors, Caravan Park and Camping Ground Managers,

Early Childhood (Pre-primary School) Teachers, Metal Casting, Forging and Finishing Trades Workers

$46,000 - $50,000 p.a.

Clerical and Office Support Workers (other), Road and Rail Drivers (other), General Clerical Workers (other), Medical Technicians, Survey Interviewers, Floor Finishers, Other Clerical and Office Support Workers, Midwifery and Nursing Professionals (other), Other Factory Process Workers, Prison and Security Officers (other), Sports and Personal Service Workers (other), Consultant, apprentice or trainee - personal service or travel, Photographic Developers and Printers, Consultant - sales assistant (retail), Gardeners, Hotel Service Managers, Cafe and Restaurant Managers, Nurserypersons, Other Farm, Forestry and Garden Workers, Caretakers, Clothing Trades Workers, Wood Machinists and Other Wood Trades Workers, Farmers and Farm Managers (other)

$41,000 - $45,000 p.a.

Personal Carers and Assistants (other), Cleaners and Laundry Workers (other), Call or Contact Centre Workers, Other Personal Service Workers, Gaming Workers, Factory Process Workers (other), Personal Care Consultants, Enrolled and Mothercraft Nurses, Other Cleaners, Ministers of Religion, Freight Handlers and Shelf Fillers (other), Apprentice or trainee - agricultural or medical technician, Garden and Nursery Labourers, Other Sales Assistants and Salespersons, Food Process Workers (other)

Other Hospitality Workers, Dental Assistants, Apprentice or trainee - mechanical trades engineering trades worker, Nursing Support and Personal Care Workers

$36,000 - $40,000 p.a.

Hospitality Workers (other), Apprentice or trainee - printer or graphic artist, Veterinary Nurses, Farm, Forestry and Garden Workers (other), Apprentice or trainee - financial services, Apprentice or trainee - metal fabrication engineering trades worker, Apprentice or trainee - floor finisher, Health and Welfare Support Workers (other), Apprentice or trainee - automotive - other

Source: Australian Taxation Office Taxation Report 20

8 Education System

Education opportunities for all

Australia's system of education provides high quality education opportunity for all. In 2010, eight million or 56% of all working-age Australian residents hold post-school qualifications. On a graduate per-capita basis, Australia is ahead of Germany, Japan, the United States, France, the United Kingdom, Korea and New Zealand.

Schooling is compulsory for children between 6 and 15 years of age.

Australian schools adopt highly interactive teaching approach, encourage active student participation and emphasize skills and confidence development. Australian school students have consistently performed well above international benchmarks

State and territory governments manage their school systems, the vocational education and training sectors and universities. The Commonwealth provides the funding for universities in all states and territories.

Distance education programs for school children are available in some states for students in remote and isolated areas and those unable to attend school.

Australian university students who are citizens and permanent residents are required to pay "student contribution" for their university education. Australian citizens may defer paying their contribution when they graduate and when their incomes reach the threshold level.

Schooling in Australia

International rankings

Australian students have consistently performed well above the international benchmarks, e.g. the OECD Programme for International Student Assessment (PISA) and the *Trends in International Mathematics and Science Study (TIMSS)* as shown in Table 8.1 and 8.2.

Table 8.1
OECD Program for International Student Assessment, 2009

	Reading Literacy	Mathematical Literacy	Scientific Literacy
Australia	515	514	527
United States	500	487	502
United Kingdom	494	492	514
Canada	524	527	529
New Zealand	521	519	532
OECD Average	493	496	501

PISA evaluates the performance of 15 year-old students within an internationally accepted common framework. Currently there are 65 countries in the survey. PISA is coordinated by the Organisation for Economic Co-operation and Development to assist governments in monitoring the outcomes of education systems in terms of student's achievement on a regular basis.

TIMSS are comprehensive state-of the-art assessments of mathematics and science for students in Year 4 and Year 8, supported with extensive data about country, school, and classroom learning environments.

Table 8.2 Trends in International Mathematics and Science Study

	Mathematics 4th Grade	Mathematics 8th Grade	Science Study 4th Grade	Science Study 8th Grade
Australia	516	496	527	515
United States	529	508	539	520
United Kingdom*	517	500	532	519
Canada**	510	518	532	519
New Zealand	492	n/a	504	n/a
TMSS Average	500	500	500	500

*Notes: * Based on averaging the scores of England and Scotland. ** Based on averaging the scores of participating Canadian provinces.*

Compulsory schooling

Schooling in Australia runs for 13 years commencing with a Preparatory or Kindergarten year and then Years 1-12 of school. It is compulsory schooling for children between 6 and 15 years of age.

Some Australian schools offer vocational training for students with skills to enter the workforce early.

Senior Certificate of Education, (known by different name in the various states), obtained after completing Year 12 is required for entry to universities and most technical and vocational training courses.

Australian schools and enrolment

In 2010, there were 2 million primary school students and 1.5 million secondary school students in 9,468 schools. The enrolment breakdown is 66% in government schools, 20% in Catholic schools and 14% in independent schools.

Government schools

Government schools (known also as state schools or public schools) are mainly co-educational and are run by state or territory governments. While government school education is free, schools do request voluntary parent contribution of between $100 to $400 for primary and $300 to $800 for secondary per annum and any expenses required for school camps, excursions and other activities.

Schools are open to students within the defined feeder areas. It is therefore not uncommon to find houses in the suburbs within the feeder areas of high performing schools to be in great demand.

In New South Wales and Victoria, there are government Selective High Schools which aim to provide a stimulating environment and high academic achievement. Admission is based on merits including performance at selective entrance examinations. The schools are as follow:

- New South Wales - Baulkham Hills High School, Caringbah High School, Fort Street High School, Girraween High School, Gosford High School, Hornsby Girls High School, Merewether High School, Normanhurst Boys High School, North Sydney Boys High School, North Sydney Girls High School, St George Girls High School, Sydney Boys High School and Sydney Girls High School;

- Victoria - MacRobertson Girls' High School, Melbourne High School, Noosa High School and Suzanne Cory High School.

Gifted, talented, and students with special needs

There are schools catering for the performing arts and music while often schools have courses and facilities for gifted and talented students. In many states there are government schools that have accelerated programs for gifted students to finish their schooling earlier.

Children with disabilities can attend special needs schools or remain in general schools, which have programs and facilities catering to their requirements.

Curriculum

Australian schools adopt highly interactive teaching approach, encourage active student participation and emphasize skills and confidence development. The main learning areas as part of the National Curriculum include English, mathematics, science, arts studies of society and environment, technology, languages other than English, personal development, health and physical education.

Students are offered a wide range of non-academic and practical learning opportunities including sports, artistic developments, excursions, field trips and camps.

Children of newly arrived migrants

For children of newly arrived migrants requiring help there are fast-track English classes available. Remedial and extensions classes are available for students with differing learning abilities.

Distance education

Distance education programs are available in a number of Australian states for students in remote and isolated areas and those unable to attend school. The School of the Air is one such example. Started in 1950, a world's first then, it now has 12 schools catering to the needs of students in remote and isolated areas.

Catholic schools

Catholic schools are mainly single sex schools and charge fees of around $3,000 per year for primary school student and $3,000 to $6,000 per year for secondary school student. While student enrolment is mainly from children of Catholic families, Catholic schools do accept students from other religions.

Independent schools (known also as private schools)

Most Independent schools have a religious affiliation, Anglican, Uniting Church, Jewish, Christian, Islamic though some are non-denominational.

Independent schools generally have a reputation for academic excellence, with a strong emphasis on sporting and other extracurricular facilities and activities. Many prestigious schools have long waiting lists for student admission.

Funding for independent schools is mainly from fees and charges while Commonwealth and State Governments provide funding in the form of subsidies and grants.

Australia's independent schools' fees are very competitive when compared to private education overseas in countries like Japan, the United States, Taiwan, United Kingdom and Singapore.   Hence, independent schools are increasingly popular with international students.

Tuition fees vary from school to school and state to state. Table 8.3 lists the fees charged by an independent school in suburban Melbourne.

Level	Annual Fee for local Student $	State and Commonwealth Grants/ Subsidies $	Net Annual Fee for local Student $
Pre-Prep	14,650	350	14,300
Prep	20,664	2,764	17,900
Year 1	20,864	2,764	18,100
Year 2	20,831	2,731	18,100
Year 3	21,797	2,697	19,100
Year 4	21,897	2,697	19,200
Year 5	23,197	2,697	20,500
Year 6	24,797	2,697	22,100
Year 7	27,348	3,448	23,900
Year 8	27,548	3,448	24,100
Year 9	27,948	3,448	24,500
Year 10	28,048	3,448	24,600
Year 11	28,348	3,448	24,900
Year 12	28,448	3,448	25,000

Table 8.3 Tuition Fee for Independent School 2013

Camberwell Grammar School, Melbourne

Many independent schools award full or partial scholarships on the basis of academic, sports, visual arts, musical achievements and performance in selection examination.

Many parents have to make considerable sacrifices in sending their children to independent schools. As the example shown in Table 8.3, the total tuition fee per child for six years of primary education cost around $130,000 and another $150,000 for six-years of secondary education. Other costs, e.g. uniforms, computer, excursions, school camps, extra-curricular activities, are additional outgoings that need to be budgeted for.

Hence, most parents send their children to independent schools after they have completed their primary education.

Boarding facilities

Some independent schools have boarding facilities for primary and secondary students. Similar facilities are also available in some government secondary schools.

School terms

The Australian school year follows the calendar year, i.e. from January to December. All Australian state schools have four terms. The end of the year summer school holiday period is the longest compared to the other term holiday periods which are normally for a fortnight.

The 2014 school terms are shown in Table 8.4. Independent schools and Catholic schools generally follow the state school term with some slight variations.

Table 8.4 2014 State School Terms

	Term 1	Term 2	Term 3	Term 4
New South Wales	28/1 – 11/4	28/4 – 27/6	14/7 – 19/9	7/10 – 19/12
Victoria	28/1 - 4/4	2/4 - 27/6	14/7 - 19/9	7/10 - 20/12
Queensland	28/1 – 4/4	22/4 – 27/6	14/7 – 19/9	7/10 – 14/12
Western Australia	3/2 – 11/4	28/4 – 4/7	21/7 – 26/9	13/10 –18/12
South Australia	28/1 – 11/4	2/4 -4/7	21/7 – 26/9	13/10 –12/12
Australia Capital Territory	31/1 – 11/4	28/4 – 6/7	21/7 – 26/9	13/10 –17/12
Tasmania	5/2 – 17/4	5/5 – 4/7	21/7 – 26/9	13/10 –18/12
Northern Territory	24/1 – 4/4	14/4 – 20/6	21/7 – 26/9	6/10 – 11/12

My school website

This is a very useful website profiling almost 9,500 Australian schools with information about the school's student population, the average achievement of students in National Assessment Program—Literacy and Numeracy. (NAPLAN) and school financial data, comparable across all Australian schools.

The Australian Curriculum, Assessment and Reporting Authority (ACARA), an Australian Government statutory authority, administers the website. ACARA is responsible for collecting and reporting data on Australian schools and administering national assessments in literacy and numeracy and developing a national curriculum.

The website address is listed on page 297.

Vocational Education and Training (VET)

Enrolments

Vocational education and training is increasingly popular with 50% of school leavers. VET training has many advantages including lower fees compared to undergraduate studies, provision of relevant industry training and good employment prospects.

Table 8.5 gives a breakdown of student enrolment by providers and type of qualifications.

Table 8.5 VET Enrolments ('000) by Qualifications and Providers 2010

AQF Qualifications	
TAFE and other government providers	1,068.2
Community education providers	64.4
Other registered providers	294.3
Students attending various providers	15.8
AQF students	1,442.7
Non-AQF Qualifications	
TAFE and other government providers	270.4
Community education providers	71.5
Other registered providers	14.2
Students attending various providers	0.2
Non-AQF students	356.3
Total	1,799.0

Source; TAFE Australia

Training providers

There are about 400 training providers with well over 300 providers being registered private training providers. Many universities, industry organisations, agricultural colleges and community organisations are also involved in the sector. There are 60 state-run Technical and Further Education (TAFE) institutes. Most of the state TAFE institutes have branch campuses and partnership arrangements with industries.

The TAFE institutes and their website addresses are listed on page 299.

Courses

Vocational education and training (VET) provides a mix of training options as shown in Table 8.6.

Modes of course delivery include on campus, online or in the workplace.

Table 8.6 Student Enrolments by Type of Course and Field of Study

	'000
AQF Qualifications	
Graduate diploma	0.2
Graduate certificate	1.4
Bachelor degree	2.2
Advanced diploma	39.3
Associate degree	.2
Diploma	189.7
Certificate IV	254.1
Certificate III	553.3
Certificate II	312.3
Certificate I	90.0
AQF students	1,442.7
Non-AQF Qualifications	
Other recognised courses	208.8
Non-award courses	71.9
Subject only	75.6
Non-AQF students	356.3
Total	1,799.0
Major courses	
Management and commerce	358.4
Engineering and related technologies	303.7
Society and culture	205.5
Mixed field programmes	195.4
Food, hospitality and personal services	182.7
Architecture and building	142.4
Health	97.5
Agriculture, environmental and related studies	77.2
Education	62.1
Creative arts	53.6
Information technology	37.3
Natural and physical sciences	7.5
Subject only - no qualification	75.6
Total	1,799

Australia Qualification Framework (AQF), first introduced in 1995, is the national education policy framework for regulating qualifications in Australian education and training. AQF qualifications are recognised right across Australia. Eighty per cent of TAFE students are enrolled in AQF courses.

For some courses, TAFE graduates can use their relevant TAFE study as partial credit for their subsequent university studies.
Courses offered include short courses, certificate level, diploma, and advanced diploma courses, and a few university undergraduate courses. Course duration ranges from half a year to four years depending on course level.

The range of subjects offered in TAFE institutes is wide though it varies from state to state and institute to institute. Subjects include accounting, international accounting, business, business administration, human resources management, marketing, advertising, property services, beauty services, aged care, children services, dental services, interior design, graphic design, digital media, agriculture, animal care, architectural, building and construction, engineering, English language program, environmental testing, equine studies, fashion technology, fine arts, ceramics and visual arts, hairdressing, horticulture, hospitality information technology, interpreting and translating, laboratory technology, hospitability, marine engineering, massage therapy, media studies, music, nursing, real estate, secretarial and office skills, sports and fitness, telecommunications, tertiary preparation and TESOL, tourism and events, visual arts, and welfare studies.

Fees

As the vocational educational and training sector is under the jurisdiction of the state and territory governments, tuition fees vary from state to state. The fees are reviewed annually.

Table 8.7 provides an indication of tuition fees charged based on TAFE NSW fees for 2013. Government benefit recipients pay a nominal fee of $100 while no fee is payable by some course attendees as shown in Table 8.7.

Table 8.7 Tuition Fees – TAFE NSW
Government Subsidised Domestic Students

Qualification Level/Category	Annual Fee ($)
Advanced Diploma	1,720
Diploma	1,432
Certificate IV	1,078
Certificate III	793
Certificate II	506
Certificate I	506
Statement/Short Courses	506
Apprentices/trainees	478
Government benefit recipients	100
Australian aboriginal and Torres Straits Islander students	Nil
Students with a disability (1st course per year)	Nil
Special access courses	Nil

Source: TAFE NSW

In addition to the tuition fees, students have to pay charges to cover the costs of materials, resources, equipment or services used directly during the course of study. Some courses also require students to purchase additional resources, e.g. protective clothing, licence fees and textbooks.

Universities

Higher education opportunity for all

Tertiary entrance for Australian citizens and permanent residents is based on merits, i.e. scores achieved at secondary examination. However, there are special considerations for mature age students and others.

Australia offers higher education opportunities for all its citizens and residents.

On a graduate per-capita basis, Australia is ahead of the Germany, Japan, the United States, France, the United Kingdom, Korea and New Zealand as shown in Table 8.8 below.

Table 8.8 Graduates per Million of Population 2008

Australia	14,040	France	10,017
New Zealand	12,871	United States	8,927
Korea	12,570	Japan	8,121
United Kingdom	10,633	Germany	4,188

Source: UNESCO Institute for Statistics, Public Reports: Education Statistics, 2009

In 2012, there were 1.1 million university student enrolments, of which 25% were from overseas as shown in Table 8.9.

Table 8.9 University Student Enrolment 2012

Degree Courses		Non-Degree Courses	
Post-graduate	311,762	Enabling courses	19,052
Undergraduate	824,756	Non-award courses	16,167
Domestic/International Students		**Type of Attendance**	
Domestic students	874,700	Full time	825,566
International students	297,037	Part time	346,171
Total			1,171,737

Source: Universities Australia

Australian universities

There are 39 universities in Australia as listed in Fact Sheet 8.1 on page 146. All, except the Bond University and Australian Catholic University are state-run institutions. Many have branch campuses within and outside Australia.

The Group of Eight (Go8)

In Australia, the eight most prestigious, oldest and leading universities – Australia National University, University of Melbourne, University of Queensland, University of Sydney, University of New South Wales, Monash University, University of Western Australia and University of Adelaide have formed a coalition of Australian universities known as the Group of Eight (Go8).

Table 8.10 shows the global rankings of the Go8 in three international studies, i.e. *2011-2012 The Times Higher Education World University Rankings* (1), *2011 QS World University Rankings* (2), and the *2011 ARWU SHJT Shanghai Jiao Tong University China Academic Ranking of world universities* (3).

Table 8.10 World Rankings of Group of Eight (Go8) Universities

	1	2	3
Australian National University	38	26	70
University of Melbourne	37	31	60
University of Queensland	74	48	86
University of Sydney	58	38	96
University of New South Wales	173	49	152-200
Monash University	117	60	151-200
University of Western Australia	189	73	102-150
University of Adelaide	201-225	92	201-300

The Go8 has listed its achievements as having nurtured every Nobel prize winner educated at an Australian university; responsible for more than two thirds of Australian university research activity, research output and research training and having 90% of Australia's university-based Federation Fellows doing their research at the Go8 universities.

Undergraduate fees

Students who are Australian citizens and permanent residents are required to pay "student contribution" for their undergraduate studies.

Australian citizens may defer paying their contribution by participating in the Higher Education Loan Program (HELP) – an interest-free loan and repay when they are working and when their income more than the threshold level ($51,309 for 2013/14 tax year).

Student contribution amount is dependent on the course of study. Students will be charged a service and amenities fee in addition to their student contribution. A 10% discount applies if fee is paid up-front. Table 8.11 provides an indication of student contribution for undergraduate courses for 2013.

Table 8.11 University of Melbourne Student Contribution Amount 2013

Band/Fee per standard year	Discipline
1 $5,868	Behavioural Science, Clinical Psychology, Education, Foreign Languages, Humanities, Nursing, Social Studies, Visual and Performing Arts
2 $8,363	Agriculture, Allied Health, Built Environment, Computing, Engineering, Mathematics, Other Health, Science, Statistics, Surveying
3 $9,792	Accounting, Administration, Commerce, Dentistry, Economics, Law, Medicine, Veterinary Science

The example below shows how the Student Contribution is being computed.

> Stephen is a domestic student who enrols for the Bachelor of Law study in 2013, commencing in Semester 1. He enrols in 8 subjects (7 Law subjects at 12.5 credit points each, 1 humanities subject at 12.5 credit points) for a total of 100 credit points or a standard full-time study load for one year of study. Stephen's contribution amount for his 2013 Bachelor of Commerce study will be $9,301.50 computed as follow:
>
> ▪   Law subjects   7 x .125 x $9,792 = $8,568.00
> ▪   Humanities subject 1 x .125 x $5,868   733.50
> $9,301.50

Most Australian universities have full-fee paying option for students intending to enter some selected courses at lower scores.

Graduate fees

Enrolments for most research degrees are exempted from tuition fee payment as they are fully funded by the Australian Government via the Research Training Scheme (RTS). This includes PhD, MPhil, Masters by research and some Professional doctorates.

However, for most other graduate programs that are Commonwealth supported places students are required to pay student contributions. As in undergraduate courses, eligible students may defer the contribution amount through HECS-HELP. The contribution amount for graduate program is the same as for undergraduate programs as shown in Table 8.1.

Fact Sheet 8.1 Universities

New South Wales
Charles Sturt University	hhtp://www.csu.edu.au/
Macquarie University	hhtp://www.mq.edu.au/
University of Newcastle	hhtp://www.newcastle.edu.au/
University of New England	hhtp://www.une.edu.au/
University of New South Wales	hhtp://www.unsw.edu.au/
Southern Cross University	hhtp://www.scu.edu.au/
University of Sydney	hhtp://www.sydney.edu.au/
University of Wollongong	hhtp://www.uow.edu.au/
University of Technology Sydney	hhtp://www.uts.edu.au/
University of Western Sydney	hhtp://www.uws.edu.au/

Victoria
Deakin University	hhtp://www.deakin.edu.au/
La Trobe University	hhtp://www.latrobe.edu.au/
Monash University	hhtp://www.monash.edu.au/
RMIT University	hhtp://www.rmit.edu.au/
Swinburne University of Technology	hhtp://www.swinburne.edu.au/
University of Ballarat	hhtp://www.ballarat.edu.au/
University of Melbourne	hhtp://www.unimelb.edu.au/
Victoria University	hhtp://www.vu.edu.au/

Queensland
Bond University	hhtp://www.bond.edu.au/
Central Queensland University	hhtp://www.cqu.edu.au/
Griffith University	hhtp://www.griffith.edu.au/
James Cook University	hhtp://www.jcu.edu.au/
Queensland University of Technology	hhtp://www.qut.edu.au/
University of Queensland	hhtp://www.uq.edu.au/
University of Southern Queensland	hhtp://www.usq.edu.au/
University of Sunshine Coast	hhtp://www.usc.edu.au/

Western Australia
Curtin University	hhtp://www.csu.curtin.au/
Edith Cowan University	hhtp://www.csu.ecu.au/
Murdoch University	hhtp://www.murdoch.edu.au/
University of Notre Dame Australia	hhtp://www.nd.edu.au/
University of Western Australia	hhtp://www.uwa.edu.au/

South Australia
Flinders University	hhtp://www.flinders.edu.au/
University of Adelaide	hhtp://www.adelaide.edu.au/
University of South Australia	hhtp://www.unisa.edu.au/

Australian Capital Territory
Australian National University	hhtp://www.anu.edu.au/
University of Canberra	hhtp://www.canberra.edu.au/

Tasmania and Northern Territory
University of Tasmania	hhtp://www.uts.edu.au/
Charles Darwin University	hhtp://www.cdu.edu.au/

National
Australian Catholic University	hhtp://www.acu.edu.au/

9 International Students

A gateway to opportunities!

Australian education is very popular with international students. In 2012, there were over 516,000 international students from 200 nations in Australian schools, colleges and universities. Since 2007, over 200,000 international students have annually lodged their visa applications to study at Australian tertiary institutions.

Australia is one of the largest providers of tertiary education for international students. In 2009, Australia was the third largest provider of international tertiary education, hosting 7% of global tertiary students. In 2010, Australia's international student tertiary enrolment ratio of 25% is the highest in the OECD countries.

Over 155,000 international students are attending universities in Australia and another 61,000 are at offshore campuses. Ninety per cent of the international tertiary students are from Asia - China, India, Republic of Korea, Malaysia, Hong Kong Japan, Thailand, Taiwan, Pakistan, Nepal, Bangladesh and Indonesia.

Many international students are attending short courses including English Language Intensive Courses for Overseas Students (ELICOS) and foundation courses (pathway to universities).

A number of Australian universities have branch or joint campuses overseas. For example, Monash has joint campuses in Suzhou in China, Prato Centre in Italy, Sunway in Kuala Lumpur Malaysia, IITB Bombay in India, and Johannesburg in South Africa. RMIT has campuses in Hanoi and Ho Chih Minh City in Vietnam and Swinburne University has its branch campus in Kuching in East Malaysia.

Why International Students Choose Australia?

Quality education system

Australian schools adopt highly interactive teaching approach, encourage active student participation and emphasize skills and confidence development. Students are offered a wide range of non-academic and practical learning opportunities including sports, artistic development, excursions, field trips and camps.

Australian universities and colleges have an excellent reputation for quality international education with several in the Top 200 Jiao Tong University Ranking. In a year-long study commissioned by the Lisbon Council ranking university systems of 17 OECD countries, Australia has emerged as having the best university system ahead of the United Kingdom, Denmark, Finland, the United States, Sweden, Ireland, Portugal, Italy, France, Poland, Hungary, Netherlands, Switzerland, Germany, Austria and Spain.

Study in a diverse environment

With its student population coming from all over the world, Australia provides international students an opportunity to experience and enrich their study and education in a diverse environment. This diversity enables individuals to get exposed to opinions and ways of life and meet people from different cultural backgrounds.

Living in a mini global environment

With its population coming from over 200 countries, Australia offers international students the unique opportunity of living in a mini global environment - a solid foundation and a prelude to their future working or business careers in the larger global environment.

Experience all things Australian

For many students, studying in Australia offers opportunities to live a unique lifestyle, explore the natural wonders of its oceans and rainforests and the buzz of its cosmopolitan cities.

Gateway to migration

Australia has long recognised that international students provide a potential if not a ready source of skilled migrants.

Since 2001, Australia has allowed foreign students in selected fields of studies to move easily into the labour market instead of requiring them to return home.

From 2013, international students graduating from Australian universities with at least 2 academic years' study in Australia will be able to apply for Australian work visas regardless of their field of study. Neither is there a need for skill assessment requirement or nomination of an occupation on the Skilled Occupation List.

Graduates with a bachelor degree, a master's degree or a doctorate will be allowed to stay and work for two years, three years or four years respectively. This is covered in greater details in Chapter 15 *Skilled Migration.*

Visa Requirements

Students and students' guardians

A student visa is required for international students intending to study in Australia. Parents or relatives can apply for a Student Guardians visa to stay in Australia as the guardian of a student who is studying in Australia.

Evidence of access to funds

Student visa applicants and their family members have to demonstrate that they have genuine access to funds to meet their annual living costs. The living costs requirement effective from 1 July 2012 are $18,610 for the main applicant, $6,515 for the student's partner, $3,720 for the student's first child and $2,790 for every other child.

Strict visa conditions

There are strict conditions attached to student visas. Students are at risk of having their enrolment and student visa cancelled for unsatisfactory class attendance or study progress. Students cannot change their education provider for the first six months of their principal/main course, unless due to provider's enrolment issue. There is also restriction on permissible hours of work, which is covered in the section *Working in Australia*.

Local guardians

All international students, regardless of age, must have a local guardian. Students who enrol below Year 9 must live with a parent. Students entering Year 9 and above can live in a homestay organised through the school.

Overseas student health cover (OSHC)

International students studying in Australia are required to have valid OSHCs for the duration of the student visas. OSHC provides basic cover for medical and hospital care costs in Australia. It is available from any government-approved provider.

Students from Belgium or Norway are considered to have health insurance comparable to OHSC through the reciprocal arrangements between the Belgium, Norwegian and Australian Governments. Similarly students from Sweden are considered to have health insurance cover if they possess valid *Kammarkolleit* or CSN International Health Insurance policy for the duration of the Student Visas.

The OSHC provides basic cover for medical and hospital care costs and limited benefits for pharmaceuticals and ambulance services in Australia.

The cost of OSHC varies according to the type of cover required. The average cost of minimum cover is $437 for 12 months singles cover, $1,222 for 12 months couples cover and $1,744 for 12 months single-parent cover and $2,022 for family cover.

Working in Australia

Working part-time offers overseas students an opportunity to understand the Australian way of life, improve social and other skills and understand the Australian work culture.

Students normally find part-time work in the retail and hospitality sectors, which offer work after hours and weekends. Students also often work as private home tutors.

According to visa requirement, students can only commence work after their course has started. They are allowed to work a maximum of 20 hours per week each term. This includes paid and voluntary work. They can work unlimited hours during holidays. The 20hours/week restriction applies throughout the year to dependent family members of all other student visa holders if granted permission to work.

Family members of students enrolled in Masters by coursework (visa 573), Masters by research or Doctoral degree (visa 574) or sponsored by AusAid or Defence (visa 576) have no restriction on working hours.

The Costs

Course fees – state schools

While fees vary from state to state, the fees listed in Table 9.1 are indicative of tuition fees charged on international students.

Table 9.1 Annual Tuition Fees ($) 2013 - Victorian Government Schools

	Student	Dependents of Student	2nd or Subsequent Children
Primary (Prep-Grade 6)	9,210	7,370	8,290
Junior Secondary (Year 7-10)	12,210	9,770	10.990
Senior Secondary (Year 11-12)	13,640	10,910	12,270

Annual tuition fees for Junior Secondary and Senior Secondary schools for Victorian College of the Arts are $16,520 and $18,550 respectively.

Course fees – private schools

Tuition fees vary from school to school and state to state. Table 9.2 is indicative of fees based on the fee schedule of a suburban independent school in Melbourne. Fees are payable in advance of the semester/semesters. Most independent schools also require an enrolment fee of around $1,000.

Table 9.2 2013 Fee Schedule for International Students

Level	Annual Fee $	Level	Annual Fee $
Pre-Prep	17,900	Year 7	28,100
Prep	21,400	Year 8	28,600
Year 1	21,400	Year 9	29,000
Year 2	21,400	Year 10	29,500
Year 3	22,300	Year 11	29,700
Year 4	22,600	Year 12	29,900
Year 5	23,900		
Year 6	25,500		

Camberwell Grammar School, Melbourne

Course fees – TAFE colleges and universities

Tuition fees vary between TAFE colleges and between private providers. As an indication, course fee is around $12,000-$16,500 per annum in state-run TAFE colleges. The duration for TAFE courses can be from 6 months to 4 years depending on course. Other sundry fees payable include service and amenity fees and materials fees.

Tuition fees - universities

Tuition fees vary between universities and are dependent on course and subject selection. Fact Sheets 9.1 and 9.2 on pages 155 and 156 show the University of Melbourne's annual undergraduate fee for international students. For further details on fees, please go to the respective university's websites listed in Fact Sheet 8.1 Universities on page 146.

Living expenses and initial establishment fees

While living expenses vary by location and are dependent on individual student's lifestyle, the per annum living costs requirement under the Migration Regulations as shown in Table 9.3 is a good indication of the living expenses one has to budget for.

Table 9.3 Financial Requirements Per Person Per Year & Evidence of Funds

Expenses	Applicant	Guardian
Travel - Return airfare	Yes	Yes
Tuition		
Applicant	Course fees	n.a.
School-age children	$8,000	n.a.
Living		
Applicant	$18,610	$18,610
Partner	$6,515	n.a.
1st child	$3,720	$3,720 aged <6
Each other child	$2,790	$2,790 aged <6

Source: DIAC – Applicable from 1 Jul 2012

The DIAC requires international students applying for student visa to demonstrate and/or declare that they have genuine access to sufficient funds for one or more years in Australia.

The initial establishment costs, e.g. rent deposit, rent in advance, utilities connection fee, furniture and household items are additional outgoings that need to be budgeted for.

Fact Sheet 9.1 University of Melbourne
– International Undergraduate Subject Fees 2013

(Based on 100 credit points or 1 year Equivalent Full Time Study Load)

Discipline	$	Discipline	$
Agriculture	33,120	Law	33,632
Computing	31,456	Medicine	66,080
Engineering	33,472	Medicine (clinical)	69,952
Information Systems	32,736	Nursing	24,096
Mathematics, Statistics	31,840	Other Health	31,840
Optometry	39,360	Physiotherapy	33,760
Science	33,760	VCA (AudioVisual)	46,688
Surveying	33,472	VCA (AVS group 1)	46,688
Veterinary Science	52,064	VCA (AVS group 2)	46,688
Built Environment	31,232	VCA (AVS group 3)	46,688
Accounting, Administration, Commerce, Economics	33,344	Arts, Foreign Languages, Humanities, Social Studies	25,120
Education	24,288	Visual and Performing Arts	23,072
Behavioural Science	31,840	VCA (Foundation Study)	16,992
Dentistry	51,840	VCA (Performing Arts)	23,072
Health (non-clinical)	31,840	VCA General	23,072

Example

Stephen, an international student, enrols for the Bachelor of Commerce study in 2013, commencing in Semester 1. He enrols in 8 subjects (7 Commerce subjects at 12.5 credit points each, 1 humanities subject at 12.5 credit points) for a total of 100 credit points or a standard full-time study load for one year of study:

Stephen's undergraduate tuition fees for his 2013 Bachelor of Commerce study will be $32,316, computed as follow:

- o   Commerce subjects   7 x .125 x $51,840 $29,176.00
- o   Humanities subject   1 x .125 x $25,120   3,140.00
                                                                   $32,316.0

Fact Sheet 9.2 University of Melbourne
Typical International Undergraduate Course Fees 2013

Course	Duration (Year)	Typical Course Fee $
Bachelor degrees		
Associate Degree I Environmental Horticulture	2	67,912
Bachelor of Agriculture	3	103,772
Bachelor of Arts	3	78,066-88,868
Bachelor of Biomedicine	3	107,362-114,032
Bachelor of Commerce	3	97,696-104,680
Bachelor of Environments	3	92,912-103,036
Bachelor of Fine Arts	3	72,272-133,634
Bachelor of Music	3	73,232-80554
Bachelor of Oral Health	3	152,176
Bachelor of Science	3	94,542-125,978
Honours degrees		
Bachelor of Agriculture	1	33,120
Bachelor of Agricultural Science	1	33,120
Bachelor of Animal Science	1	52,064
Bachelor of Animal Science and Management	1	33,120
Bachelor of Arts	1	25,120
Bachelor of Arts with studies in Psychology		31,840
Bachelor of Biomedicine	1	33,760
Bachelor of Commerce	1	33,344
Bachelor of Dance	1	23,072
Bachelor of Environments	1	33,120
Bachelor of Films and Television	1	46,688
Bachelor of Fine Arts	1	23,072
Bachelor of Food Science	1	33,120
Bachelor of Forest Science	1	33,120
Bachelor of Horticulture	1	33,120
Bachelor of Information Systems	1	32,736
Bachelor of Music	1	23,072
Bachelor of Natural Resource Management	1	33,120
Bachelor of Production	1	23,072
Bachelor of Science	1	33,760
Bachelor of Science (Psychology)	1	31,840
Concurrent diplomas		
Diploma	1	23,072 - 32,736
Foundation1		
Foundation Program (Music Performance)	1	16,992

10 Healthcare System
It works, it is fair and good quality

Australia's healthcare system has consistently ranked high in many OECD studies.

Australia achieved impressive outcomes and ranked third overall based on measures of quality, equity, accessibility, efficiency, and attainment of long and healthy lives according to a recent U.S. study on health care performance of seven countries - Australia, Canada, Germany, the Netherlands, New Zealand and the United States.[24]

Australians are outliving most of the world. Australian life expectancy, at 84 years for females and 79 years for male, ranks third in the world.[25]

While there are a number of contributing factors, e.g. lifestyle, environment, food safety, socioeconomic factors, occupational health and safety, a health system that works with accessibility based on needs is another important factor. Australia has all that.

In 2010-11, Australian health care expenditure amounted to $130 billion, an average of $5,800 per Australian. This is among the highest in OECD countries. The Commonwealth, state, territory and local governments accounted for 69% of the expenditure.[26]

---

[24] K. Davis, C Schoen, and K. Stremikis, *Mirror, Mirror on the Wall: How the Performance of the U.S. Health Care System Compares Internationally 2010 Update*, The Commonwealth Fund, Jun 2010
[25] Australian Institute of Health and Welfare, *Australian Health 2012*
[26] See (2)

The Public Health System

Medicare

Medicare, introduced in 1983, provides all eligible Australian residents access to free or low-cost medical, optometric and public hospital care Australia-wide. Medicare is based on the principles of universal coverage for medical services and access to care based on health needs rather than based on an individual's ability to pay.

Medicare cards are issued to people who enrol in Medicare. Persons aged 15 or older are issued with individual cards. Children under 15 are listed on their parents' cards.

Persons eligible

Individuals residing in Australia, other than in Norfolk Island, are eligible if they are:

- Australian citizens,

- Australian permanent residents (unless specially excluded or waiting period specified),

- New Zealand citizens,

- Persons who have applied for permanent visa (excludes an application for a parent visa), and

- Visitors and temporary residents from countries with which Australia has reciprocal health care agreements.

Extensive benefits

Medicare covers the following expenses incurred in Australia:

- Free in-patient, out-patient and emergency services as a public patient in a public hospital,

- Part or fully free
    - Consultation fees of general practitioners (GPs) and specialists,
    - Cost of tests and examinations by doctors needed to treat illnesses, including X-rays and pathology tests,
    - Cost of eye tests performed by optometrists,
    - Cost of some surgical procedures performed by approved dentists,
    - Cost of specified items under the Cleft Lip and Palate Scheme
    - Cost of specified items for allied health services as part of the Chronic Disease Management program
    - Most surgical and other therapeutic procedures performed by doctors,

- Part of the cost of medicines covered by the Pharmaceutical Benefits Scheme,

- 75 per cent of the Medicare Schedule fee for services and procedures provided by the treating doctor if admitted as a private patient in a public hospital or private hospital.

Medicare in practice

Medicare covers medical consultations, procedures and tests that are listed on the Medical Benefits Schedule (MBS). The fee (schedule fee) for each item is determined by the Australian

Government and is listed in the MBS. The schedule fee is like a 'recommended retail price'. Medical practitioners and service providers may charge the patient the schedule fee (bulk-bill) or above the schedule fee. Bulk billing is a common practice among general practitioners, optometrists and other service providers.

Medicare reimburses expenses incurred by patients on medical consultations and other services listed in the MBS. The reimbursement (Medicare rebate) is 100% of the schedule fee for a consulting visit at the general practitioner, and 85% of the schedule fee for a consulting visit to a specialist and 75% if admitted as a private patient in hospital.

The following two examples illustrate how this works in practice.

Example 9.1
A patient visits his general practitioner who charges $52 for a standard consultation. The patient's out-of-pocket expense of $15.25 is calculated as shown below:

GP's consultation fee	$52.00
Medicare Schedule fee	$36.75
Medicare rebate (100% of schedule fee)	$36.75
Out-of –pocket expense for patient	$15.25

If the general practitioner bulk-bills, the patient will incur nil out-of-pocket expense.

Example 9.2
A patient visits a Consultant Physician whose fee for initial consultation is $200. The patient's out-of-pocket expense of $74.10 is calculated as shown below:

Consultant Physician consultation fee	$200.00
Medicare Schedule fee	$148.10
Medicare rebate (85% of Schedule fee)	$125.90
Out-of –pocket expense for patient	$74.10

If the consultant physician bulk-bills, the out-of-pocket expense for the patient will be $22.20 ($148.10 less $125.90).

Patients generally have to pay the full consultation fee (unless the practice bulk bills), and get reimbursement from Medicare at a Medicare office or by mail.

When the consulting clinic has Medicare electronic claiming facility, the patient rebate can be claimed when the patient settles the account at the clinic. The rebate will be credited to the patient's nominated bank account almost immediately (when the clinic uses EFTPOS system) or within a few days (when the clinic uses the internet-based system).

Medicare safety net

An individual may incur high medical costs if he or she needs to see a doctor often or have regular tests.

Under Medicare Safety Net arrangement, when these costs reach the Medicare Safety Net thresholds, an individual may be eligible for additional Medicare benefits known as Medicare Safety Net Benefits.

Medicare levy

Medicare is funded by general taxation and Medicare levy. Medicare levy of 1.5% is charged on an individual's taxable income and another 1% Medicare Levy Surcharge if the individual's annual income is greater than $80,000, or the family's income is greater than $160,000.

A person is not liable for Medicare levy if the person's taxable income is equal or less than the lower tax threshold amount (about $30,685 for seniors, $30,451for pensioners and $19,404 for all other taxpayers).

Public hospitals

Public hospitals include hospitals established by governments and those initially started by religious or charitable institutions but have since been funded by the government. The state and territory governments mainly own and manage public hospitals. Large urban public hospitals handle most of the complex hospital care cases, e.g. intensive care, major surgery, organ transplants and renal dialysis. Acute care beds and emergency outpatient clinics are in public hospitals.

Many public hospitals have a private section catering to individuals with private health insurance.

In 201-12, there were 753 public hospitals in Australia as shown in Table 10.1.[27]

Table 10.1 Number of Public Hospitals by State 2011-12

New South Wales	225	South Australia	80
Victoria	151	Australian Capital Territory	3
Queensland	170	Tasmania	23
Western Australia	96	Northern Territory	5
Total			753

The public hospitals are very diverse both in size and the range of available services as shown overleaf:

- *Principal referral* hospitals
  They provide a wide range of services. They are mainly located in major cities and there is at least one in each state and territory.

---

[27] AIHW 2013, *Australia's hospitals 2010-11 at a glance*, Health services series no. 44. Cat. no. HSE 118. Canberra: AIHW

- *Specialist women's and children's* hospitals
  They specialise in maternity and other women services and/or paediatric services.

  They are in Sydney, Melbourne, Brisbane, Perth and Adelaide. *Large* hospitals have emergency departments, outpatient and admitted patient services but the range of activities is less than that of the Principal referral hospitals.

- The *Medium, Small acute* and *Small non-acute* hospitals
  They provide a narrower range of services and do not have emergency departments while *Other* hospitals consist of small hospitals and hospices.

- *Multipurpose services* hospitals
  They provide mainly non-acute admitted patient care and generally include residential aged care.

Health care for remote areas

More than 30% of Australians live in regional and remote areas. The Royal Flying Doctor Service provides a 24-hours-a-day, all year round aero-medical emergency and health care service to people who live, work or travel in Australia's remote areas.

From 21 bases, the service's 61 aircrafts fly more than 26.8 million kilometres over an area of 7,150,000 square kilometres. The service conducted 14,412 health care clinics and 88,530 *telehealth* contacts.[28]

---

[28] Royal Flying Doctor Service *Annual Report 11/12*

The Private Health System

Private health insurance cover

Australians have a choice of a variety of private health insurance covers, e.g. private hospital cover, cover for allied health and other professional services.

About half of the population supplement the public health cover by taking up private health insurance. The tax rebate on private health insurance cover scheme introduced in 1999 is a further incentive to encourage private health insurance cover.

In Australia, private health insurers are mandated by legislation to adopt the principle of community rating. The insured are to be charged the same premiums for similar health cover regardless of sex, health status, or claims history. The right to policy renewal is guaranteed and no insurer can refuse to insure a person.

This is a departure from normal insurance products where premiums are charged according to claims experience and potential risks, and exclusion or refusal of cover is not uncommon.

Private health insurance providers

Twenty-six private health insurers offer private health insurance cover to the public. Another 14 offer to restricted groups, e.g. doctors, teachers, and police. All 40 private heath insurers are registered under the *Private Insurance Act 2007*.

Private health insurance cover

About half of the Australian population take out private health insurance to have more health care options and to have cover on items not covered by Medicare, e.g. the following items:

- Dental examination and treatment
- Physiotherapy, occupational therapy, speech therapy, chiropractic, podiatry services
- Psychology services (unless as part of an agreed procedure referred by GP, psychiatrist or paediatrician)
- Acupuncture (unless as part of a doctor's consultation)
- Ambulance service
- Home nursing
- Hearing aids and other appliances
- Glasses and contact lenses
- Private patient hospital costs (e.g. theatre costs and accommodation)

Cost of private health insurance

Policies and premiums vary between health insurance providers depending on cover, e.g. whether just hospital cover, or extras cover (physiotherapy, optical, dental, podiatry, osteopathy, chiropractic, acupuncture), or combined cover. Annual premium can amount to:

- $800 to $2,800 for single,
- $2,500 to $4,500 for couples, and
- $2,500 to $4,500 for family.

Private hospitals

In 2012, there were 592 private hospitals in Australia. They are owned and operated by large corporations, private health funds and not-for-profit religious organisations.

Private hospitals handle the less complex non-emergency care, including simple elective surgery, though some have since included complex and high technology services.

Medical and Health Professionals

World-class training

Australian medical schools have consistently ranked high in world's university rankings for medicine. In 2012, nine universities in the Asia Pacific region made it to the world top 50 List. Five were from Australia, with the University of Melbourne tops the list from the region.[29] The five Australian universities and their world rankings (in brackets) were:

- University of Melbourne (9),
- University of Sydney (17),
- Monash University (29),
- University of Queensland (33), and
- University of New South Wales (37).

The Australian National University, University of Adelaide and the University of Western Australia were included in the world top 100 List.

---

[29] *QS World University Rankings for Medicine 2012*

Australia has 19 universities with medical schools and 43 teaching hospitals.

Pool of qualified health professionals

In 2011, there were 70,200 medical practitioners comprising 43,400 general practitioners and 25,400 specialist medical practitioners. The 257,200 nurses working in 2011 comprised of registered nurses (80%), enrolled and mothercraft nurses (7%) and midwives (5%). There were 120,000 allied health professionals.

Australia beckons overseas-trained health professionals

Australia continues to attract many overseas trained doctors. The Department of Immigration & Citizenship has, over the period 2007-11, issued 20,310 entry visas to overseas-trained medical practitioners. In 2011-2012, of the total 3,560 visas granted to medical practitioners 40% were issued to those from the United Kingdom, Republic of Ireland and Canada and 30% were issued to those from India, Malaysia, Sri Lanka, Pakistan, Philippines and Singapore. In 2011, 56% of general practitioners, 47% of the specialists and 33% of nurses in Australia were born overseas.[30]

Newly Arrived Migrants and Visitors

Medicare benefits for newly arrived migrants

The Medicare eligibility of migrants is dependent on condition in the visa sub-class. Most newly arrived migrants under permanent residence basis are eligible for Medicare benefits. However,

---

[30] ABS 4102.0 - *Australian Social Trends*, April 2013

holders of provisional and temporary residence visas are normally ineligible for Medicare benefits.

Visitors

Australia has reciprocal health care agreements with the United Kingdom, Republic of Ireland, Finland, Italy, Malta, Norway, the Netherlands, New Zealand, Slovenia and Sweden. Visitors from countries that have reciprocal health care arrangements have restricted access to Medicare assistance for medically necessary treatment (but not for prearranged treatment) and subsidised medicine under the Pharmaceutical Benefits Scheme.

Australians travelling overseas

As Medicare does not cover medical expenses incurred overseas. Australians travelling to countries with which Australia has reciprocal health care agreements have restricted access to the host country's public health care system.

However, travellers would normally purchase travel insurance cover even if they were travelling to these countries as transit to or from these countries are not covered under the reciprocal health care agreements.

11 Social Security System
The catchall social safety net, just in case

Australia's social security benefits, with the aim of supporting the standard of living of the disadvantaged and vulnerable groups, are generally means tested – income, assets, or activity based tests.

Benefits are available to low-income households, students and trainees, the unemployed, disabled, sick, seniors and retirees, families and individuals raising children and persons affected by crisis or disasters.

Australia's annual social expenditure including public pension is around 20% of the country's GDP. This is below that of the United Kingdom (25%), New Zealand (22%), Canada (21%), but ahead of the United States (14%). Australia's budgeted expenditure for 2013 on social security and welfare amounts to $132 billion.

Centrelink, an agency under the Commonwealth Department of Human Services, is responsible for administering and delivering the range of social security payments and services; providing other specialist services for clients including claiming foreign pension, income management, services for the homeless and those at risks of homelessness and job search facilities and arranging workshops and seminars including those for impending retirees, the unemployed and persons returning to work.

Australia has entered social security agreements with 27 countries whereby countries will share the social security burden for those who have migrated between countries. Each country will pay part-pension to these people.

Social Security Benefits

A wide range of benefits

Australia's social security benefits cover a wide range of areas and purposes, including the following:

- Students and trainees pursuing their studies or receiving training,
- Job seekers in transition to employment,
- Sick, injured and persons with disability,
- Carers looking after their loved ones, and
- Parents or guardians bringing up children,
- Seniors and retirees in their retirement years.

Fact Sheets 11.1 on pages 174 to178 provides further details on each of the social security benefits. The payment rates shown for the respective benefits are the latest before their next reviews.

Disaster relief and other payments

These are payments made to farmers, small businesses and individuals affected by natural disasters and government policy change and initiatives.

Concession cards and others

The recipients of social security benefits are often eligible for cards that entitle them to discount from utilities, transport, local council rates, pharmaceutical and services. The available cards include Concession cards, Health Care Card, Pensioner Concession Card. Other benefits available include pharmaceutical allowance, rent assistance, telephone allowance and utilities.

Extra assistance for household expenses

These are payments and services to help households responding to a number of government policy changes. They include the following:

- Digital TV Switchover Household Assistance Scheme
- Telephone Allowance
- LPG Vehicle Scheme
- Household Assistance Package
- Clean Energy Advance and Clean Energy Supplement
- Low Income Supplement
- Low Income Family Supplement
- Single Income Family Supplement
- Essential Medical Equipment Payment

Eligibility requirements

Most social security payments are means tested, i.e. eligibility is subjected to income, assets, activity tests and other requirements including residence requirement.

The social security benefit rates

Most of the social security benefits are means tested and the maximum eligible payment will be adjusted accordingly depending on income and the type of benefit.

The benefits are generally paid fortnightly while some are one-off payments.

Newly-Arrived Migrants

For newly arrived permanent residents, other than refugees, Australian citizens and their family members and people who have previously lived in Australia for 104 weeks, there is a waiting period of 104 weeks before they are eligible for certain payments as shown in Table 11.1.

Table 11.1 Newly Arrived Permanent Residents

Eligible Payments and Services on Becoming Permanent Resident	Eligible payments only after the Waiting Period
Family Tax Benefit	Newstart allowance
Baby Bonus	Youth Allowance
Maternity Immunisation Allowance	Sickness Allowance
Child Care Benefit	Carer Payment
Health Care Card (may be)	Austudy
Carer Allowance	Mobility Allowance
Exceptional Circumstances Relief Payment	Special Benefit
Australian Disaster Recovery Payment	
Employment services	

Obligations of social security recipients

All social security payment or service recipients have to inform Centrelink immediately of any change of circumstances and other factors that may impact on their payment and eligibility.

By not informing Centrelink about changes in one's circumstances, individual runs the risk of in debt for the overpayment, or if the non-disclosure is deliberate, the risk of being charged with fraud.

International Social Security Agreements

Australia has social security agreements with 27 countries, namely Austria, Belgium, Canada, Chile, Croatia, Cyprus, Czech

Republic, Denmark, Finland, Germany, Greece, Republic of Ireland, Italy, Japan, Republic of Korea, the former Yugoslav Republic of Macedonia, Malta, the Netherlands, New Zealand, Norway, Poland, Portugal, Slovenia, Spain, Switzerland and the United States of America.

Generally under the agreements, countries will share the social security burden for those who have migrated between countries. Each country will pay part-pension to these people.

Fact Sheet 11.1 Social Security Benefits

Students and Trainees

Youth Allowance	Youth who is studying, undertaking training or receiving an Australian Apprenticeship, looking for work, or sick. Range - $223 to $533.80 fortnightly
AUSTUDY	Persons aged ≥ 25 years studying at an approved institution or undertaking an Australian Apprenticeship full-time. Range - $407.50 to $533.80 fortnightly
Education Entry Payment	Individuals returning to study. $208 one-of
ABSTUDY	Indigenous secondary or tertiary students or full-time apprentices. Range - $30.80 to $537.80 fortnightly Masters or doctorate students $945.60 maximum fortnightly *Other payments including school fee allowance, incidental allowance and fare allowance.*
Assistance for Isolated Children	Families with primary or secondary student unable to attend school because of geographical isolation, disability or special health need. Boarding allowance (maximum $8919 p.a.), 2nd home allowance $218.09/student/fortnight (maximum 3/family), Distance education allowance $3,743 p.a., Assistance for Isolated Children Pensioner Education Supplement $62.40 fortnightly
Fare Allowance	Individuals living away from permanent home to study.
Pensioner Education Supplement	Certain current benefit recipients to help with the costs of full-time or part-time study.

Job Seekers	
Youth Allowance	Youth who is studying, undertaking training or receiving an Australian Apprenticeship, looking for work, or sick. Range - $223 to $533.80 fortnightly
Newstart Allowance	Individuals aged 21 years or over, but under Age Pension age, looking for paid work, and prepared to enter into an Employment Pathway Plan, meet activity test requirements, and not involved in industrial action. Range - $448.70 to $683.50 fortnightly.

Sicked, Injured or Persons with Disability	
Sickness Allowance	Individuals who are employed, or self-employed, and temporarily unable to work because of a medical condition. Range - $444.70 to $533 fortnightly
Disability Support Pension	Individuals who have a physical, intellectual, or psychiatric condition that stops them from working or who are permanently blind. Range $338.40 to $733.70 fortnightly.
Mobility Allowance	Individuals with disabilities who are involved in qualifying activities and use public transport only with substantial assistance. Range - $87 to $121.80 fortnightly
Special Benefit	Individuals with severe financial need due to circumstances beyond their control and are unable to receive other Centrelink benefit.
Youth Disability Supplement	Extra assistance to youths aged below 21 years of age with a disability. Maximum $114 fortnightly.

Parents/Guardians

Baby Bonus	Birth or adoption of a child. $5,000 for first children and multiple births and $3,000 for subsequent children.
Child Care Benefit	Long day care, family day care, occasional care, outside school hour care, vacation care and registered care. A non-school aged child at $3.99 maximum 50 hours, i.e. $199.50/week. Payment for a school-aged child is at 85% of the non-school rate.
Child Care Rebate	Parents or guardians for approved childcare if they are working, training or studying. Payment rate is 50% of out-of-pocket expenses subject to maximum of $7,500/child/year.
Child Support Scheme	For either or both parents who are separated and the child or children aged < 18.
Double Orphan Pension	Individuals caring for children or children who are unable to be cared for by their parents in certain circumstances. $57.90/week.
Family Tax Benefit A	Families with dependent child or secondary student children aged under 20 (child receives no other payment, or benefit). Range from $55.16 to $224 per child fortnightly.
Family Tax Benefit B	An extra payment for single parents and families with one main income. $102.20 or $146.44 per child per fortnight.
Maternity Immunisation Allowance	Parents to immunise their children. Two separate payments amount of $129 each.
Paid Parental Leave	Payment support for up to 18 weeks to help working parents take time off work to care for a newborn or recently adopted child. $622.10/week up to a maximum 18 weeks. Payment can be paid by Centrelink or one's employer.
Parenting Payment	Parent, grandparent or foster carer, if individual is single and care for ≥ one child aged < 8, or if individual has a partner they care for ≥ one child aged < 6. Ranges from $448.70 to $683.50 fortnightly.

Seniors and Retirees

Benefit	Eligibility	Payment Rates		
Aged Pension	Female age 64.5, male age 65. Residence, income and assets tests	Fortnightly Single – $733.70, Couple – $1,106.20 or 733.70 each for couple separated due to ill health		
Commonwealth Seniors Health Card	Seniors of age pension age but not qualified for Age Pension.	N/A		
Pension Bonus Scheme	Individuals, though qualified for Age Pension or service pension before 20 September 2009, defer claiming. Registered for scheme, has not received any other income support payment and meet the work test rule	Bonus Amount based on number of years deferred (*Rates are updated 20/3 and 20/9 each year*)		
		Year deferred	Single ($)	Couple ($)
		1	1,845.20	1,395.30
		2	7,380.90	5,581.10
		3	16,607.00	12,557.50
		4	29,523.50	22,324.50
		5	46,130.50	34,882.00
Pension Loan Scheme (secured by Australian real estate)	Individuals of pensionable age with capital tied up in assets and who need more income to live on.	Individual nominate fortnightly amount up to the maximum Age Pension amount.		

Carers

Carer Allowance	A supplementary payment for carers who provide additional daily care and attention for someone with a disability or medical condition, or who is frail aged. Rate - $115.40/fortnight.
Carer Payment	Individual unable to support oneself through paid employment because of fulltime care for someone with a severe disability, medical condition or frail-aged. Rate - $553.10 to $733.70 fortnightly.

Partners, Bereaved

Widow Allowance	Individuals born on or before 1 July 1995 who become widowed, divorced or separated later in life and have no recent workforce experience. Rate - $492.60 or $533 fortnightly.
Bereavement Allowance	A short-term income support payment for individual recently widowed. Maximum rate $712/fortnightly up to 14 weeks.
Bereavement Payment	Individual after the death of one's partner or child, or someone one cared for. Rate is dependent on individual circumstances.

12 Doing Business
No hidden surprises

Australia, the world 12th largest economy, is one of the global safest trade and investment destinations.

Australia's financial system is well-developed and ranked 5th out of the world 57 leading financial systems and capital markets

The ease of doing business has remained strong in Australia according to an international study.

There are no hidden surprises. The business environment is well supported by legal and ethics structures, transparent public policies and regulations and skilled and literate workforce. All three levels of government provide support in funding and other initiatives for business to expand and transform.

Australia continues to attract foreign investments. At the end of 2012, foreign investment in Australia totalled $2 trillion including $550 billion direct investment.

There are many Australian business success stories. Many Australian businesses have since become global players, outgrowing the domestic market.

Australia's business migration program continues to attract many business migrants to the country. The program targets successful business people to settle in Australia and to develop business activity and growth for the Australian economy.

Business in Australia

60% are SMEs

Table 12.1 shows the 2 million businesses by turnover and staff employed. More than 60% of them are small and medium enterprises.

Table 12.1 Businesses by Turnover Staff Employed 30 June 2012

Annual turnover	Number of businesses '000	Number of staff employed	Number of businesses '000
0 - < $50k	598	0	1,306
$50k - < $200k	740	1- 4	515
$200k - < $2m	673	5 - 19	232
≥ $2m	131	20 - 199	82
		200+	7
Total	2,142	Total	2,142

Business by industry

The businesses are in a range of industries as shown in Table 12.2.

Table 12.2 Businesses (in '000) by Industry 30 June 2012

Construction	347	Administrative and support	82
Professional/scientific/technical	251	Wholesale trade	79
Rental/hiring/real estate	225	Arts and recreation	27
Agriculture/forestry/fishing	192	Education and training	26
Financial/insurance	167	Information/media/telecom.	19
Retail trade	142	Public administration/safety	8
Transport/postal/warehousing	130	Mining	8
Health care/social assistance	104	Electricity/gas/water/waste	6
Manufacturing	88	Others	158
Accommodation and food s	83		
Total			2,142

Business structure

Sole proprietorship, partnership and trusts are the business structure chosen by 65% of the businesses as shown in Table 12.3.

Table 12.3 Business Structure 30 June 2012			
	'000		'000
Companies	728	Partnerships	328
Sole proprietor	607	Trusts	479
Total			2,142

Starting and Running a Business

The Regulators

There are industry specific regulations. The following lists the major regulators and the legislations they administer.

- The Australian Competition and Consumer Commission (ACCC)
  The ACCC administers the *Competition and Consumer Act 2010*. The Act aims to promote competition, fair-trading and provide consumer protection.

- Australian Securities and Investment Commission (ASIC)
  ASIC administers the *Australian Securities and Investment Commission Act 2001*. It carries out most of the work under the *Corporation Act 2001*, regulating Australian registered companies.

  It also administers many other legislations including *Business Names Registration Act 2011*, *Business Names Registration (Transitional and Consequential Provisions) Act 2011*, *Insurance*

Contracts Act 1984, Superannuation (Resolution of Complaints) Act 1993 and *Superannuation Industry (Supervision) Act 1993.*

Together with the Australian Prudential Regulation Authority, ASIC regulates certain sections of the *Retirement Savings Accounts Act 1997, Life Insurance Act 1995, National Consumer Credit Protection Act 2009 and Medical Indemnity (Prudential Supervision and Product Standards) Act 2003.*

- Australian Taxation Office (ATO)
  The ATO administers Australia's federal taxation system including *Income Tax Assessment Act 1936, Income Tax Assessment Act 1997, Taxation Administration Act 1953, Fringe Benefits Tax Assessment Act 1986* and *A New Tax System (Goods and Services Tax) Act 1999.*

- Foreign Investment Review Board (FIRB)
  The FIRB examines foreign direct investment proposals and make recommendations to the Treasurer on the compatibility of the proposals with *Foreign Acquisitions and Takeovers Act 1975* and Australia's foreign investment policy.

Australian Securities Exchange Limited (ASX)
The ASX oversees compliance with ASX operating rules and promotes standards of corporate governance among the listed companies. The ASX has markets trading in equities, derivatives, futures and fixed interest securities. The ASX has offices in Sydney, Melbourne, Brisbane, Adelaide, Perth and Hobart.

Australia's equity market is the 8th largest in the world and the 2nd largest in the Asia-Pacific, with a $1.2 trillion market capitalisation. Its bond and derivatives markets are ranked 3rd and 1st respectively in the Asia Pacific.

- Australian Prudential Regulation Authority (APRA)
  APRA is the prudential regulator of the Australian financial services industry. It oversees banks, credit unions, buildings societies, general insurance and reinsurance companies, life insurance and most superannuation funds.

- IP Australia
  IP Australia - an agency within the Department of Industry, Innovation, Science, Research and Tertiary Education - administers intellectual property rights and legislation relating to patents, trademarks, designs and plant breeder's rights.

Employment essentials

Table 12.4 outlines the basic employment requirements that businesses have to comply.

Table 12.4 Employment Essentials

Age of employee	Not < 15 years old unless with special permit.
Pay rate and conditions	At least minimum pay rate and minimum conditions according to job and industry
Superannuation	Contribute 9% of gross wage of staff member's gross salary into a complying superannuation fund or retirement saving account No super contribution if member: • Receives less than $450 a month in salary or wages • Is < 18 years old and works < than 30 hours a week • Is aged ≥ 70 years
Working environment	Safe, free of harassment, bullying and discrimination
Workplace injury insurance	Workplace insurance is required for businesses incurring wages above a certain threshold.

Please refer Table 7.5 on page 114 and Fact Sheet 7.1 on page 124 in Chapter 7 *Working in Australia* for details of minimum wage and requirements under the *National Employment Standards* which regulate maximum work hours, leave entitlement, flexible working arrangements, notice of termination, and redundancy pay.

Income tax essentials

Table 12.5 outlines the income tax basics applicable to businesses.

Table 12.5 Income Tax Essentials

Tax and legal obligations	Vary depending on business structure.
Tax file number	Separate business tax file number for partnership, company or trust. Sole trader can use personal tax file number.
Goods and services tax (GST)	GST registration required for annual business turnover ≥ $75,000 or ≥$150,000 for non-profit organisation; taxi driver, limousine or car hire business.
Australian Business Number (ABN)	Need to apply for an ABN if the business is required to register for GST.
Pay as you go (PAYG) registration and remittance	Register with ATO and remit any tax deducted from payments of salary to employees and fees to directors.
Business Activity Statement (BAS) and tax payment	Most businesses must lodge quarterly BAS with the tax payment. Large businesses have to lodge BAS monthly. Small businesses can lodge BAS annually.
Superannuation contribution	Employer must contribute superannuation for each eligible employee minimum 9% of their ordinary time earnings.
Fringe benefit tax (FBT) and annual return	Businesses providing non-cash benefits to employees or employees' associates (e.g. family members) may have to pay FBT and lodge an annual fringe benefits tax return. Individual who is an employee of own company or trust, fringe benefits tax can apply to benefits the individual receives.
Small business tax concessions	A range of concessions is available to eligible businesses with <$2 million annual turnover.
Running business from home	Beware of tax effect on CGT exemption normally applies to private residence.
Record keeping	Generally required to keep records for 5 years.
Annual tax return l	Required for business even if no tax liability.

Payroll tax

Payroll tax is a state tax collected by the respective state and territory governments. Employers employing staff in the state or territory are liable to payroll tax to the state and territory government if the total wages exceed the applicable exemption threshold. Table 12.6 lists the applicable threshold and payroll tax rate.

Table 12.6 Payroll Tax Threshold & Tax Rate 2013

Payroll tax exemption threshold (annual total wage)	State	Threshold	Tax rate
	New South Wales	$0.689m	5.45
	Victoria	$0.550m	4.90
	Queensland	$1.100m	4.75
	South Australia	$0.600m	4.95
	Western Australia	$0.750m	5.50
	ACT	$1.750m	6.85
	Tasmania	$1.010m	6.10
	Northern Territory	$1.500m	5.50
Payroll tax due	7 days after the end of the month		

Other requirements

Some businesses, e.g. those in the food retailing, packaging, manufacturing must comply with strict food and safety requirements by local council and health authorities before the business can commence operation. For businesses like childcare and elderly care there are strict accreditation rules and registration requirements.

Governments' support

The Australian federal, state and territory and local governments provide hundreds and millions of dollars annually in funding and other initiatives for businesses expansion and transformation. They include capital expansion, business development and trade shows, research and development, consulting/financial services, marketing, product development/improvement, new business startup, training/certification/wage support, feasibility study/business plan, renovation/maintenance/upgrade and import/export assistance.

The funding and assistance include grants (non repayable), low and no interest loans, guaranteed loans, tax refunds and tax credits, business risk insurance, relocation incentive, access to resources (state-of-the-art expertise, resources and facilities), one-time and renewable, conditionally repayable, equity financing and many more.

The three tiers of government (Commonwealth, state and local) have many agencies and initiatives supporting Australian businesses. For example, the Australian Trade Commission *Austrade* through its network of offices in 50 countries has been assisting Australian companies to grow their international business, encourage and facilitate foreign direct investment to Australia and promote Australia's education sector overseas. All the state and territory governments have dedicated business units providing business support and promoting foreign direct investment to their states.

Australian success stories

Australia's business landscape is full of home grown success stories. The list includes *Boost Juice, Cochlear, Computershares, Flight Centre, Harrvey Norman, JB Hi-Fi, Linfox, Lend Lease, Lonely Planet, MYOB, Kathmandu, Oriental Merchant, Servcorp, Transfield Holdings, QBE Insurance, Village Roadshow, Westfarmers, Westfield Holdings* and many more. Many of these companies have since outgrown their home base and have businesses across many continents.

The entries for the many annual business awards in Australia, e.g. *Australian Business Awards, Ethnic Business Awards, Telstra Business Awards*, are examples of business success stories.

Annually, the *Business Review Weekly* (BRW) publishes the 'Rich 200', 'Young Rich List', 'Top 1000 companies' and 'Fast Starters' ranking and showcasing some of the business success stories.

Foreign Direct Investments

$550b foreign direct investment

Australia continues to attract considerable foreign direct investments. Foreign direct investment (FDI) has grown by more than 50% over the 5-year period to 2012. The United States, the United Kingdom and Japan are the major foreign investors holding almost 50% of the total FDI as shown in Table 12.7.

Table 12.7 Stock of FDI ($b) in Australia by Country, 2012

USA	131.3	Hong Kong	7.3
UK	79.4	Bermuda	6.4
Japan	61.2	Belgium	6.1
Netherlands	32.3	Malaysia	5.7
Singapore	23.8	New Zealand	4.3
Switzerland	22.5	Luxemburg	4.3
Canada	21.2	South Korea	2.1
British Virgin Islands	19.2	Sweden	1.6
China	16.7	India	1.3
Germany	13.6	Others	81.7
France	7.6		
Total			549.6

The scale of FDI from China and Singapore has grown significantly over the last decade. Australia has been the most significant recipient of Chinese outbound direct investment since

2006. China registers a compound annual growth rate of 46% over the 5-year period to 2012.

Sixty-percent of the foreign direct investments are in mining, manufacturing, finance and insurance and wholesale and retail trades.

Why Australia?

Many factors have attributed to the increase in foreign investments in Australia. These include the following:

- Deregulation and liberalisation
  The deregulation of the finance, telecommunications and the utilities sectors and the liberalisation of airline ownership rules, investment in the resource sector and a robust share market have contributed to the growth of foreign investments.

- Safe trade and investment destination
  Australia ranks together Canada, Germany, Norway, Sweden and Switzerland as the safest trade and investment destinations according to the Dun & Bradstreet's *Global Risk Indicator* (GRI). The study provides a comparative, cross-border assessment of the political, commercial, economic and external risk of doing business.

- Ease of doing business
  A recent study *Doing Business* 2013 by the World Bank and the International Finance Corporation, found the ease of doing business in Australia remains strong. Australia ranks 10 out of the 185 economies and 4 out of 62 economies with large population.

- Proximity to Asia

  Australia's proximity to Asia, the world's fastest growing region, is a unique advantage that Australia has been able to maximise. Australia's economy has received tremendous boost first from Japan's post-war reconstruction and its subsequent economic expansion, Korean post-1980 economic growth and subsequently the opening of China.

  Australia is set to benefit from India's long-term growth potential. India, after two decades of economic reforms, is now the world's 4th largest economy. In the first decade of the 21st century, Australia's merchandise trade exports to India have risen by 800%. While there are challenges ahead, India's economic transformation will provide opportunities for many sectors of the Australian economy, i.e. resources and energy, education, tourism, agriculture and infrastructure.

- Multi-cultural, skilled work force

  More than 3 million Australians or 25% of the work force speak a language other than English at home. More than a million are fluent in a European language other than English and over 1.5 million are fluent in a major Asian language including Mandarin, Cantonese, Vietnamese, Hindi, Punjabi, Indonesian, Tagalog and Japanese.

  This linguistic diversity provides companies and organisations with the workforce that is multilingual and understands multicultural sensitivities. Many international companies and organisations have taken advantage of what Australia has on offer and establish regional centres here.

Setting up a business

Foreign company can establish an Australian subsidiary or establish a branch office and carry on business in the name of the foreign company. Table 12.8 highlights the differences in the two business structures.

Table 12.8 Business Structure - Differences

	Australian Subsidiary	Branch Office
Company Law	Separate legal entity registered with (ASIC)	Not a separate legal entity Foreign company is registered with the ASI C directors
Liabilities	Subsidiary liable unless parent company has provided a guarantee or subsidiary has been trading whilst insolvent	Liabilities remain with the foreign company
Tax	Taxed on global income at resident tax rate Must apply for Australian Business Number (ABN), Tax File Number (TFN)	Taxed as a separate entity in Australia. Must apply for Australian Business Number (ABN) and Tax File Number (TFN)
Debt/equity ratio	Not >3:1 if funded by debt owed to a foreign parent to qualify for tax deductions for interest paid to parent	Not >3:1 if funded by debt owed to a foreign parent to qualify for tax deductions for interest paid to parent

Foreign Investment Review Board

The Foreign Investment Review Board (FIRB) examines foreign investment proposals and makes recommendations to the Treasurer on the compatibility of the proposals with *Foreign Acquisitions and Takeovers Act 1975* and Australia's foreign investment policy.

Foreign interests include individuals not ordinarily resident in Australia, corporation or trust where there is 15% or more foreign interest or where several foreigners have 40% or more interest in aggregate.

There are rules governing notification and approval of foreign investment in Australia. Notification of foreign acquisition is required depending on the nature and value of the investments and the industrial sectors as shown in Fact Sheet 12.1 on page 192. However, notification and approval is not required in a number of instances as shown in Fact Sheet 12.2 on page 193.

Certain industry sectors, e.g. banking, telecommunications, shipping, civil aviation and airports, are subjected to other additional industry specific restrictions.

Business Migration

Australia has been actively encouraging business migrants to set up businesses and invest in the country especially in regional, rural or low growth areas. The state and territory governments have established dedicated business investment sections enticing business migrants to their states.

Annually, Australia issues around 7,000 visas to business migrants intending to establish business or investments in Australia. While the number is slightly less than 10% of the skilled migrant intake, its impact on the business scene is visible especially in capital cities and some regional centres.

Business migration will be covered in greater details in Chapter 16 *Business Skills Migration.*

Fact Sheet 12.1 Acquisitions by Foreign Investors Requiring Notification to FIRB

	Non-US Investor	US Investor
Business investments		
Direct investments or new businesses by foreign governments or their agencies	Notification required	Notification required
An interest in an Australian corporation or assets of Australian business	$248m	Private investor (sensitive sectors[1]) $248m
Offshore takeover of a company with assets or business in Australia		Private investors (other sectors) $1,078m
Real estate investments		
All vacant non-residential land	Notification required	Notification required
All residential real estate	Notification required	Notification required
All shares or units in Australian urban land corporations or trusts	Notification required	Notification required
Developed non-residential commercial real estate subject to heritage listing	$5m	$1,078m
Developed non-residential commercial real estate not subject to heritage listing	$54m	$1,078m

[1]Media, telecommunications, transport, military, encryption / security technology and communications, uranium / plutonium extraction, nuclear facilities

Fact Sheet 12.2 Acquisitions by Foreign Investors No Notification No Approval Required

Real estate acquisitions

- Australian property by Australian citizen living abroad;
- Property in joint names and the spouse is an Australian citizen;
- Residential property by New Zealand citizen;
- Residential property by permanent resident;
- New dwellings from developer who has preapproval to sell the dwellings to foreign persons;
- An interest in a time share scheme which does not allow the purchaser to more than 4 weeks entitlement annually;
- Certain residential real estate in an Integrated Tourism Resort (ITR);
- An interest in developed commercial property valued below the relevant threshold;
- An interest in developed commercial property and the property is to be used immediately and in its present state for industrial or non residential commercial purposes;
- An interest acquired by will or by operation of law (e.g. court order in a divorce settlement);
- Purchase of property from the government.

Non-real estate investments

No application for approval for acquisitions is required for existing Australian corporations or businesses and proposals to establish new businesses if the transactions are below the relevant monetary thresholds.

13 Australian Taxation

No hidden surprises, just pay your dues

Australia's taxation revenue as a percentage of GDP remained unchanged in 2011-12 at 26% and it spent a third of its GDP.

Australia's taxation revenue as a percentage of GDP remained unchanged in 2011-12 at 26% and it spent a third of its GDP.

This makes Australia one of the lowest-taxed countries in the Western world and among the lowest-spending countries of the 34 advanced economies.

Among the other lowest-spending countries are Hong Kong SAR, Singapore, Republic of Korea and Taiwan where welfare is individual's responsibility. In terms of leaner government, Australia, New Zealand and Switzerland are the three countries with the smallest governments in the Western world.

The three levels of Australian government collected $390 billion of tax revenue in 2011-12. The Commonwealth Government accounted for 81% of the tax revenue while the State and Territory Governments raised $60 billion or 16% of the total Australia's tax revenue. Australia's local governments collected $13 billion or 3% of the total Australia's tax revenue in 2011-12.

The Commonwealth Government tax revenue is mainly from personal income tax, company income tax, goods and services tax, excise, fringe benefits tax, tax on superannuation and custom duty.

The state and territories imposed taxes include payroll tax, stamp duty, land and property tax, taxes on gambling, taxes on insurance and motor vehicle taxes.

Commonwealth Government Taxes

Personal income taxes

Individuals are taxed on their personal income including wages and salaries, business income (their share of partnership or trust profits), investment income and capital gains.

Tax on capital gains is not a separate tax but part of the income tax, though it is generally referred to as capital gains tax (CGT).

A person working in Australia needs to establish whether he or she is an Australian resident for tax purposes as different rules apply to non-residents as shown in Table 13.1.

Table 13.1 Tax Residence & Taxable Income

Australian Tax Residence	<ul><li>Always lived in Australia, or</li><li>Moved to Australia and lives permanently, or</li><li>Lived in Australia continuously for ≥6 months, or most of the time in the same job and living in the same place, or</li><li>In Australia ≥1/2 of financial year and intends to live in Australia</li></ul>
Tax on Australian Resident	Tax on global income<ul><li>Australian income (other than those derived before becoming an Australian resident and non-resident tax has been withheld), and</li><li>Foreign source income</li></ul>
Tax on Non-Resident	Tax on Australian income only

The Australian tax year runs from 1 July to 30 June. The personal income tax rates for 2013-14 are as shown in Table 13.2 overleaf.

Table 13.2 Personal Income Tax Rates 2013-14

Residents		Non-Residents	
Taxable Income	Tax Rate (%)	Taxable Income	Tax Rate (%)
$0 - $18,200	Nil	$0 - $80,000	32.5
$18,201 - $37,000	19		
$37,001 - $80,000	32.5		
$80,001 - $180,000	37	$80,001 - $180,000	37
≥$180,001	45	≥$180,000	45

Low income tax offset

An Australian resident taxpayer with taxable income of less than $67,500 is entitled to a low income tax offset of up to $1,500 as shown in Table 13.3.

Table 13.3 Low Income Tax Offset 2013-14

Taxable Income	Low Income Tax Offset
$0 - $37,000	$445
$37,001 - $66,666	$445 less 1.5% of excess over $37,000
≥ $66,667	Nil

Senior Australians and pensioner tax offsets (SAPTO)

Senior Australians, pensioners or mature workers may be eligible for SAPTO and Mature Age Worker Tax Offset if they meet certain conditions.

Medicare levy

Medicare levy, at 1.5% of individual taxable income, is payable by most taxpayers, with the following exceptions:

- Medicare levy reduction for people with low income, e.g. income below a certain threshold

- Medicare levy exemption, e.g. a foreign resident, a resident of Norfolk Island, not entitled to Medicare benefits, or person meeting certain medical requirements

- Additional Medicare levy surcharge is payable for people with income above a certain threshold and the person and any of the person's dependents don't have appropriate private patient hospital insurance cover.

Tax on capital gains

Tax on capital gains is not a separate tax but part of the income tax, though it is generally referred to as capital gains tax (CGT). CGT was introduced in Australia on 20 September 1985.

CGT applies to the global assets owned by an Australian tax resident. CGT applies to share, real estate and business goodwill. Some personal assets including home, car and personal use assets like furniture are exempt from CGT.

Any capital loss is used to offset against capital gains and not against other income and can be carried forward to future years.

Company tax

Companies, including incorporated and unincorporated associations, limited partnerships, certain unit trusts and public trading trusts, are subjected to a tax rate of 30% on all earned income. Pooled developments funds, credit unions, non-profit companies, retirement saving account providers and life insurance companies are subject to special tax rates.

Tax on superannuation funds

Complying superannuation funds are taxed at the rate of 15% on contribution, realised capital gains and investment income. This same rate of tax applies to superannuation products of life insurers and retirement savings account providers.

Fringe benefits tax (FBT)

Employers are liable to pay FBT at 46.5% of the gross-up taxable value of certain non-cash benefits that are provided to their employees. These benefits include free or discounted use of motor vehicles, payments for housing, meals, entertainment, health insurance, childcare and education. The FBT rate will increase to 47% from 1 April 2014.

Resource rent taxes

The Petroleum Resource Rent Tax, at a rate of 40%, is levied on taxable income relating to offshore petroleum projects other than some of North-West production area, which are subject to excise and royalties. A 30% Minerals Resource Rent Tax (MRRT) applies to taxable profit of all iron ore and coal projects from 1 July 2012.

Sales tax

The Goods and Service Tax (GST), introduced in 2000, is the main revenue component of the sales tax. It is levied at 10% on most goods and services consumed in Australia. Basic food items, health care, child-care, rent, and education are excluded

Wine equalisation tax at the rate of 29% is levied on all alcoholic beverages including grape wine, including sparkling and fortified wine, grape wine products, fruit wines or vegetable wines, cider, perry, mead and sake, if they have more than 1.15% by volume of ethyl alcohol.

Luxury car tax (LCT) at 33% is levied on car purchase that exceeds the luxury threshold of $60,316 or $75,375 for fuel-efficient models for financial year 2013-14. LCT is addition to any GST payable on purchase of luxury car.

Excise duty

Excise duty is imposed on local products including petroleum and fuel products, crude oil, oils and lubricants, tobacco and alcoholic beverages (other than wine). Customs duties are levied on these products when imported.

Customs duty

Australia has been implementing a trade liberalisation program with gradual tariff reduction since 2005. By 1/01/2015, the general tariff rate and that of passenger motor vehicles, clothing and finished textiles, cotton sheeting fabric, carpet and footwear, sleeping bags, table linen and footwear, sleeping bags, table linen will be 5%.

Other indirect taxes

Other indirect taxes include agriculture levies and charges that are used to fund various industry initiatives, including research and development, marketing and promotion; broadcasting licence fees paid by commercial radio and television licensees; passenger movement charges and import processing and depot charges administered by the Australian Customs.

State/Territory Government Taxes

The state and territory governments supplemented funding from the Commonwealth government with states imposed taxes mainly from payroll tax, stamp duty, land and property tax, taxes on gambling, taxes on insurance and motor vehicle taxes. Motor vehicle taxes are vehicle registration fees and licence driving licence fees.

Payroll tax

Payroll tax is levied on employers based on wages paid or payable when the wages exceed the exemption threshold. Table 13.4 lists the 2013 payroll tax rates and the exemption thresholds.

Table 13.4 Payroll Tax – Rates and Exemption Threshold 2013

State	Payroll Tax		Top Stamp Duty Rate
	Payroll tax rate	Exemption threshold	
New South Wales	5.45%	$689,000	5.50%
Victoria	4.90%	$550,000	5.50%
Queensland	4.75%	$1,100,000	5.75%
Western Australia	5.50%	$750,000	5.15%
South Australia	4.95%	$600,000	5.50%
Australian Capital Territory	6.85%	$1,750,000	7.25%
Tasmania	6.10%	$1,010,000	4.50%
Northern Territory	5.50%	$1,500,000	4.95%

Stamp duty

Stamp duty is charged on transactions including land transfers, certain leasing arrangements, motor vehicle transfers, declarations of trust, livestock sales, life insurance, general insurance and transport accident charge. Stamp duty is charged at a flat rate or based on transaction value. There are concessions and exemptions depending on the nature of the transactions. Table 13.5 below shows the top rate of stamp duty.

Land tax

All Australian states and territory governments, except Northern Territory, impose land tax on all owners based on the site value and land use.

There are exemptions, including owner's principal place of residence, most land used for primary production and a range of other uses. There is also a tax exemption threshold as shown in Table 13.5.

Table 13.5 Land Tax Threshold for State and Territories 2013

New South Wales	$406,000	South Australia	$316,000
Victoria	$249,999	ACT	Nil
Queensland	$599,999	Tasmania	$24,999
Western Australia	$300,000	Northern Territory	Not applicable

Local Government Taxes

The revenue collected mainly from council rates and licence and other fees to supplement funding from Commonwealth and State/Territory governments. Rates revenue, together with other income, is the main direct revenue source of councils to fund the services and facilities for local community.

14 Migration Program
Entering the third century!

Since the arrival of the *First Fleet* with convicts and free settlers from the British Isles more than 220 years ago, migration to Australia has continued unabated except for the short periods during the 1920s *Great Depression* years and the two world wars.

Seven million people have migrated to Australia since the 1945's slogan of *Populate or Perish* by Arthur Calwell Australia's first Minister for Immigration. Three-quarter a million people have come to Australia under the humanitarian stream.

Net overseas migration has become the number one contributor, overtaking natural increase, to Australia's population growth for almost 3 decades since the 1980s.

The focus of Australia's migration program has evolved from migrants primarily from the United Kingdom, for the purpose of increasing Australia's population, to a non-racial basis aimed at attracting workers and temporary (skilled) migrants in meeting the skilled labour needs of the economy.

A Nation of Immigrants since 1788

First the convicts and free settlers

Australia has been a nation of immigrants since British colonisation in 1788. Between 1788 and the late 1860s, over 160,000 convicts were transported to the penal settlements in New South Wales, Van Diemen's land (present day Tasmania), and Western

Australia. Other earlier settlers included free settlers seeking a better life and soldiers who stayed on when their term of service was over.

Before federation in 1901, individual colonial administration of the six colonies managed its immigration affairs. The many schemes aiming to attract and assist migrants resulted in more than 700,000 arrivals. The focus was on migration from Europe, with preference for those from the British Isles.

Gold rush and population influx

The discovery of gold outside Bathurst, New South Wales in 1851 and later in Ballarat and Bendigo in Victoria provided the impetus to sizeable arrivals. Some 600,000 people arrived within a decade of the gold discovery. The majority was from Britain and Ireland while other substantial groups included 60,000 from the rest of Europe, 42,000 from China, 10,000 from the United States and 5,000 from New Zealand and the South Pacific.

By 1861, foreign-born accounted for over 60% of the total population in the colonies. Gold discovery in the mid 1890s in Western Australia further boosted the population in that state.

Birth of a nation and the 'White Australia' policy

In 1901, the six colonies in Australia came together to form the Commonwealth of Australia. By then, the new nation had a population of 3.8 million with 23% of the population foreign born and 80% were from the British Isles.

A number of legislations were enacted to formally exclude non-European migrants. The *Immigration Restriction Act 1901* marked the start of the 'White Australian Policy' formally excluding non-European migrants with the infamous 'Dictation Test' requiring applicants to pass the written test in any European language. The natives of Asia, Africa and the Pacific Islands (except New Zealand) were excluded from becoming naturalised by the *Commonwealth Naturalisation Act 1903*.

Almost 400,000 settlers arrived between 1905 and the beginning of World War I. They were mostly from the British Isles. Migration virtually ceased during World War I

Vigorous migration programs post World War I

Australia embarked on a vigorous migration program, including the 'Empire Settlement Scheme' after World War I which resulted in more than 300,000 new settlers arriving between 1919 and 1929. Two-thirds of them were 'assisted' and mostly from Britain.

Migration virtually ceased during the Great Depression years (1929-1937) and thereafter during World War II except for the arrival of 7,000 refugees, mainly Jews of German and Austrian descent from Nazi Germany.

Post World War II immigration expansion

Arthur Calwell, the first Minister for Immigration, promoted mass migration with the slogan *Populate or Perish*. During the period 1945 to 1965, Australia embarked on a post-war reconstruction and immigration expansion program.

Once again, the program was mainly Europe-centric. The programs initiated included:

- Free, assisted passage for British ex-servicemen and their dependents and other selected British migrants, Polish ex-servicemen; schemes for freedom fighters from the USA, Netherlands, Norway, France, Belgium and Denmark; assisted migration scheme with Austria, Belgium, Spain, West Germany, USA, Switzerland, Denmark, Norway, Sweden and Finland.

- 'Bring out a Briton' campaign

- 'Net Egg' scheme for Britons

- The signing of peace treaties with Italy, Romania, Bulgaria and Hungary facilitated migrant arrivals thereafter

- 'Operation Reunion' scheme bringing in settlers from Yugoslavia, Poland, Hungary, USSR, Romania, Czechoslovakia and Bulgaria, to reunite with relatives in Australia

- Resettlement of refugees from Hungary after an uprising there.

The *Immigration Restriction Act 1901* was partly relaxed in 1947 allowing non-European business persons who have lived continuously for 15 years to stay without periodic application for permit.

From 'White Australia' to Multicultural Australia

The end of the 'White Australia Policy'

In 1972, seventy-one years after the enactment of the *Immigration Restriction Act 1901*, Australia completely dismantled the 'White Australia Policy'. The Whitlam Labour government took further steps in the following year to gradually remove race as a factor in Australia's immigration policies.

In the late 1970s, Malcolm Fraser, the then Prime Minister opened Australia's door to Vietnamese refugees after the first boatload of refugees arrived in Darwin.

Effects of the ending of the 'White Australia Policy'

The ending of the 'White Australia Policy' has significant impact on Australia's demographic. The Australian population born in Asia has increased many folds.

Table 14.1 shows that, over the last three decades, there were 11-fold increase in those born in China 10-fold increase from the Philippines, 9-fold increase from Korea, and 5-fold increase from those born in India.

Table 14.1 Australian Population ('000) by Country of Birth
Selected Asian Countries

Country of Birth	1981 Census	2011 Census
China (excludes SAR's and Taiwan)	26.8	319.0
India	43.7	295.4
Vietnam	43.4	185.0
Philippines	15.8	175.2
Malaysia	32.5	116.0
Indonesia	16.4	67.6
Hong Kong and Macau	16.3	56.3
Korea	4.1	41.4
Sri Lanka	17.9	56.0
Singapore	12.4	30.7

Source: ABS – Population Census 1981, 2011

The 2011 population census reported 866,000 people are of Chinese ancestry and 391,000 are of Indian ancestry.

Seven Asian countries have consistently been on the list of the Top 10 Citizenship Countries of migrants. The total annual migration from these countries has exceeded that from the United Kingdom as shown in Table 14.2.

Table 14.2 Migrant Numbers ('000) from Seven Asian Countries

	2008-09	2009-10	2010-11	2011-12
China	21.8	24.8	29.6	25.5
India	25.0	23.1	21.8	29.0
Philippines	9.0	10.2	10.8	12.9
Sri Lanka	5.1	5.1	4.6	5.6
Malaysia	5.0	5.2	5.1	5.5
South Korea	4.9	4.4	4.3	4.9
Vietnam	3.3	3.9	4.7	4.8
Sub-total	74.2	76.7	80.9	88.2
United Kingdom	30.6	25.7	24.0	25.3

Source: DIAC - Migration Program Report

Australian Migration Program

A million migrants a decade since 1945

Australia's migration program has continued unabated since the 1945's slogan of *Populate or Perish* by the first Minister for Immigration. Since then, seven million people have migrated to Australia.

The focus of the Migration Program has evolved from attracting migrants primarily from the United Kingdom, for the purpose of increasing Australia's population, to a non-racial basis aimed at attracting workers and temporary (skilled) migrants in meeting the skilled labour needs of the economy.

For almost 3 decades since the 1980s, net overseas migration has become the number one contributor, overtaking natural increase, to Australia's population growth.

Rights and privileges

Australian permanent residents enjoy many of the rights and privileges of citizens, including access to free or subsidised legal and health services, social security benefits (waiting period and special conditions apply), education and the right to sponsor close relatives for permanent residency.

Children born in Australia of permanent residents are Australian citizens by birth. There are few employment restrictions though some state or federal government jobs do require Australian citizenship.

Permanent residents may remain in Australia indefinitely and multiple entries during the initial 5-year visa. After the expiry of the initial visa the holder is required to have a Resident Return Visa if the individual plans to travel to and from Australia.

Permanent residency may be revoked at the discretion of the Minister for Immigration and Citizenship. However this does not normally happen except in cases of criminal misconduct.

Australia's migration program

As part of its planned migration program, the Australian government annually allocates places for people who want to migrate permanently to Australia.

Australian migration program today consists of three main streams – skilled stream, family stream and humanitarian stream.

- Skilled stream
  Selection of skilled workers and business migrants is based on qualifications, skills, work experience or business and entrepreneurial experience

- Family stream
  Family migration is for Australian citizens or permanent residents to sponsor a close family relative, partner or fiancé to migrate to Australia.

- Humanitarian stream
  This includes offshore refugee visas, offshore humanitarian visas and onshore protection visas.

Table 14.3 shows the recent migrant intake for the last 5 years.

Table 14.3 Australia's Annual Migrant Intake ('000) 2010-2014

Migration Stream	2010 Actual	2011 Actual	2012 Actual	2013 Actual	2014 Plan
Skilled	107.9	113.7	125.7	129.2	128.6
Family	60.2	54.5	58.6	60.2	60.9
Total	168.6	168.2	184.3	189.4	189.5

Source: Department of Immigration and Citizenship 2013 and 2014 are planned data.

The above table does not include the annual intake of migrants under the humanitarian stream (13,800 persons) and the special eligible category (500 persons).

Almost 500,000 Kiwis

New Zealand citizens coming to Australia to take up permanent or long-term stay are not included as part of Australia's migration program. For many decades, annually more than 20,000 New

Zealand citizens moved to Australia to take up permanent or long-term stay.

The Australia's 2011 population census recorded more than 483,000 people are New Zealand born.

Subclass 457 Business Visa

The Subclass 457 visa holders are skilled workers from overseas sponsored and nominated by Australian employers to work in Australia temporarily. Subclass 457 visa holders are not included in the annual migration statistics in Table 14.3. It has since been renamed to subclass 457 Temporary Work (Skilled) visa.

Citizenships of top 10 source countries of migrants

Table 14.4 shows the citizenships of the top 10 countries for the various migration streams and categories.

Table 14.4 Australia's Migration Programs - Top Source Countries 2011-12

Rank	General Skilled Migration	Employer Sponsored Migration	Total Skilled Migration	Business Long Stay (457)	Family Migration
1	India	UK	India	UK	PRC
2	UK	Philippines	UK	India	UK
3	PRC	India	PRC	Ireland	India
4	Sri Lanka	Philippines	Philippines	Philippines	Philippines
5	Malaysia	South Africa	South Africa	USA	Vietnam
6	South Africa	South Africa	Sri Lanka	PRC	Thailand
7	Pakistan	ROK	Malaysia	South Africa	USA
8	Philippines	USA	Ireland	Canada	ROK
9	Iran	Nepal	ROK	France	Indonesia
10	Bangladesh	Sri Lanka	Pakistan	Germany	Lebanon

Source: DI&C

States migrants intend to settle

New South Wales, Victoria, Queensland and Western Australia consistently attracted 90% of the new settlers as shown in Table 14.5.

State/territory	2008-09	2009-10	2010-11	2011-12
Percentage of Total	%	%	%	%
New South Wales	30	30	31	29
Victoria	24	24	25	25
Queensland	20	18	18	18
Western Australia	16	17	16	18
South Australia	6	7	6	6
Australian Capital Territory	1	2	1	2
Tasmania	1	1	1	1
Northern Territory	1	1	1	1
AUSTRALIA ('000)*	223.9	206.7	211.1	242.1

Table 14.5 State/territory of Intended Residence

Source: DI&C Based on annual arrivals who indicated their intention

Settlement Outcomes

The Department of Immigration and Citizenship commissioned regular studies on settlement outcomes of new arrivals.

Fact Sheet 14.1 on page 213 lists the findings from a recent study on settlement outcomes including employment, income, accommodation, level of comfort of living, confidence in making choices and social connection.

If citizenship status and intention is an indication of their overall satisfaction, 36% of skilled visa holders and 11% of Family visa holders have taken up Australian citizenship and 60% of skilled visa holders and 82% of Family visa holders hope to become Australian citizens.

Fact Sheet 14.1 Settlement Outcomes of Migrants (% of total respondents)

		Skilled Stream	Family Stream
Living in Australia Comfortable most of the time	Self	82	80
	Children	90	93
	Other family members	73	81
Very confident/ confident	In making choices about life in Australia	87	84
	In finding out about places, organisations and activities	84	78
Employment	Employed or own business	85	49
	Study	9	16
	Looking after family	5	25
	Retired	-	5
	Technicians and trade	14	10
	Community/personal service	7	14
	Clerical and administrative	13	16
	Sales	5	9
	Machine operators/drivers	3	5
	Labourers	5	18
Income	≥ $62,605	39	16
	$42,988 - $62,604	26	19
	$34,381 - $42,988	13	18
	$26,086 - $34,380	7	14
	≤$26,085	5	21
Health Excellent/Good	Physical health	89	86
	Mental health	89	87
Well connected to other/ community	Before arriving in Australia	45	24
	After arriving in Australia	50	54
Accommodation	Rent	49	35
	Owned with mortgage	39	30
	Own with no mortgage	6	6
	Live with family/friends rent free	4	26

Happy with accommodation	Size of accommodation	74	71
	Close to shops	80	79
	Close to medical centres	74	73
	Close to workplace	48	37
	Close to public transport	67	67
	Close to schools	56	53
	Close to childcare	56	53
	Safety of area	70	72
	Friendliness of neighbours	62	66
Community activities	Meeting with family/friends	87	89
	Religious group	31	28
	Cultural group	19	22
	School where children attend	26	15
	Community/voluntary work	10	12
	Sporting club/group	31	21
	Hobby group	25	23

DIAC - Settlement Outcomes of New Arrivals – Report of findings April 2011

15 Skilled Migration

>200,000 intakes annually

Since the 1980s, skilled migration has been an important and effective strategy for Australia to address its skill shortage. Annually, over the last three decades, Australia issued between 100,000 to 200,000 skilled visas.

These specific purpose visas aiming at attracting skilled migrants based on occupations, qualifications, skills, work experience, business and entrepreneurial experience are under constant reviews and refinements to ensure smooth transition by migrants and their effective contribution to Australia's prosperity.

The 3 main options for skilled migrants are General Skilled Migration, Employer Sponsored Migration and Business Skills Migration. Business Skills Migration will be covered in Chapter 15.

Employer Sponsored Migration, especially subclass 457 visa is increasingly an important option and has also attracted considerable media attention in recent years.

The changes in last couple of years include substantial changes to visa options and the establishment of *SkillSelect* an online service enabling skilled workers and business people interested to migrate to Australia to record their details through an expression of interest (EOI). From 1 January 2013, a number of previously available subclasses have been closed to new applications.

From 2013, international students graduating with a bachelor degree, a master's degree or a doctorate will be allowed to stay and work for two years, three years or four years respectively.

Main Categories

The Skilled Migration categories for professional and skilled workers to migrate to Australia are listed in Table 15.1.

Table 15.1 Skilled Migration Visa Options

General Skilled Migration	Skilled Independent (Permanent) 189
	Skilled Nominated (Permanent) 190
	Skilled Regional Nominated or Sponsored (Provisional) 489
Employer Sponsored	Employer Nominated Scheme 186
	• Direct entry
	• Agreement
	• Temporary residence transition
	Regional Sponsored Migration Scheme 187
	• Direct entry
	• Agreement
	• Temporary residence transition
	Temporary Work (Skilled) 457

Annual intake

Table 15.2 shows the skilled migrant intake by visa categories.

Table 15.2 Skilled Migrant Intake ('000) by Categories 2010-2014

Category	2010	2011	2012	2013	2014
General Skilled Migration					
Skilled Independent	37.3	36.1	44.3	45.6	45.0
Skilled - Australian Sponsored	3.7	9.1	4.1	4.2	
Skilled - State/Territory Sponsored	18.9	16.2	24.0	24.6	28.9
Employer Sponsored Migration					
ENS	30.2	33.1	30.0	31.2	47.2
RSMS	10.2	11.1	16.0	16.0	
Labour Agreements	0.5	0.2	-	-	-
Business skills	6.8	7.8	7.2	7.4	7.2
Distinguished Talents	0.2	0.1	0.2	0.2	0.2
Total	107.8	113.7	125.8	129.2	128.5

Source: DIAC (2013 and 2014 are planned data)

Table 15.2 does not include intake under subclass 457 visa as it is not subjected to annual *cap* (planning places) and does not form part of the annual migration plan. The annual intake (primary and secondary applicants) in thousands under 457 is very substantial as shown below:

	2008	2009	2010	2011	2012
Subclass 457	110.6	101.3	67.9	90.1	125.1

Skilled occupations

The skilled occupations that have appeared in the top 10 occupation list of skilled migrants over the last 4 years include accountant, business professional, civil engineer, computer professional, cook, electrical engineer, general electrician, general manager, general medical practitioner, hairdresser, marketing specialist, mechanical engineer, motor mechanic and registered nurse.

Basic requirements

The basic requirements are:

- *Age*
  The age requirement of less than 50 year old applies to all General Skilled Migration subclasses and Employer Sponsored or Nominated Classes except for subclass 457 where the age requirement is < 55 year old.

- *English language requirement*
  This requirement applies to all subclasses.

- *Point Test*

  All applicants for visa subclass 189, 489, *Direct Entry* and *Temporary Transition* streams for 186 and 187 need to have a pass score of 60 based on the *Point Test Table*. Points are awarded for age, qualifications, work experience, English language ability, nomination/sponsorship and other criteria as shown in Fact Sheet 15.1 on page 228.

- *Nominated occupation*

  The skills that Australia needs for migration purpose are listed in Skilled Occupation List (SOL) or the Consolidated Sponsored Occupation List (CSOL). These lists are updated annually to reflect the skills in demand in Australia. Currently, the SOL has 192 'high value occupations' listed and the CSOL has 642 occupations listed. The SOL and CSOL are listed on the DIAC's website at *http://www.immi.gov.au/skilled/sol.*

  All intending skilled migrants will need to nominate an occupation that best matches his or her qualifications and skills on the relevant skilled occupation list.

  Individuals applying for General Skilled Migration visa not nominated by a state or territory government must nominate an occupation on Schedule 1 of SOL.

  Individuals applying for a General Skilled Migration visa and are nominated by a State or Territory Government, or a direct entry stream Employer Nomination Scheme visa and a Subclass 457 visa must nominate an occupation from either Schedule 1 of SOL or Schedule 1 and 2 of CSOL.

- *Skills assessment*

  This is required for many skilled migration visa subclasses. Individuals will need to contact the relevant assessing authorities to have their skills assessed as suitable for the nominated occupations. The SOL and CSOL list the relevant assessing authority for each nominated occupation. A listing of the relevant assessing authorities is provided in Fact Sheet 15.2 on page 229.

- *Expression of interest*
  Individuals interested in all the three general skilled migration subclasses (189, 190, 489) must first complete and lodge an *Expression of interest* (EOI) via *SkillSelect* an online portal of the DIAC. In the EOIs, individuals outline their skills and experience, their interest in employer sponsorship, the states and territories they are willing to live and work in and their willingness to work outside capital cities and in regional areas.

Though EOI is not mandatory for employer-sponsored visas (subclasses 186, 187 and 457), individuals, by expressing their interest in employer nomination or sponsorship, may be contacted by prospective employers thus widening their migration options.

The information in the EOIs facilitates the state or territory governments to invite individuals to lodge their visa applications when the individuals meet the state or territory government's assessment criteria.

There may be an occupational ceiling limiting the number of invitations to be issued for a particular occupation group. When the ceiling is reached, no further invitations would be issued for that year.

Individuals may be invited to submit online visa application via *SkillSelect* based on their EOI. Once invited, an applicant has 60 days to lodge the application online. Applications received past the timeframe will be invalid. Applicants who fail to apply for a visa after receiving two invitations will have their EOIs removed from *SkillSelect*.

- *Health and character requirements*
  All visa applicants for permanent visas, i.e. the main applicant, secondary applicants and any dependents have to satisfy the health and character requirements.

General Skilled Migration

Professional and skilled workers who are not nominated or sponsored by employers apply for the 3 visa subclasses as shown in Table15.3.

Table 15.3 General Skilled Migration Subclasses

Skilled Independent (Permanent) subclass 189	Apply independently
Skilled Nominated (Permanent) subclass 190	Nominated by state/territory government
Skilled Regional Nominated or Sponsored (Provisional) Subclass 489	Nominated by a state or territory government and sponsored by a close relative to live and work in regional area - anywhere in Australia other than the Gold Coast, Brisbane, Newcastle, Sydney, Wollongong and Melbourne.

Fact Sheet 15.3 on page 230 outlines the visa requirements and entitlements for the various General Skilled Migration visa subclasses.

Further details are available in *Booklet 6 Points Based Skilled Migration (subclasses 189, 190 and 489) visa* on the DIAC's website *http://www.immi.gov.au*.

Employer-nominated/Sponsored Skilled Migration

The three main subclasses of employer nominated/sponsored migration are shown in Table 15.4. Subclasses 186 and 187 are permanent residency visas and subclass 457 is a provisional visa.

Table 15.4 Employer Nominated/Sponsored Skilled Migration

Employer Nominated Scheme subclass 186	Direct entry
	Agreements
	Temporary residence transition
Regional Sponsored Migration Scheme subclass 187	Direct entry
	Agreements
	Temporary residence transition
Temporary Work (Skilled) subclass 457	

Subclasses 186 and 187

These are permanent resident visas. There are 3 streams in each of the sub-classes 186 and 187:

- Direct entry stream
  For applicants who have not been subclass 457 visa holders for the last 2 years or are applying from overseas,

- Agreement stream
  For employers to bring in overseas skilled workers to Australia pursuant to the labour agreements or regional migration agreements that have been tailored and negotiated by employers with the government to bring in workers on a temporary or permanent basis,

- Temporary transition stream
  For existing subclass 457 visa-holders, who have been offered permanent employment by their sponsoring employers

Fact Sheets 15.4 and 15.5 on pages 231 and 232 outline the visa requirements and entitlements for the various Employer Nominated/Sponsored visa subclasses.

Further details are available in *Booklet 5 Employer Sponsored Migration (Permanent)* on the DIAC's website.

Subclass 457 visas

The 457 visas is the most commonly used temporary visa category for employers to recruit temporary skilled workers from overseas. The subclass 457 visa has been renamed as Temporary Work (Skilled) subclass 457 visa in November 2012.

For many permanent resident aspirants, the 457 visas, allowing temporary stay for a period form 1 day to 4 years, is an important and popular pathway to permanent residency. Many 457 visa-holders subsequently qualified for permanent residence after some years in Australia.

In 2013 (11 months ending 31 May), 35,320 of them were granted permanent visas under the Skilled streams and 1,820 obtained permanent residence under the Family stream. In the same period, 62,810 subclass 457 visas were granted to primary applicants and almost 4,000 of these were sponsored for employment with the three levels of government.

Fact Sheets 15.6 on page 233 outlines the visa requirements and entitlements. Further details are available in *Booklet 9 Temporary Work (Skilled) Subclass 457 visa* on the DIAC's website.

Temporary Graduate Visas

Australia has long recognised that international students provide a potential source of skilled migrants. Since 2001, Australia has allowed foreign students in selected fields of studies to move easily into the labour market instead of requiring them to return home.

This initiative has attracted a significant number of international students to Australian tertiary institutions. Since 2007, over 200,000 international students have annually lodged their visa applications to study at Australian tertiary institutions.

However, the DIAC has reminded students to choose a course of study based on their own interest and the quality of the course rather than solely on hoping to achieve a particular migration outcome as Australia's skilled migration program changes in response to the country's economic needs.

With the recent changes, international students graduating from Australian universities and who have at least 2 academic years of study in Australia are able to apply for Australian work visas regardless of their field of study. Neither is there a need for skill assessment requirement or nomination of an occupation on the SOL. Graduates with a bachelor degree, a master's degree or a doctorate will be allowed to stay and work for two years, three years or four years respectively.

Subclass 476 visa

The subclass 476 visa *Recognised Graduate (Temporary)* is currently available to recent engineering graduates aged under 31 years of selected overseas universities to work in Australia for 18 months.

Holders of the visa may apply for permanent residence whenever they are able to meet the requirements.

The recognised institutions from countries, including Argentina, Brazil, Canada, Chile, Finland, Germany, Hong Kong SAR, Hungary, India, Indonesia, Iran, Ireland, Japan, Lebanon, Malaysia, Mexico, Netherlands, New Zealand, People's Republic of China, Philippines, Poland, Russia, Republic of Kazakhstan, Singapore, Slovakia, South Africa, Republic of Korea, Sweden, Taiwan, Tanzania, Turkey, United Arab Emirates, United Kingdom and United States of America, are listed on the DIAC's website.[31]

Subclass 485 visa

The subclass 485 *Temporary Graduate* visa has two streams:

- Graduate work stream
  This is for international students who graduate with skills and qualifications relating to an occupation on the Skilled Occupation List Schedule 1. The temporary visa is for 18 months.

- Post-study work stream
  This is for international students who were granted their first Student visa on or after 5 November 2011. International students graduating from Australian universities and who have at least 2 academic years of study in Australia will be able to apply for Australian work visas regardless of their field of study. Neither is there a need for skill assessment requirement or nomination of an occupation on the SOL.

---

[31] *http://www.immi.gov.au/skilled/general-skilled-migration/476/recognised-institutions.htm*

Graduates with a bachelor degree, a master's degree or a doctorate will be allowed to stay and work for two years, three years or four years respectively.

Fact Sheet 15.7 on page 234 outlines the visa requirements and entitlements for the Graduate Visa subclasses.

Application

SkillSelect

All applications for skilled migration visas have to be lodged via *SkillSelect* accessible at *http://www.immi.gov.au/skills/skillselect/*. Further details are available in *Booklet 11 SkillSelect* at the DIAC's website.

Processing priority

The current processing priority, in order of priority, is as follow:

1. Applications under the RSMS program or under Skilled – Regional (subclass 887)
2. Applications under ENS program
3. Applications nominated by state and territory government agency for occupations on the agency's migration plan
4. Applications with nominated occupations on the Skilled Occupation List (SOL)
5. All other applications

Visa application fees

The visa application fees are as shown in Table 15.5. The first instalment is payable when submitting the application. It is non-refundable.

The second instalment is payable after the visa application has been assessed as successful and the applicant has decided to take up the offer.

Table 15.5 Visa Charges ($)– Skilled Migration Visas

Subclass	Base Application Charge	Additional Applicant Charge ≥18	Additional Applicant Charge <18	2nd Instalment
186	3,060	1,530	765	8,520[1] 4,250[2]
187	3,060	1,530	765	8,520[1] 4,250[2]
189	3,060	1,530	765	4,250[2]
190	3,060	1,530	765	4,250[2]
457	900	900	225	Nil
489	3,060	1,530	765	4,250[2]
485	1,250	625	315	Nil
476	315	160	80	Nil

Visa processing time

The Department of Immigration and Citizenship (DIAC) has established service standards for processing visa applications. It aims to process 75% of the applications within these service standards. However, processing time does vary depending on complexity and requirements in each case.

The processing time schedule for the skilled migration subclasses is:

- Subclasses 186, 187 – 6 months
- Subclass 190, 489 (state sponsored) - 6 months
- Subclasses 189, 489 (family sponsored) – 12 months

Low risk countries are countries that issue Electronic Travel Authority (ETA). High risk countries are countries that do not issue ETA.

Employment Outcomes

The DIAC commissions regular studies on settlement outcomes of new arrivals. The employment outcomes for skilled migrants based on the study conducted in 2009 on recent settlers (arrived from offshore 6 months ago or visa granted onshore within the last 6 months) is shown in Table 15.6.

Table 15.6 Employment Outcomes (in %) for Recent Skilled Migrants

	Participation Rate	Unemployed Rate	Full-time employed	Employed in Skilled Job (% of employed)	Median Earnings ($'000)
Points tested independent	97.6	5.6	83.0	80.0	60.0
Points tested sponsored	97.6	9.8	75.0	62.7	48.7
Employer nominated	98.3	0.3	95.0	94.1	80.0
Skilled graduate	96.3	5.6	76.0	56.2	40.0
Overall skilled stream	95.0	5.0	83.6	75.0	60.0
AUSTRALIA aged ≥15	65.2	5.7	70.2	49.2	56

Source: DIAC Continuous Survey of Australian Migrants

Fact Sheet 15.1 Points Test Table (subclasses 189, 190 and 489)

			Points
Age		18-24	25
		25-32	30
		33-39	25
		40-44	15
		45-49	0
Qualification		Doctorate	20
		At least an undergraduate degree	15
		Diploma/ trade qualification	10
Experience (maximum. 20 points)	Inside Australia	≥3 but < 5 years	5
		≥5 but ≤ 8 years	10
		≥8 and up to 10 years	15
	Outside Australia	≥1 but ≤ 3 years	5
		≥ 3 but < 5 years	10
		≥ 5 but < 8 yearr	15
		≥8 and up to 10 years	20
English language		Competent IELTS 6 OET B	0
		Proficient IELTS 7 OET B	10
		Superior IELTS 8 OETA	20
Nomination/ sponsorship		Nominated by state or territory government or sponsored by an eligible family member, to reside and work in a specified /designated area (visa subclass 489 only)	10
Others		Credential community language qualifications	5
		Study in regional Australia or a low population growth metropolitan area (distance education excluded)	5
		Partner skill qualifications	5
		Professional Year[3] in Australia for at least 1 year in the previous 4 years	5
		Nomination by state or territory government (visa subclass 190 only)	5
		Australian Study	5

[1] *In nominated or closely related occupation* [2] *From an Australian educational institution or other of recognised standard*[3] *Qualifying professional year courses are offered by Australian Computer Society, CPA Australia, Institute of Chartered Accountants of Australia, Institute of Public Accountants and Engineers Australia.*

Fact Sheet 15.2 Assessing Authorities for Skilled Occupations

Architects Accreditation Council of Australia (AACA)

Australian Association of Social Workers (AASW)

Australasian College of Physical Scientists and Engineers in Medicine (ACPSEM)

Australian Computer Society (ACS)

Australian Dental Council (ADC)

Australian Institute of Management (AIM)

Australian Institute of Medical Scientists (AIMS)

Australian Institute of Quantity Surveyors (AIQS)

Australian Institute of Radiography (AIR)

Australian Institute of Teaching and School Leadership (AITSL)

Australian Community Workers Association (ACWA)

Australian Maritime Safety Authority (AMSA)

Australian Nursing and Midwifery Accreditation Council (ANMAC)

Australian and New Zealand Osteopathic Council (ANZOC)

Australian and New Zealand Podiatry Accreditation Council (ANZPAC)

Australian and New Zealand Society of Nuclear Medicine (ANZSNM)

Australian Pharmacy Council (APharmC)

Australian Physiotherapy Council (APC)

Australian Psychological Society (APS)

Australasian Veterinary Boards Council (AVBC)

Certified Practising Accountants of Australia (CPAA)

Chinese Medicine Board of Australia (CMBA)

Council on Chiropractic Education Australasia (CCEA)

Civil Aviation Safety Authority (CASA)

Dieticians Association of Australia (DAA)

Engineers Australia

Institute of Chartered Accountants in Australia (ICAA)

Medical Board of Australia (MBA)

National Accreditation Authority for Translators and Interpreters (NAATI)

Occupational Therapy Council (OTC)

Optometry Council of Australia and New Zealand (OCANZ)

Institute of Public Accountants (IPA),

State Legal Admissions Authority (SLAA)

Speech Pathology Association of Australia (SPA)

Surveying and Spatial Sciences Institute (SSSI)

Trades Recognition Australia (TRA)

Vocational Education and Training Assessment Services (VETASSESS)

Fact Sheet 15.3 General Skilled Visas

	189	190	489
Expression of Interest	Y	Y	Y
Invited to apply	Y	Y	Y
Age	<50	<50	<50
Points test score	≥60	N/A	≥60
Nominated occupation on Skilled Occupation List	Y	Y	Y
Nominated by state or territory government	N/A	Y	Y
Skills assessment	Y	Y	Y
English language	Y	Y	Y
Health, character	Y	Y	Y
Visa allows:			
Live and work permanently in Australia, designated regional area (489)	Y	Y	Y
Study in Australia, designated regional area (489)	Y	Y	Y
Enrol in Medicare	Y	Y	N/A
Some social security benefits (subject to waiting periods)	Y	Y	N/A
Apply for Australian citizenship (subject to residency criteria)	Y	Y	N/A
Sponsor family members for permanent residence	Y	Y	N/A

189 Skilled Independent, 190 Skilled Nominated, 489 Skilled Regional Sponsored (Provisional)

Fact Sheet 15.4 Employer Nominated Visas (subclass 186)

	Direct Entry	Agreement	Temporary Residence Transition
Expression of Interest	Y	Y	Y
Invited to apply	Y	Y	Y
Age	<50	<50	<50
Points test score	≥60	N/A	≥60
Nominated occupation on Skilled Occupation List	Y	Y	Y
Nominated by state or territory government	N/A	Y	Y
Skills assessment	Y	Y	Y
English language	Y	Y	Y
Health, character	Y	Y	Y
Visa allows:			
Live and work permanently in Australia	Y	Y	Y
Study in Australia	Y	Y	Y
Enrol in Medicare	Y	Y	Y
Some social security benefits (subject to waiting periods)	Y	Y	Y
Apply for Australian citizenship (subject to residency criteria)	Y	Y	Y
Sponsor family members for permanent residence	Y	Y	Y

Fact Sheet 15.5 Regional Sponsored Migration Scheme Visas (subclass 187)

	Direct Entry	Agreement	Temporary Residence Transition
Expression of Interest	Y	Y	Y
Invited to apply	Y	Y	Y
Age	<50	<50	<50
Points test score	≥60	N/A	≥60
Nominated occupation on Skilled Occupation List	Y	Y	Y
Nominated by state or territory government	N/A	Y	Y
Skills assessment	Y	Y	Y
English language	Y	Y	Y
Health, character	Y	Y	Y
Visa allows:			
Live and work permanently in Australia, designated regional area (489)	Y	Y	Y
Study in Australia, designated regional area (489)	Y	Y	Y
Enrol in Medicare	Y	Y	Y
Some social security benefits (subject to waiting periods)	Y	Y	Y
Apply for Australian citizenship (subject to residency criteria)	Y	Y	Y
Sponsor family members for permanent residence	Y	Y	y

Fact Sheet 15.6 Temporary Work (Skilled) subclass 457

Age	< 55
English - IELTS 5 (standard business sponsor), or per labour agreement *	Y
Nominated by an approved employer	Y
Eligible occupation on Consolidated sponsored occupation list	Y
Skill and experience; trade occupation needs skills assessment	Y
Health insurance while in Australia	Y
Exemption for holder of subclass 457 visa 'service seller' stream, or the 'privileges and immunities' stream	
Health, character	Y

Visa allows:

- 4 years residence for applicant and accompanying family members
- work in Australia during visa duration
- family member can work and study
- travel in and out of Australia for 4 years

Obligations:

- work in the nominated occupation
- work for the sponsor or the associated entity in nominated position
- not to cease employment for a period of > 28 days
- if cease employment, must within 28 days, do one of the following:
  - find another employer to sponsor (employer has to lodge a nomination)
  - apply for another type of substantive visa
  - make arrangements to depart Australia
- arrange for health insurance cover while in Australia, unless holding a subclass 457 visa under either the 'service sellers' stream or the 'privileges and immunities' stream
- notify DIAC of any child born in Australia, child will automatically receive a 457 visa
- notify DIAC of change of employer or occupation but not to work before the nomination is approved; failure to do so will result in visa cancellation

* *English exemption if Gross annual salary $92k, if nominated occupation does not need English for registration, licence or membership, passport holders of Canada, New Zealand, Ireland, UK and USA, 5 years of continuous fulltime study in secondary/tertiary institution with instruction in English, occupation in diplomatic or consular commissio*

Fact Sheet 15.7 Temporary Graduate Visas (subclass 485)

	Graduate Work Stream	Post Work Stream
Visa duration (*See note*)	18 months	≥2 years
Age	<50	<50
Nominated skilled occupation on Skilled Occupation List	Y	N/A
Skills assessment	Y	N/A
Holder of eligible visa	Y	Y
Meet the Australian study requirement in the last 6 months	Y	N/A
Meet the 2 year study requirement last 6 months	N/A	Y
In Australia	Y	Y
English language	Y	Y
Health insurance cover	Y	Y
Nominated occupation on Skilled Occupation List	Y	Y
No outstanding debts to Australian government or have made settlement arrangement	Y	Y
Health, character	Y	Y
Visa allows:		
Applicant and accompanied family members temporary stay travel, work and study	Y	Y

Note: *Post-study work stream Bachelor/honour/master degree (coursework) 2 years Master degree by research 3 years, Doctoral degree 4 years*

16 Business Skills Migration

Around 7,000 visas annually

Since the 1980s, Australia has been addressing its skill shortage by developing policies and implementing programs including specific purpose visas aiming at attracting skilled migrants with business and entrepreneurial experience.

Australia issues around 7,000 Business Skills visas annually over the last three decades. Business Skills visas continue to be popular with annual applications outstripping the approvals. In 2012, there was a 34% increase for Business Skills visas. There were more than 11,000 applications awaiting finalisation at the end of June 2012.

The Business Skills visa subclasses have gone through many changes over the years. The most recent changes took effect over the last couple of years.

Annual intake

Table 16.1 shows the skilled migrant intake by visa categories for the last 5 years and the 2013 and the 2014 plan intake.

Table 16.1 Business Migrant Intake ('000) 2008 -2014

2008	2009	2010	2011	2012	2013	2014
6.6	7.4	6.8	7.8	7.2	7.4	7.2

Source: Department of Immigration and Citizenship (2013 and 2014 are planned data)

The top 10 source countries, based on visas granted in 2010-2011, are People's Republic of China, Republic of Korea Malaysia, UK, South Africa, Taiwan, Hong Kong, Pakistan, Iran and Sri Lanka.

Two main options

There are two main options for business migrants, i.e. Business Talent (subclass 132) and Business Innovation and Investment (subclasses 188 and 888) as shown in Table 16.2 overleaf.

Table 16.2 Business Migration Options

Business Talent (Permanent)	Significant Business History
subclass 132	Venture Capital
Business Innovation and Investment	Business Innovation
(Provisional)	Investor
subclass 188	Significant Investor
Business Innovation and Investment	Business Innovation
(Permanent)	Investor
subclass 888	Significant Investor

Business Innovation and Investment visa is a 2-stage option. Individuals first apply for provisional visa subclass 188. Later, after having held subclass 188 visas for sometime, they apply for subclass 888 permanent visas.

Basic requirements

The basic requirements are:

- *Expression of interest*
  All applicants first record their interest in Expression of Interest (EOI) via *SkillSelect* – an online portal established by the DIAC. Individuals may be invited to submit online visa application via *SkillSelect* based on their EOI.

- *Nomination by state/territory government*
  All applications for business skills migration visa subclasses have to be supported by nomination from an Australian state or territory government.

- *Age < 55 years*
  The age requirement of less than 55 years old applies to subclasses 132 and 188.

- *English language requirement*
  This requirement applies to subclasses 132 and 188.

- *Assets*
  There are specific asset requirements on applicant's net worth, prior business experience, amount transferrable to Australia and Australian investment depending on the visa subclasses.

- *Innovation Point Test*
  All applicants for 188 visa subclass need to have a pass score of 65 based on the Innovation Point Test Table.

  Points are awarded for age, English language ability, qualifications, business or investment experience, net personal and business assets, business turnover, and innovation as shown in Fact Sheet 16.1 on page 241.

- *Health and character requirements*
  All visa applicants for permanent visas, i.e. the main applicant, secondary applicants and any dependents have to satisfy the health and character requirements.

Business Talent subclass 132

Business Talent (Permanent) subclass 132 has 2 streams:
- Significant business history stream – for owners or part-owners of a business wanting a major management role in a new or existing business,

- Venture capital stream – for people who have secured ≥ $1m funding from an Australian venture capital firm

Fact Sheet 16.2 on page 242 outlines the visa requirements, entitlements and obligations for subclass 132.

Further details are available in *Booklet 7 Business Skill Entry* on the DIAC's website.

Business Innovation and Investment subclasses 188, 888

Both the provisional visa (subclass 188) and permanent visa (subclass 888) have 3 streams:

* Business Innovation stream – for people wanting to own and manage a new or existing business in Australia,

* Investor stream – for people wanting to make a designated investment in Australia and maintain business and investment after investment maturity,

* Significant Investor – for people wanting to invest ≥$5m in complying business in Australia and continue the business or investment after the investment matured.

Fact Sheets 16.3 to 16.6 on pages 243 to 246 outline the visa requirements and entitlements for the various 188 and 888 visa subclasses. Further details are available in *Booklet 10 Business Innovation and Investment* on the DIAC's website.

Application

SkillSelect

All applications for Business Skills migration visas have to be lodged via *SkillSelect*. Individuals may be invited to submit online visa application via *SkillSelect* based on their EOI. Once invited, an applicant has 60 days to lodge the application online. Applications received past the timeframe will be invalid.

Applicants who fail to apply for a visa after receiving two invitations will have their EOIs removed from SkillSelect.

Visa application fees

The visa application fees are as shown in Table 16.3. The first instalment is payable when submitting the application. It is non-refundable. The second instalment may be payable (e.g. when applicants or/and their dependents have less than than functional English) after the visa application has been assessed as successful and the applicant has decided to take up the offer.

Subclass	Base Application Charge	Additional Applicant Charge ≥18	Additional Applicant Charge <18	2nd Instalment
Table 16.3 Visa Charges ($) - Business Skills Visas				
132	5,940	2,970	1,485	8,520
				4,250
188	4,065	2,035	1,015	8,520
				4,250
888	1,960	980	490[3]	4,250

Visa processing time

The Department of Immigration and Citizenship (DIAC) has established service standards for processing visa applications. It aims to process 75% of the applications within these service standards.

The processing time for all business skills migration subclasses is as shown below:

- Low risk countries (countries that issue Electronic Travel Authority)
  - o Lodged in Australia – 11 months
  - o Lodged outside Australia – 9 months
- High risk countries (countries that do not issue ETA)
  - o Lodged in Australia – 22 months
  - o Lodged outside Australia – 28 months

The processing time does vary depending on complexity and requirements in each case.

Fact Sheet 16.1 Innovation Points Test Table

(For visa subclass 188 Innovation and Investment streams)

		Points
Age	18-24	20
	25-32	30
	33-39	25
	40-44	20
	45-54	15
Business experience	> 4 years	10
	> 7 years	15
Investment experience	> 4 years	10
	> 7 years	15
English language	Vocational or higher	5
	Proficient or higher	10
State/territory nomination	Special endorsement (limited places)	10
Qualification	Australian trade certificate, diploma or bachelor degree	5
	Bachelor degree in business, science or technology	10
Net business and Personal Assets	$800,000	5
	$1.3 million	15
	$1.8 million	25
	$2.235 million	35
Business turnover	$500,000	5
	$1 million	15
	$1.5 million	25
	$2 million	35
Innovation	Registered patents or designs	15
	Evidence of trademarks	10
	Evidence of joint venture agreements	5
	Evidence of export trade	15
	Gazelle business	10
	Evidence of receipt of grants or venture capital funding	10

Applicants aged 55 or older may be nominated by a state or territory government agency if their business is of exceptional economic benefit

Fact Sheet 16.2 Business Talent Permanent (subclass 132) Visas

	Significant History Stream	Venture Capital Stream
Visa period	Permanent	Permanent
Expression of Interest	Y	Y
Invited to apply	Y	Y
Age	<55	<55
English	Y	Y
Nominated by state or territory government	Y	Y
Total assets transferrable to Australia within 2 years of granting the visa	$1.5m	N/A
Net assets in qualifying business 2 out of 4 years immediately before application	$400k	N/A
Annual business turnover (1 or more businesses) 2 out of 4 years prior to application	$3m	N/A
Business ownership: Either 51% if business turnover <$400k/annum, or 30% if business turnover >$400k/annum, or 10% of publicly-listed company	Y	Y
Venture capital of from AVCAL venture capital member, funding agreement	N/A	$1m
Desire to own and manage a business in Australia	Y	N/A
Health, character	Y	Y
Visa allows:		
Permanent residence	Y	Y
Establish a new or develop an existing business in Australia	Y	Y
Medicare benefits	Y	Y
Some social security benefits (subject to waiting periods)	Y	Y
Apply for Australian citizenship (subject to residency criteria)	Y	Y
Sponsor family members for permanent residence	Y	Y

Fact Sheet 16.3 Business Innovation and Investment Provisional (subclass 188) Visas

Business Innovation Stream	
Visa period	4 yrs
Expression of Interest	Y
Invited to apply	Y
Age	<55
Innovation Point Test	65
English	Y
Nominated by state or territory government	Y
Total assets transferrable to Australia within 2 years of granting the visa	$800k
Net assets in qualifying business 2 out of 4 years immediately before application	$400k
Annual business turnover (1 or more businesses) 2 out of 4 years prior to application	$3m
Business ownership: Either 51% if business turnover <$400k/annum, or 30% if business turnover >$400k/annum, or 10% of publicly-listed company	Y
Have managed a business but <50% of time in professional, technical or trade services	Y
Desire to own and manage a business in Australia	Y
Health, character	Y
Visa allows:	
Permanent residence	Y
Establish a new or develop an existing business in Australia	Y
Medicare benefits	
Some social security benefits (subject to waiting periods)	
Apply for Australian citizenship (subject to residency criteria)	
Sponsor family members for permanent residence	Y

Obligations:
- Applicant must enter Australia by specified date
- Any dependants included in the application may not be able to marry before they enter Australia
- Obtain and maintain substantial ownership in a business in Australia
- Participate, at a senior level, in the daily management of that business
- The business must also do at least one of these - develop business links with international markets; create or maintain employment in Australia; export Australian goods; produce goods or services that would otherwise be imported; introduce new or improved technology; add to commercial activity and competitiveness within sectors of the Australian economy.

Fact Sheet 16.4 Business Innovation and Investment (subclass 188) Visas

Investor Stream	
Visa period	4 yrs
Expression of Interest	Y
Invited to apply	Y
Age	<55
Innovation Point Test	65
English	Y
Nominated by state or territory government	Y
Skills:	

- High level of management skill in relation to eligible investments or qualifying business activity
- ≥ 3 years' experience of direct involvement in managing one or more qualifying businesses or eligible investments

Total assets for ≥ 2 financial years before invitation to apply and transferrable to Australia within 2 years of grant of visa	$2.25m
Prepared to invest for at least 1 of the 5 years before invitation to apply in one of:	$1.5m

- Managing eligible investments that total at least $1.5 million, or
- Managing a qualifying business (≥ 10%ownership of the total value of the business.

Genuine and realistic commitment to continuing business and investment activity in Australia after the original investment has matured	Y
Health, character	Y

Visa allows:

- 4 years residence including accompanying family members
- Establish a new or develop an existing business in Australia, make a designated investment with an Australian state or territory government, or make and maintain complying investments in Australia
- May apply for permanent residence by applying for a Business Innovation and Investment (Permanent) visa (subclass 888) after 2 years
- May renew for another 2 years if need time to meet the criteria for Business Innovation and Investment (Permanent) visa (subclass 888) Permanent residence

Obligations:

- After entering Australia, must hold the complying investments continuously for the life of the visa

Fact Sheet 16.5 Business Innovation and Investment (subclass 188) Visas

Significant Investor Stream	
Visa period	4 yrs
Expression of Interest	Y
Invited to apply	Y
Age	<55
English	Y
Nominated by state or territory government	Y
Total assets unencumbered, and are available to be used to make the 'complying investment' in Australia	$5m
Prepared to invest in at least one of the 'complying investments': <ul><li>Government bonds,</li><li>ASIC regulated managed funds,</li><li>Direct ownership interest in Australian private company that genuinely operates a qualifying business in Australia.</li></ul>	$5m
Prepared to invest for at least 1 of the 5 years before invitation to apply in one of: <ul><li>Managing eligible investments that total at least $1.5 million, or</li><li>Managing a qualifying business (≥ 10%ownership of the total value of the business.</li></ul>	$1.5m
Genuine and realistic commitment to continuing business and investment activity in Australia after the original investment has matured	Y
Health, character	Y

Visa allows:
- 4 years residence including accompanying family members
- Establish a new or develop an existing business in Australia, make a designated investment with an Australian state or territory government, or make and maintain complying investments in Australia
- May apply for permanent residence by applying for a Business Innovation and Investment (Permanent) visa (subclass 888) after 2 years
- May renew for another 2 years if need time to meet the criteria for Business Innovation and Investment (Permanent) visa (subclass 888) Permanent residence

Obligations:
- After entering Australia, must maintain the designated investment for ≥4 years
- May switch between complying investments provided funds withdrawn from complying investments are reinvested into other complying investments within 30 days of withdrawing them, and the sum withdrawn corresponds with the sum reinvested

Fact Sheet 16.6 Business Innovation and Investment (Permanent) subclass 888

	BI	I	SI
Hold subclass 188 visa	Y	Y	Y
Have met all requirements in provisional visa	Y	Y	Y
Nominated by state/territory government	?	Y	Y
Lived in Australia 1 out of 2 preceding years	Y	-	-
Lived in Australia 2 out of 4 preceding years	-	Y	-
Lived in Australia as 188 Significant Investor visa holder (160 days in the past 4 years), 188 Significant Investor Extension stream visa holder (240 days in the past 6 years, 2 provisional visas in Significant Investor Extension stream visa holder (320 days in the past 8 years	-	-	-
Nominated by state/territory government	Y	Y	Y
Have had and continue to directly manage the main business (or 2 main businesses) for ≥2 years	Y	-	-
Turnover ≥$300k in the year before application	Y	-	-
Ownership of business	Y	-	-
• 51% if business turnover <$400k/annum, or			
• 30% if business turnover >$400k/annum, or			
• 10% of publicly-listed company			
Bbusiness not acquired from applicant or holder of permanent (subclass 888) visa, holder of permanent skills visa (subclasses 890, 891, 892 or 893) other than having a joint interest in the business for ≥1 year before application	Y	-	-
Throughout the year immediately before application	Y	-	-
• net assets in main business (or 2 main businesses) ≥$200k			
• net personal and business assets ≥$600k/annum,			
• employed 2 full-time equivalent employees who are Australian citizens, Australian permanent residents and not family members			
Desire to own and manage a business in Australia	Y	-	-
Held designated investment (years) as provisional visa holder	-	4	2
Health, character	Y	Y	Y
Satisfactory compliance record with Australian laws, including those relating to taxation, superannuation, workplace relations and other laws relevant to the business	?	Y	Y
Strong commitment to continue business and investment activity in Australia	?	Y	Y

Visa allows:
- permanent residence for applicant and accompanied family members
- own and manage a business in Australia, or continue investment activity in Australia
- travel in and out of Australia for five years
- live and work in Australia permanently
- enrol in Medicare

Obligations:
- applicant must enter Australia by specified date
- any dependants included in application may not be able to marry before they enter Australia

BI – Business Innovation, I – Investor, SI – Significant Investor

17 Family Migration

Getting the family together

Australian citizens and permanent residents are able to sponsor their close relatives including their partners, parents, child and other family members to reside in Australia permanently. Partner visas account for 75% of the Family Migration visas issued.

The sponsored applicants have to meet the eligibility requirements including health and character requirements. The character requirement is also applicable to persons sponsoring children under 18 years of age in Child Visa application.

A number of Family visa subclasses require an Assurance of Support (AoS) from an eligible assurer. For some subclasses, a financial bond is required.

The Department of Immigration and Citizenship (DIAC) has established processing service standards (except for Parent and Other Family Member subclasses) according to applicant's country-risk classification.

Parent and Other Family Members visa subclasses are subjected to annual limit or 'cap'.

There is a long waiting list for Non-Contributory Parent visa. It will take the DIAC 13 years to clear the existing applications basing on the current intake level. Just a couple of years ago, the waiting period was 19 years.

Main categories

Table 17.1 lists the Family Migration categories that Australian citizens and permanent residents are able to sponsor their close relatives to reside in Australia.

Table 17.1 Family Migration Categories

Partner	Prospective marriage
	Partner
Parent	Non-contributory
	Contributory
Child	Orphan relative
	Adoptive relative
	Dependent child
Other Family Members	Remaining relative
	Aged dependent relative
	Carer

Annual limit in some subclasses

The Parent and Other Family Member subclasses are subjected to annual limit or 'cap'. Once the cap is reached in a year, no further visas will be issued for the year. The other applications outside the 'cap' are then placed in a queue and carried forward to the following year.

The DIAC indicated a delay of up to 13 years is expected for Parent (non-contributory) visas.

Contributory parent visa applicants have a shorter waiting period and can expect their applications to be finalised within 2 years.

Annual intake

The annual Family Migration visas granted over the last three years and the planned intake for 2013 and 2014 are shown in Table 17.2.

Table 17.2 Family Stream Intake ('000) 2010-14

Category	2010 Actual	2011 Actual	2012 Actual	2013 Plan	2014 Plan
Partner:					
Prospective Marriage	7.0	6.6	6.5		
Partner	37.8	35.4	38.6		
Subtotal	44.8	42.0	45.1	46.3	47.5
Parent:					
Non-Contributory	2.0	1.0	2.0		
Contributory	7.5	7.5	6.5		
Sub-total	9.5	8.5	8.5	8.7	8.9
Child	3.5	3.3	3.7	3.8	3.8
Other family members:					
Remaining Relative	1.1	0.2	0.3		
Aged Dependent Relative	0.2	-	-		
Carer	1.1	0.4	0.9		
Sub-total	2.4	0.7	1.2	1.3	0.6
Total	60.2	54.5	58.5	60.1	60.8

Source: Department of Immigration and Citizenship

Basic requirements

The basic requirements are:

- *Sponsorship*
All Family Visa applications require sponsorship by a close family relative, partner or fiancé depending on the visa subclass. The sponsor must be an Australian citizen, or a permanent resident or an eligible New Zealand citizen. In some subclasses, there are restrictions on who can be sponsor.

The sponsor is required to furnish an undertaking to provide support, financial assistance, accommodation and other assistance for a specified period.

- *Health and character requirements*
  All visa applicants for permanent visas, i.e. the main applicant, secondary applicants and any dependents have to satisfy the health and character requirements.

  The character requirement is also applicable to Child Visas sponsor in sponsoring children under 18 years of age. The sponsor and his or her spouse or de facto partner, are required to submit an Australian Federal Police (AFP) National Police Check and/or foreign police certificate/s, depending on their circumstances.

- *Assurance of support (AoS)*
  The AoS is a legal commitment by the assurer (not necessarily the sponsor) to repay to the Australian Government if certain payments have been made to the visa applicant during the AoS period. A financial bond is required during the AoS period for a number of Family visa subclasses as shown in Table 17.3. For other Family Visa subclasses, AoS is at the discretion of the DIAC based on departmental assessment.

Table 17.3 Financial Bond

Visa Subclass	Financial Bond
Parent visa 103, Aged Parent visa 804 Aged Dependent Relative visa 114, 838 Remaining Relative visa 115, 835	$5,000 for main applicant + $2,500 for each secondary adult applicant Assurance period 2 years
Contributory Parent visa 143 Aged Parent visa 864	$10,000 for main applicant + $4,000 for each adult secondary applicant Assurance period 10 years

Partner Visa

Partner visa subclasses

Marrying an Australian citizen or permanent resident does not lead to automatic residency in Australia. A person who is engaged, married or intends to marry an Australian citizen, Australian permanent resident or eligible New Zealand citizen has to apply for a Partner visa to reside in Australia permanently. Table 17.4 lists the applicable visa subclasses.

Table 17.4 Partner Visa Subclasses

Prospective Marriage (subclass 300)	Individuals applying from overseas to enter Australia before marrying their fiances
Partner (subclass 309, 100)	Individuals from overseas in married or de-facto relationship with partners in Australia First apply for 309 visa and thereafter eligible to apply for 100 visa after a waiting period
Partner (subclass 820, 801)	Onshore application for individuals in a married or de-facto relationship with partners in Australia, First apply for 820 visa and thereafter for 801 visa after a waiting period.

Application for Partner visa

Application for Partner visa requires sponsorship by the fiancé, partner, or in certain cases a parent or guardian of the partner. Application may include dependent children and other dependent family members.

An applicant for Partner visa has to be aged 18 or over. An applicant aged 16 or over but less than 18 years will require an

Australian court order allowing the marriage or both will be of marriageable age at time of intended marriage.

Applicant applies for both Partner temporary and permanent visas at the same time. Temporary visa allows the visa holders to remain in Australia until a decision is made on the permanent visa. A temporary visa holder, after a waiting period (normally 2 years), will be granted permanent visa, if the individual meets the requirements.

An applicant may be granted permanent visa without the waiting period if the individual:

- has been married or in a de facto relationship with the partner for 3 years or more
- has been married or in a de facto relationship with the partner for 2 years or more and there is a dependent child from the relationship
- had a relationship before the Protection visa or permanent visa under the humanitarian visa was granted.

An applicant granted Prospective Marriage visa has to enter Australia at least once before the marriage, and the marriage must take place 9 months after receiving the visa approval. The marriage can take place in Australia or overseas.

Persons ineligible for Onshore Partner visa

Individuals may not be eligible for the Onshore Temporary and Permanent (subclasses 820 and 801) visas if the individuals or the individual's accompanying dependent family members:

- hold Contributory Parent (subclass 173 or 814) visa, or visa with a *No Further Stay* condition, or Sponsored visitor visa or Criminal Justice Entry visa

- since last entry to Australia, hold or last held a Skilled-Independent Regional (Provisional) visa (Subclass 495); or a Skilled-Regional Sponsored (Subclass 475) visa; or a Skilled-Regional Sponsored (Subclass 487) visa and the visa has ceased for at least two years

- have not made satisfactory arrangements to repay the debt owing to the Australian Government

- do not hold a substantive visa, i.e. a visa that is not a Bridging visa or a Criminal Justice visa

- have been refused a partner category visa in the last 21 days and hold a Partner (subclass 820) visa or a Partner (subclass 309) visa.

Who can be sponsor?

Table 17.5 outlines persons who may or may not be sponsors.

Table 17.5 Sponsorship Eligibility

Sponsor	Australian citizen
	Australian permanent resident
	Eligible New Zealand citizen
	≥ 18 years old
	if age 16 or 17, parent becomes sponsor
Person who may not be sponsor	Had sponsored 2 other partners previously, or had sponsored another partner within the last 5 years, or hold a Woman at Risk visa (subclass 204), has a conviction or an outstanding charge for child offence, or has a Contributory Parent visa on or before 1/7/2009 and was married or in de facto relationship
Circumstances may still be sponsor though has previously sponsored	Individual's previous partner has died or abandoned the relationship leaving young children. Individual and current partner have a long-standing relationship (≥2 years) and have dependent children from the relationship.

Sponsor's undertaking

Sponsor of Prospective Marriage visa is to be responsible for all financial obligations to the Commonwealth government that the fiancé might incur while in Australia.

Sponsor of Partner visa agrees to provide:

- adequate accommodation and financial assistance required to meet the partner's reasonable living needs for the initial 2 years in Australia (for application outside Australia) or 2 years after the issuance of visa (for application inside Australia) and

- other support, including childcare for the partner to attend appropriate English classes.

Visa requirements, fees and entitlements

Fact Sheet 17.1 on page 261 provides an overview of the visa requirements, fees and entitlements for the various Partner visa subclasses.

Further information is available in *Booklet 1 Partner Migration* at the DIAC's website http://www.immi.gov.au.

Parent Visa

Parent visa subclasses

Parent visa is for eligible parents of Australian citizens, Australian permanent residents or eligible New Zealand citizens to apply to live in Australia. Table 17.6 lists the two main categories of Parent visas.

Table 17.6 Parent Visa Subclasses

Non-contributing Parent	Parent visa subclass 103
	Aged Parent visa subclass 804
Contributing Parent	Parent visa subclass 173
	Parent visa subclass 143
	Aged Parent visa subclass 884
	Aged Parent visa 864

An applicant for the contributory parent category has two options, i.e. applying directly for permanent residency or first apply for temporary residency and thereafter for permanent residency. By making a two-step application, an applicant is effectively staggering the visa application cost and the AoS bond. An AoS and AoS bond is not required for temporary parent visa subclasses.

Visa requirements, fees and entitlements

Table 17.7 list the visa requirements for Parent visa.

Table 17.7 Parent Visa Requirements

Balance of family test	≥ 50% applicant children living permanently in Australia, or More children are living in Australia than in any single country
Sponsorship	By applicant's child If applicant's child is < 18 years old, then the child's partner, or a relative or guardina of the child, or a relative or guardian of the child's partner, or a community organization
Age of applicant	For Aged Parent subclasses, aged 65 for men and 60-65 for women depending on year of birth Age requirement not applicable to other Parent visa subclasses

Limitations on applications

An individual in Australia may be prevented from applying for this visa if one of the following applies to the individual:

- does not hold a substantive visa (which is any visa other than a bridging visa, a criminal justice visa or an enforcement visa) and had a visa cancelled or refused since last entry into Australia

- last visa was granted on the condition that the individual would not be granted a substantive visa while remaining in Australia

- holder of sponsored visitor visa

- the individual is in immigration detention.

Sponsorship obligations and undertaking

The sponsor must continue to help the applicant and accompanying family members to settle in Australia by providing support, accommodation and financial assistance for the first 2 years in Australia.

Assurance of support (AoS)

Applicants have to provide an AoS from an eligible assurer in their applications.

A person providing the AoS has to pay a refundable bond before the visa is granted. The assurer must provide financial support to the applicant so that the individual does not have to rely on any government forms of support. The assurer has to repay to the

Australian Government for any recoverable social security payments made by Centrelink to the persons covered by the AoS.

Fact Sheet 17.2 on page 262 provides an overview of the visa requirements, fees and entitlements for the various Parent Visa subclasses.

Further details are available in *Booklet 3 Parent Migration* at the DIAC's website.

Long waiting period

It will take 13 years before the DIAC can consider recent Non-Contributory Parent visa applications as there are many existing applications remaining in the queue. For Contributory Parent visa, the wait is 1 to 2 years.

Child Visa

Why child visa?

Children born in Australia automatically acquire Australian citizenship if at least one parent is an Australian citizen or permanent resident at the time of the child's birth.

However, children born overseas to Australian permanent residents must apply for a child visa if the child intends to reside permanently in Australia.

Child visa is also required for Australian citizens, permanent residents and eligible New Zealand citizens to sponsor an orphan relative or an adopted child to reside in Australia.

Child visa subclasses

Table 17.8 list the main Child visa categories and subclasses.

Table 17.8 Child Visa Subclasses

Child	Child visa subclass 101
	Child visa subclass 802
Orphan Relative	Orphan Relative visa subclass 117
	Orphan Relative visa subclass 837
Adoptive Child	Adoptive Child visa subclass 102
Dependent Child	Dependent Child visa subclass 445

Visa requirements, fees and entitlements

Sponsorship, character requirement and assurance of support are the requirements as shown in Table 17.9.

Table 17.9 Visa Requirements for Child Visa

Sponsorship (required for all child visas)	Sponsor by parent, relative or guardian (some subclasses)
	Sponsor must be Australian citizen, or permanent resident, or eligible NZ citizen
	Sponsor aged ≥18 years
Character requirement of sponsor	Required if sponsoring children aged <18 years
Assurance of support (discretionary)	May be required if a risk of financial burden on Australia identified on processing
	Person/s providing AoS usually reside in Australia and financially able

The requirements, entitlements and visa fees for the various Child Visa subclasses are listed in Fact Sheet 17.3 on page 263.

Further information is available in *Booklet 2 Child Migration* at the DIAC's website.

Other Family Members

Other family member visa subclasses

The four visa subclasses are as shown in Table 17.10.

Table 17.10 Other Family Member Visa Subclasses

Remaining Relative (brothers, sisters or parents)	Remaining Relative visa subclass 115 Remaining Relative visa subclass 835)
Aged Dependent Relative	Aged Dependent Relative visa subclass 114 Aged Dependent Relative visa subclass 838
Carer (carer for Australian relative with medical condition)	Carer visa subclass 116 Carer visa subclass 836
NZ Family Relationship (non NZ citizens to reside in Australian with NZ citizen)	New Zealand Family Relationship visa subclass 461

Priority for Carer visa

Applicants for Carer visa have priority over applicants for other subclasses within the Other Family category. Almost 80% of the Other Family visa category is allotted to Carer visas.

Annual limit or 'cap'

Other Family Member subclasses are subjected to annual limit or 'cap'. Once the cap is reached in a year, no further visa will be issued for the year. The other applications are then placed in a queue and carried forward to the following year.

The DIAC estimated that the Remaining Relative and Aged Dependent Relative visa applications that have not yet been assessed and queued as at 1 July 2012 are likely to take up to 15 years to be released for final processing.

Visa requirements, fees and entitlements

Fact Sheet 17.4 on page 264 provides an overview of the visa requirements, fees and entitlements for the various Other Family visa subclasses.

Further details are available in *Booklet 4 Other Family Migration* at the DIAC's website.

Fact Sheet 17.1 Partner Visas

	Offshore Application			Onshore Application	
	300	309	100	820	801
Visa period – P (Permanent Residence)	9 mths	2 yrs	P	2 yrs	P
Legally marriageable age (300) Legally married (others)	Y	Y	Y	Y	Y
Intent to marry	Y	N/A	N/A	N/A	N/A
Sponsorship	Y	Y	Y	Y	Y
Relationship					
- ≥3 years married or de facto relationship	N/A	N/A	Y	N/A	Y
- ≥2 years married or de-facto relationship with 1 dependent child	N/A	N/A	Y	N/A	Y
- Personally met the intended spouse	Y	N/A	N/A	N/A	N/A
Health requirement	Y	Y	Y	Y	Y
Character requirement	Y	Y	Y	Y	Y
Australian value statement	Y	Y	Y	Y	Y
Visa allows one to:					
Live and work in Australia	Y	Y	Y	Y	Y
Study in Australia - own fund for tertiary study (309, 300)	Y	Y	Y	Y	Y
Medicare/PBS (subclass 300 must have applied for Partner Visa)	Y	Y	Y	Y	Y
Social security, 100 subclass (some)	N	N	Y	N	Y
Citizenship subject to eligibility criteria	N/A	N/A	Y	N/A	Y
Visa fees – Base application charge ($)	2,680	2,680	2,680	3,975	1,995
Additional applicant charge aged ≥18	1,340	1,340	1,340	1,990	1,990
Additional applicant charge aged < 18	670	670	670	995	995

300 Prospective Marriage 309 Partner temporary visa, 100 Partner permanent visa, 820 Partner temporary visa, 801 Partner permanent visa. Please refer to Booklet 1 Partner Migration published by the DIAC for further details.

Fact Sheet 17.2 Parent Visas

	Offshore Application			Onshore Application		
	103	143	173	804	864	884
Visa period – P (permanent) T (temporary 2 yars)	P	P	T	P	P	T
Balance of family test	Y	Y	Y	Y	Y	Y
Age – minimum 65 for male and 63 to 65 for female[1]	N/A	N/A	N/A	Y	Y	Y
Sponsorship	Y	Y	Y	Y	Y	Y
Assurance of support (in years)	2	10	2	2	10	2
Financial bond	Y	Y	N/A	Y	Y	N/A
Health and character requirement	Y	Y	Y	Y	Y	Y
Australian value statement	Y	Y	Y	Y	Y	Y
Live and work in Australia	Y	Y	Y	Y	Y	Y
Study in Australia – no Austudy for 173 and 884	Y	Y	Y	Y	Y	Y
Medicare/PBS	Y	Y	Y	Y	Y	Y
Most social security benefits - 2 years waiting period	Y	Y	Y	Y	Y	Y
Age and disability pension – 10 years waiting period	Y	Y	Y	Y	Y	Y
Citizenship subject to eligibility criteria	Y	Y	N/A	Y	Y	N/A
Sponsor people to permanent residence	Y	Y	Y	Y	Y	Y
Visa fees – Base application charge ($)	2,060	2,060	2,060	3,060	3,060	3,060
Holder of 173 visa or 884 visa	-	280	-	-	280	-
Additional applicant charge aged ≥18 years	1,030	1,030	1,030	1,530	1,530	1,530
Holder of 173 visa or 884 visa	-	140	-	-	140	-
Additional applicant charge aged <18 years	515	515	515	765	765	765
Holder of 173 visa	-	70	-	-	70	-
Visa fees – 2nd instalment ($) for each person	1,795	42,220	25,330	1,795	42,220	25,330
2nd instalment holder of 173 visa or 884 visa	-	16,885	-	-	16,885	-
Visa fees – 2nd instalment ($) – applicant aged < 18 years	1,795	1,825	1,825	1,795	1,825	1,825

103 Non-Contributory Parent, 143 Contributory Parent, 173 Contributory Parent (Temporary), 804 Non-Contributory Aged Parent, 864 Contributory Aged Parent, 884 Contributory Aged Parent (Temporary) *Please refer to Booklet 3 Parent Migration published by the DIAC for further details.*

Fact Sheet 17.3 Child Visas

	Offshore Application				Onshore Application		
	101	102	117	445	802	837	445
Visa period – P (Permanent Residence), T (Temporary)	P	P	P	T	P	P	T
Age under 25 and single, under 18 (102, 117)	Y	Y	Y	Y	Y	Y	Y
Sponsor – Parent of child, step-child	Y	Y	Y	Y	Y	Y	Y
Sponsorship undertaking	Y	Y	Y	Y	Y	Y	Y
Assurance of support by sponsor	Y	Y	Y	Y	Y	Y	Y
Health requirement	Y	Y	Y	Y	Y	Y	Y
Character requirement if age ≥16 years	Y	Y	Y	Y	Y	Y	Y
Character requirement of sponsor	Y	Y	Y	Y	Y	Y	Y
Settle/arrange to settle any o/s debts	Y	Y	Y	Y	Y	Y	Y
Australian value statement	Y	Y	Y	Y	Y	Y	Y
Limitations on application apply	Y	Y	Y	Y	Y	Y	Y
Visa allows one to:							
Live, work and study in Australia	Y	Y	Y		Y	Y	
Medicare/PBS	Y	Y	Y	See Note	Y	Y	See Note
Most social security benefits (waiting period)	Y	Y	Y		Y	Y	
Visa fees – Base application charge ($)	2,060	2,060	1,260	2,060	3,060	1,260	2,060
Additional application charge aged ≥18	1,030	1,030	630	1,030	1,530	630	1,030
Additional applicant charge aged <18 ($)	515	515	315	515	765	315	515

101 Child visa, 102 Adoptive Child visa, 117 Orphan Relative visa, 445 Dependent Child visa, 802 Child visa, 837 Orphan Relative visa, 445 Dependent Child visa. Please refer to Booklet 2 Child Migration published by the DIAC for further details.

Note: 445 visa-holders can travel to and from, or remain in Australia for as long as their parent's temporary visa is valid, or until the parent's permanent visa application is finalised.

Fact Sheet 17.4 Other Family Member Visas

	Offshore Application			Onshore Application		
	114	115	116	838	835	836
Visa period – P (Permanent Residence)	P	P	P	P	P	P
Dependency on sponsor	Y	N/A	N/A	Y	N/A	N/A
Age requirement	Y	N/A	N/A	Y	N/A	N/A
Sponsorship undertaking (no. of yrs)	2	2	2	2	2	2
Assurance of support by sponsor/other (no. of yrs)	2	2	2	2	2	2
Health requirement	Y	Y	Y	Y	Y	Y
Settle/arrange to settle any o/s debts	Y	Y	Y	Y	Y	Y
Australian value statement	Y	Y	Y	Y	Y	Y
Visa allows one to:						
Live, work and study in Australia	Y	Y	Y	Y	Y	Y
Medicare/PBS	Y	Y	Y	Y	Y	Y
Most social security benefits (waiting period)	Y	Y	Y	Y	Y	Y
Apply for citizenship (eligibility criteria)	Y	Y	Y	Y	Y	Y
Sponsor others for permanent residence (waiting period)	Y	Y	Y	Y	Y	Y
Visa fees – Base application charge ($)	2,060	2,060	1,260	3,060	3,060	1,260
Additional applicant charge ≥18	1,030	1,030	630	1,530	1,530	630
Additional applicant charge <18	515	515	315	765	765	315
– 2nd instalment for each person included on application ($)	1,795	1,795	1,795	1,795	1,795	1,795

114 Aged Dependent Relative, 115 Remaining Relative, 116 Carer visa, 838 Aged Dependent Relative visa, 835 Remaining Relative visa,
836 Carer visa. Please refer to Booklet 4 Other Family Migration published by the DIAC for further details.

18 Working Holiday Program

Travel, work and holiday opportunities

Since 1975, Australia has reciprocal Working Holiday Maker (WHM) arrangement with partner countries to foster closer ties and cultural exchange between Australia and these countries.

Under the program, eligible young people aged 18-30 (at the time of applying) are allowed to work while holidaying in Australia.

The program helps Australian employers in regional areas to meet their short-term and casual staff requirements. It also enables Australian youths to work while holidaying in countries with which Australia has reciprocal arrangements.

WHM Program

About the program

The program began in 1975 aiming to foster closer ties and cultural exchange between Australia and partner countries, with emphasis on young adults.

Under the program, eligible young people aged 18-30 (at the time of applying) are allowed to work while holidaying in Australia.

The program helps Australian employers in regional areas to meet their short-term and casual staff requirements.

The reciprocal program also enables Australian youths to work while holidaying in countries with which Australia has reciprocal arrangements.

WHM partner countries

The countries that Australia has the reciprocal WHM program are as shown in Table 18.1.

Table 18.1 WHM Program Countries

Working Holiday visa (subclass 417)	Belgium, Canada, Cyprus, Denmark, Estonia, Finland, France, Germany, Hong Kong SAR, Hungary, Ireland, Italy, Japan, Republic of Korea, Malta, Netherlands, Norway, Sweden, Taiwan, United Kingdom
Working and Holiday visa (subclass 462)	Argentina, Bangladesh, Chile, Indonesia, Malaysia, Papua New Guinea. Thailand, Turkey, USA

More countries will come on board the WHM program as Australia concludes its negotiations with Andorra, Czech Republic, Greece, Israel, Latvia, Mexico, Poland, Portugal, San Marino, Slovak Republic, Spain and Vietnam.

Popular program

The WHM program is very popular with young adults. Over the last decade, the number of 417 visas issued annually ranged from 150,000 to over 180,000. The annual number of 462 visas issued ranges from 3,000 to around 7,000.

At the end of 2012, there were over 160,000 WHM visa holders in Australia. The number of visa holders by citizenship countries at the end of 2012 for subclass 417 and 462 is listed in Tables 18.2 and 18.3

**Table 18.2 Number ('000) of Subclass 417 Visa Holders in Australia
By Citizenship Countries 31/12/12**

United Kingdom	28.1	Canada	4.3
South Korea	23.1	Sweden	3.4
Taiwan	22.0	Netherlands	2.6
Germany	17.4	Estonia	1.7
Ireland	15.0	Belgium	1.1
France	14.4	Finland	0.8
Italy	9.1	Denmark	0.8
Japan	7.0	Norway	0.2
Hong Kong	6.4	Others	0.1
Total			157.5

Source: DIAC Working Holiday Maker Visa Program Report 2012

**Table 18.3 Number of Subclass 426 Visa Holders in Australia
By Citizenship Countries 31/12/12**

USA	3,678	Malaysia	60
Chile	500	Bangladesh	52
Thailand	323	Turkey	37
Argentina	238	Indonesia	21
Total			4,909

Source: DIAC Working Holiday Maker Visa Program Report 2012

Visa holder's entitlements

Holders of visa subclass 417 and 462 are entitled to:

- Reside in Australia for 1 year from the date of entry
- Multiple entries into Australia during the visa duration
- Work with each employer for up to 6 months
- Study in Australia up to 4 months

Visa eligibility requirements

Table 18.4 lists the requirements for visa subclass 417 and 462.

Table 18.4 Visa Eligibility Requirements

Basic Requirements for subclasses 417 and 462	<ul><li>Aged 18-30 at time of application</li><li>Health, character, financial requirements</li><li>Not accompanied by dependent children in Australia</li><li>Apply within 1 year of intended travel</li></ul>
Additional Requirements for subclass 462	<ul><li>Functional English</li><li>Successful completion of 2 year of undergraduate study</li><li>Letter of support from home government with visa application</li></ul>

The education requirements for Work and Holiday visa application vary according to countries as shown in Fact Sheet 18.1 on page 270. For example, a Senior Secondary Certificate of Education or equivalent will suffice for applicants from the United States of America while an Associate Degree is required for applicants from Malaysia.

Application and Visa charge

Both online and paper applications are available for the two WHM visa subclasses. Visa charge of $280 is payable on application.

Short processing time

The service-processing standards established by the DI&C for WHM visas are as follow:

- Finalise subclass 417 applications Finalise within 6 calendar days of lodgement for 75% of

- Finalise within 6 calendar days of online lodgement for 75% of subclass 426 by US nationals
- Finalise within 14 calendar days of lodgement of paper application for subclass 426.

Second Working Holiday visa

Working Holiday visa (subclass 417) holders who have completed 88 days of 'specified work' in regional Australia are eligible to apply for a second visa.

The second Working Holiday visa has been very popular with over 30,000 second visas granted in 2011-12. This is an eleven-fold increase since its introduction.

Specified work includes work in agriculture, construction and mining. Regional Australia consists of mainly rural and regional areas identified by post-codes, and listed on the DIAC's website at *www.immi.gov.au./visitors/working-holidays/417/postcodes.html.*

Fact Sheet 18.1 Education Requirements - (subclass 462) Visa

Education Requirements	Argentina	Bangladesh	Chile	Indonesia	Iran	Malaysia	Thailand	Turkey	United States
Senior Secondary Certificate of Education or equivalent	N	N	N	N	N	N	N	N	Y
Tertiary qualifications/or ≥2 years of university undergraduate study.	Y	Y	Y	Y	Y	Y	Y	Y	N
Doctoral degree	Y	Y	Y	Y	Y	Y	Y	Y	N
Masters degree	Y	Y	Y	Y	Y	Y	Y	Y	N
Graduate diploma	Y	Y	Y	Y	Y	Y	Y	Y	N
Graduate certificate	Y	Y	Y	Y	Y	Y	Y	Y	N
Bachelor degree	Y	Y	Y	Y	Y	Y	Y	Y	N
Associate degree	Y	Y	Y	Y	Y	Y	Y	Y	N
Advanced diploma	Y	Y	Y	Y	Y	N	Y	Y	N
Diploma	Y	Y	Y	Y	Y	N	Y	Y	N
Certificate IV	N	N	Y	N	N	N	N	N	N
Certificate III	N	N	Y	N	N	N	N	N	N

19 Are You Ready?

Ready, get set…

Migration is a major life event and is often associated with pre-migration stress and post-migration adjustments.

It is crucial for one to be clear of the 'push' and 'pull' factors behind their decision to migrate. It is equally important that one is prepared for the challenges ahead in a new environment.

An adequate research and assessment will certainly be helpful in deciding the intended migration destination.

A good understanding of the eligibility requirements, visa entitlements and the application process is useful even if one engages the services of a migration agent.

Once the migration application is lodged, it is never too early to plan the move, get personal affairs organised and review any existing and future commitments financial and non-financial.

Consider All Factors

Personal circumstances

Leaving one's country of origin to start life in another country is a major decision not to be taken lightly. By migrating to another country, one is leaving behind familiar environment, families and friends. One has to consider the impact on family members – those who emigrate together and those left behind.

Persons, with plans of sponsoring their parents to Australia at a later stage, need to be aware of the eligibility requirements, the long waiting period and the limited places for Parent visas. For some elderly persons, moving to a new environment may pose challenges and require considerable adjustments. There may be significant personal, cultural, social and lifestyle impacts not to mention the costs for both the applicant and the sponsored family.

'Push' and/or 'pull' factors

One has to be very clear of the reason/s for making the move and have adequately researched the available options before taking the emigration path and choosing Australia. It is equally important that enough discussions have been made and consensus reached with those affected.

It is not uncommon for some newly arrived migrants to doubt their decisions especially in early years as they try to establish or adapt themselves to the new country. When doubts occur, they can remind themselves the 'push' or 'pull' factors that initiated the migration path so that they can focus on the big picture.

Is Australia the answer?

Individuals need to do adequate research and read and learn as much about Australia – employment and business opportunities, its geography, its climate, its economy, its government, its multicultural society, its education system, its health care services, the lifestyle and much more before making the plunge.

It is not a bad idea for a person to re-visit all the relevant chapters in this book if it helps to decide whether Australia is the right destination.

Beware of challenges

Migration is a stressful life event. All intending migrants need to be prepared for the challenges ahead.

There are challenges in starting life in a new land, in seeking employment or in establishing a business. For example, a qualified and experienced accountant in the old country may have to content with a much lower position initially to acquire the local experience and understand the work culture. It takes time to adapt to a new environment and to understand the employment market requirements.

Initial migration expenses

There are many initial migration expenses that have to be budgeted for. The following are just some of them:

- Migration application fees payable to the Australian government
- Other fees e.g. fees payable to assessing authorities, fees for medical check up, translation services, etc.
- Fees and charges of migration agent if one is engaged
- Airfares to Australia
- Shipping costs of household and other items
- Settling-in costs in Australia
- Living costs prior to receiving an Australian income

Where to reside?

In deciding where to reside, one tries to look for a match based on individual and family circumstances and aspirations with what are available in the various states, territories, cities, and regional centres and towns.

A checklist ranking items that are important may be helpful in deciding where to reside. Items to be included in the checklist include geography, weather, economy, employment, business opportunities, housing, schools, tertiary institutions, health care facilities, public transport, demographics, population size, community services and organizations, entertainment, sports and recreation facilities.

When to emigrate?

This is dependent on individual and family circumstances.

However, there are many good reasons for intending migrants to start life in Australia early. Individuals, by coming to Australia earlier in life, will have a longer lead-time to establish themselves. It also means an earlier matching of Australian income with Australian expenses. For the children, it means earlier exposure to the Australian education system. It also allows the family to enjoy the many splendid things that Australia has to offer.

When an opportunity arises, e.g. an occupation or skill comes on the Skilled Occupation List (SOL), one should consider the opportunity seriously as occupations and skills on demand change according to market demand and supply. Moreover, for points based skilled migration subclasses, there are annual occupation ceilings for some occupations. Once the annual ceilings are reached, no further invitation will be issued for the year. The state and territory government will not be able to nominate the individual for that year once the nominated occupation has reached the annual occupational ceiling.

For business migrants, establishing a business takes time. An early start for those with innovative business ideas could be the beginning of a successful business career in Australia. The business scene in Australia is laden with many of these success stories. Moreover, the available business migration subclasses are subject to review and similar opportunity might not arise in future.

Talk to those who are in Australia

You may want to talk to those who are in Australia and learn from their experiences and observations. They may provide invaluable support and connections.

Make a trip

A fact-finding mission to Australia is certainly worth considering.

Self-Assessment on Eligibility

It pays to self-assess

It pays to self assess one's visa eligibility even if one intends to engage the service of a migration agent. Initial visa application fee, ranges from $3,000 to $6,000, is payable when submitting the application form. It is non-refundable if the application is unsuccessful.

Explore all visa options

Individuals may want to explore all available visa options in the initial self-assessment exercise. As indicated in Chapter 15 *Skilled*

Migration and Chapter 17 *Family Migration,* there are differences between the subclasses as to the eligibility requirements, available places, processing priority and processing time.

Applying to Migrate

Gather information and documents

All visa applications for migration subclasses require documentation and evidence to substantiate the information provided in the application form. Generally, only certified copies of documents are required. Documents that are in a language other than English have to be translated by accredited translator.

Gathering the required information and documentation requires personal effort irrespective of whether the visa application is through a migration agent or D-I-Y application.

It helps to start gather the information and the required documentations early. It is not uncommon for an individual to take time to locate the information and records even though they are 'somewhere in the house'. Intending migrants often have to spend a fair bit of time and effort in gathering the required information and supporting documents to complete the migration application form.

Many visa Skilled Migration subclasses - general skilled migration visa subclasses (189, 190 and 489) and the business skills migration visa subclasses (132 and 188) - require intending migrants to submit an *Expression of Interest* (EOI) before they are invited to submit a visa application. Once invited to apply, an individual has to submit the visa application within 60 days – not a long time for one to start gathering the required documents.

One also needs to make allowance for time in securing the sponsorship if the application requires sponsorship by the state and territory governments.

Fact Sheet 19.1 on page 286 is indicative of the extent of information and documentation required to complete an application for Business Innovation and Investment (Provisional) subclass 188 visa.

Fact Sheet 19.2 on page 288 lists some of the information and documentation required for an application for Skilled Independent (subclass 189) visa.

Migration Agents

Registered migration agents

The migration advice industry in Australia has been a regulated industry since September 1992, with the introduction of the Migration Agents Registration Scheme.

Persons, other than 'exempt people', giving advice or render immigration assistance on migration to Australia have to be registered with the Office of the Migration Agents Registration Authority (Office of MARA). Legal practitioners giving migration assistance have to be registered with the Office of MARA. Education agents and employment recruiters in Australia cannot provide immigration assistance unless they are registered migration agents.

As at 30/06/2012, there were 4,687 registered migration agents in Australia - 4,363 of them were operating on a commercial basis while 324 registered as not-for-profit and 1,435 migration agents were lawyers with legal practising certificates.

The regulator

The Office of MARA, attached to the Department of Immigration and Citizenship, has been regulating the industry from 1 July 2009. It ensures the migration agents have and maintain good knowledge of immigration requirements, run the businesses professionally, have professional indemnity insurance, passed criminal history checks and behave according to the Code of Conduct (Code) for registered migration agents.

While the Code has no criminal sanctions, MARA may impose a range of administrative sanctions, i.e. caution, suspension or cancellation of registration for a breach of the Code by the registered migration agent. The Migration Act and the Migration Regulations have provisions dealing with misleading statements, unregistered migration practice and misrepresentation. Other Commonwealth legislations, e.g. Crime Act, Criminal Code Act and Trade Practice deal with any criminal or illegal practices.

According to MARA, as at 30 June 2012, majority (75%) of the agents had never had a complaint made against them.

Engaging migration agent

In engaging the service of a migration agent, one should:

- Check the agent's registration status on MARA's website at https://www.mara.gov.au/ to ensure that it is still current, and not one that has been cancelled, lapsed or currently suspended and whether the migration agent has been cautioned, suspended or cancelled previously for misconduct,

- Understand the services provided, the costs and charges,

- Stay involved throughout the application process,

- Retain originals of required documents, as certified copies are normally sufficient,

- Keep records of all dealings with the agent and confirm in writing all discussions and instructions.

Fees and charges

There are no set fees. Fees charged may vary according to the agent's experience, complexities of the case, extent of service and many other factors. Table 19.1 shows the average range of fees charged by 70% of registered migration agents.

Table 19.1 Average Range of Fees Charged by Migration Agents

		Fees (GST included)
Permanent residency service	General Skills	$1,500 - $4,000
	Business Skills	$3,850 - $10,000
	Employer Sponsored	$2,750 - $5,500
	Partner Migration	$1,500 - $3,520
	Child Migration	$1,500 - $3,500
	Parent Migration	$1,500 - $3,850
	Other Family Migration	$1,500 - $4,000
	Special Migration	$2,000 - $5,000
	Humanitarian Offshore	$1,000 - $3,400
	Onshore Protection	$1,000 - $4,000
Temporary residency service	Temporary non-business	$500 - $2,950
	Temporary business	$1,500 - $4,500
	Students	$440 - $1,800
Others	Review application	$1,400 - $4,000
	Other	$440 - $3,000

Source: MARA1 based on information for December 2012 quarter

Beware of fraud or scams

The DIAC advises individuals to take steps to avoid becoming victims of migration fraud or scams.

The DIAC's publication, *Protect yourself from Migration Fraud* lists the warning signs and myths to protect one from being taken advantage of. These are listed in Table 19.2.

Table 19.2 Protect Yourself from Migration Fraud

Warning Signs
X   Does not provide Migration Agent Registration Number
X   Post office box or mobile phone number instead of an office address
X   Meeting at café, pub or other public area
X   Upfront fees and charges in cash only with no receipt
X   Extremely high fees compared to that charged by most registered migration agent
X   Fails to provide a contract or statement of services and fees

The DIAC further lists some of the misleading information or *myths* used by fraudulent operators:

Myths
X   Guaranteed a visa to Australia
X   Pay now to register for the migration program
X   A 'once in a lifetime opportunity',
X   Your 'only' chance to travel or migrate to Australia
X   Only I can pay the department's fees. Give me the money and I will pay the department's fees for you
X   Individual has a special relationship with the department
X   Don't worry—the department is still processing the visa
X   Keeping your original documents (that is, passport, birth certificate or marriage certificate) to give to the department

Victim Stories, the DIAC's other publication, provides stories of victims of migration fraud and warns intending migrants to avoid the same thing happening to them. *Don't Get Caught Out*, a DIAC produced video, shows how easily anyone can become a victim of fraud and stresses that if an offer sounds too good to be true, it probably is.

Submission

Bogus documents and false and misleading statements

Where an applicant is found to have supplied bogus documents or provided false or misleading information, the visa application will be refused and the applicant will be barred for 3 years. This refusal also applies to all persons included in that application including dependent (secondary) applicants who were under 18 years of age at time of application.

Document checklists

The DIAC has established *Document checklist* for each visa subclass to help applicants in lodging a fully documented application. The document checklists are on the DIAC's website.

Individual visa application form too has a *Checklist* section for applicant to indicate the documents that are included in the application.

Online and hard copy submission

Submission is online via SkillSelect or via DIAC website for Skilled Migration subclasses., Supporting documents for some skilled migration subclasses have to be scanned and loaded online via SkillSelect.

In the case of Business Skills subclasses, the supporting documents have to be sent by registered post to the Adelaide Business Skills Processing Centre. Applicants who usually reside in Taiwan or the People's Republic of China (including Hong Kong and Macau) are required to send the documents to the office of the Australian Consulate General in Hong Kong. The documents have to be sent immediately after lodging the online application.

Applications for Family Migration visa subclasses are based on hardcopy forms.

DIAC's assessment

The DIAC follows the priority processing rules. It has also established service standards on processing time for assessing migration visa applications.

The DIAC has indicated, as covered earlier in Chapter 14 *Migration Program*, for Skilled Migration subclasses, the processing priority, in order of priority, is as follow:

- Applications under the RSMS program or under Skilled – Regional (subclass 887)
- Applications under ENS program
- Applications nominated by state and territory government agency for occupations on the agency's migration plan
- Applications with nominated occupations on the Skilled Occupation List (SOL)
- All other applications

It aims to process 75% of the applications within these service standards. However, processing time does vary depending on complexity and requirements in each case. The processing time schedule for the skilled migration subclasses is:

- Subclass 187 – 6 months
- Subclass 186 – 6 months
- Subclass 190, 489 (state sponsored) - 6 months
- Subclasses 189, 489 (family sponsored) – 12 months
- All business skills visas (132, 188, 888)
  - o Low risk countries
    - Lodged in Australia – 11 months
    - Lodged outside Australia – 9 months
  - o High risk countries
    - Lodged in Australia – 22 months
    - Lodged outside Australia – 28 months

Low risk countries are countries that issue Electronic Travel Authority (ETA) High risk countries are countries that do not issue ETA.

For Family Migration subclasses, Partner, Contributory Parent, Child, and Carer visa sub-classes are given higher processing priority by the DIAC.

Health and character requirements

The DIAC will inform the applicant when to arrange the health examinations for the applicant and the accompanying family members.

It will also inform offshore applicant to obtain police certificates for the applicant and each of the dependents (whether migrating or not) aged 16 years or older from each country the applicant and the family members have lived in for 12 months or more over the last 10 years or for those below 26 years old, since they turned 16. Onshore applicant who has been in Australia for ≥12 months is required to provide an Australian National Police Check when submitting the visa application.

Get Organised While Waiting

There are a number of things and tasks that an individual can initiate while waiting for the outcome.

Plan and organise

Start organising one's personal affairs – financial and non-financial. One may want to revisit those commitments that have medium and long-term implications.

Inventory of things to bring

Have an inventory of the items one intends to ship to Australia and those to be disposed of or given away. Individual's finance, availability and replacement costs of the items in Australia, shipping, storage and removalist costs will be the considerations in helping one to arrive at a decision.

Where to reside

Preparatory works including research on the city or town one intends to reside in will ease and facilitate the eventual move. The information on the suburb, public transport, housing, property prices, job or business opportunities and schools are all useful data. Please refer to *Useful Web Addresses* page 305 for addresses to enable you to get further information.

Add or upgrade skills

Most Australian households manage their household chores instead of relying on paid workers. It is useful for family members to top up the skill levels in the meantime.

Stay informed

Follow news from Australia, especially those relating to one's intended place of residence and those concerning employment or business. Table 19.3 lists some of the major newspapers in Australia.

Table 19.3 Major Newspapers

Newspapers/TV Stations	Website
Major Newspapers	
The Australian	http://www.theaustralian.com.au/
The Australian Financial Review	http://www.afr.com/
Sydney Morning Herald	http://www.smh.com.au/
The Daily Telegraph	http://www.dailytelegraph.com.au/
The Age	http://www.theage.com.au/
Herald Sun	http://www.heraldsun.com.au/
The Courier Mail	http://www.couriermail.com.au/
The West Australian	http://www.thewest.com.au
The Advertiser	http://www.adelaidenow.com.au/
The Canberra Times	http://www.canberratimes.com.au/
The Mercury	http://www.themercury.com.au/
Northern Territory News	http://www.ntnews.com.au/
Major TV Stations	
Australian Broadcasting Corporation	http://www.abc.net.au/tv/
Special Broadcasting Corporation	http://www.sbs.com.au/sbsone/
Seven Network	http://au.tv.yahoo.com/
Nine Network	http://ninemsn.com.au/
Ten Network	http://ten.com.au/

Fact Sheet 19.1 Information and Documentation for Business Innovation and Investment (Provisional) Subclass 188 – Business Innovation Stream Visa

1	Business documents
	• Overview of business career and intentions in Australia
	• Evidence of participation in daily management of the business for 2 out of 4 financial years prior to invitation to apply
	• Evidence of business ownership
	• Full set of financial statements for 2 out of the 4 financial years prior to invitation to apply
	• 1 page organisation chart showing applicant's position in the business
	• ≤ 6 photographs of business premises and business activities
	• if relevant details of businesses that has/have operated at a loss, that has/have been subjected to insolvency, receivership or liquidation
	• if relevant, evidence of bankruptcy
2	Net assets of applicant and/or partner (spouse/de-facto) available for transfer to Australia within 2 years
	• 1 page summary of assets and liabilities at any date in the 3 months preceding the invitation and details on evidence of source of funds
	• Evidence of ownership of net assets ≥A\$800,000 and additional assets for settling in Australia
	o cash assets – bank statements on the same day in the 3 months preceding invitation to apply
	o real estate assets – title deeds, accredited property valuation report, mortgage
	o business net assets – full set of financial statements
	o personal/business loans – loan agreement, loan statements indicating loan amount and repayment schedule
	o stocks and bonds – share or bond registers, share/fixed interest securities/debentures certificates, transfer certificates, market value

3	Personal documents (certified copies)

- Passport (biological pages)
- Birth registration
- Birth certificates/or/the family book showing the names of both parents for all applicant's children
- Adoption papers, if applicable, for children aged <18 included in the application
- Evidence of custody arrangements for any children included in the application where one parent is not migrating, including consent from the non-migrating parent for the children to migrate
- Evidence of dependency, if applicable, for any dependent children aged ≥18 included in the application
- Marriage certificates or relationship registrations
- Separation certificates, divorce decrees or death certificates of deceased partners, of any name change
- Military service records, discharge papers

3	English language

- Evidence that each applicant meets the relevant English language requirements

4	Character requirement (if applying onshore)

- Results of character checks

Fact Sheet 19.2 Information and Documentation for Skilled Independent (subclass 189) Visa

1	Point test and skills assessment
	▪ Point test – evidence against each criterion
	▪ Skills assessment
2	Personal documents (certified copies)
	▪ Passport (biological pages)
	▪ Birth registration
	▪ Birth certificates/or/the family book showing the names of both parents for all applicant's children
	▪ Adoption papers, if applicable, for children aged <18 included in the application
	▪ Evidence of custody arrangements for any children included in the application where one parent is not migrating, including consent from the non-migrating parent for the children to migrate
	▪ Evidence of dependency, if applicable, for any dependent children aged ≥18 included in the application
	▪ Marriage certificates or relationship registrations
	▪ Separation certificates, divorce decrees or death certificates of deceased partners, of any name change
	▪ Military service records, discharge papers
3	English language
	▪ Evidence that each applicant meets the relevant English language requirements
4	Character requirement (if applying onshore)
	▪ Results of character checks

20 So Off You Go!

Get organised and start your journey

Having the visa application approved is certainly an excellent first step in starting life in Australia. It is also the start of organising and implementing all the departure plans.

It is time to update one's research about Australia, job and business opportunities, house prices, costs of living, schools for the children, etc. It is also decision and action time in the choice of suburb and schools for the children.

In deciding what to bring to Australia, an individual needs to be aware of the customs and quarantine regulations in force at the time of arrival.

Getting Ready to Leave

Know about the visa

Successful applicants need to go through the grant notification and note the conditions and obligations that they and their accompanying family members have to comply with.

Get organised

A relocation checklist listing tasks to be done will be helpful in minimising the stress. The tasks include disposing assets, organising finance, notices to be given, sorting out paperwork and other visa-related tasks, e.g. organising medical tests, police clearance, payment of visa and other fees, organising air travel, obtaining copies of medical or health records and organising temporary accommodation in Australia.

Sort out important documents

It is a good idea for incoming migrants to bring in their carry-on luggage the originals of several important documents. They include birth certificates or baptismal certificates, marriage certificate, separation or divorce papers, adoption papers, school records, diplomas or certificates for each family member, trade or professional certificates and licences, immunization, vaccination, dental and other health records for each member of the family and driver's licence.

Many decisions to be made

With the visa approval, an individual has to make a number of decisions. They include choosing the city and suburb to settle in and narrowing down the school for the children. Any earlier research on these matters comes in useful in facilitating the decision making process. Some of the earlier researches may have to be updated.

Personal and Household Effects

Items to bring to Australia

A decision has to be made about bringing any existing personal and household items into Australia.

Personal and household effects for first time migrants and returning Australian residents are not subject to duty or GST if the items have been owned and used for the entire year preceding the departure for Australia.

Customs and quarantine regulations

Australia has strict custom and import regulations on goods, currency and quarantine rules. The following information will be helpful for intending migrants:

- Duty-free concessions for inbound travellers
  Travellers aged 18 and over can bring in free of duty 50 cigarettes or 50grams of cigars or tobacco products, general goods up to $900 worth and 2.25 litres of alcohol. Families travelling together can pool their duty free concessions.

- Prohibited drugs
  Marijuana, cannabis heroin, cocaine and amphetamines are prohibited drugs. There are severe penalties for drug offences.

- Declaration and completion of Incoming Passenger Card
  All inbound passengers must complete an Incoming Passenger Card. In completing the required information, one should exercise care. Fact Sheet 20.1 on page 296 lists the restricted items that must be declared.

G'day and Welcome to Australia

Fresh Start and Right Attitude

Starting a new life can be both exciting and daunting. There are bound to be trials and tribulations. There will also be occasions of triumph and celebrations. It requires support from family and one's ability to adapt, commit, and the determination to make a success of life in Australia.

It is certainly helpful to leave behind any negative 'baggage from the old country', and forge full steam ahead in starting life in Australia. When in doubt, one might need to remember the 'push' and/or 'pull' factors that first initiated the migration journey.

A balanced view and a positive can-do attitude will certainly be helpful as individuals go through their journey in Australia. Many have done just that and have done very well.

First things first

Some of the suggested tasks for a newly arrived migrant soon after arrival are listed in Table 20.1.

Table 20.1 Required Tasks Soon After Arrival

A place to live	In choosing a place to live, an individual has to consider schooling for their children, as some schools have zoned specific catchment area. A checklist will be helpful especially if one is buying the property to avoid costly decision and unnecessary disruption arising from constant relocation.
Apply for a tax file number (TFN)	This should be done first as any individual receiving income, government payments and investment income will need a tax file number. It can be done online, in person at the Australian Tax Office (ATO) shop-front location, or call the ATO for a form to be sent to the home address.
Open a bank account	Most payments in Australia, e.g. salary and government payments are credited directly to a bank account.

Register with Medicare	Individuals eligible to join Medicare should immediately join the scheme and gain access to the health care program.
Private medical insurance	Individuals may want to consider private medical insurance scheme covers, e.g. treatment as a private patient in private or public hospitals and some services not covered by Medicare.
Register for English classes	Newly arrived migrants may be eligible to receive 510 hours of free English language courses provided under the Adult Migrant English Program (AMEP).
Register with Centrelink	Newly arrived migrants, though not immediately eligible for certain social security payments (except those holding refugee or humanitarian visas) have access to government employment services and permanent residents, may be eligible to access some services.
Enrol children in school	Some state schools are zoned serving a specific catchment area and enrolment from outside the area may not be permitted or may need to meet certain criteria. Hence, an individual needs to bear this in mind when choosing where to reside.
Apply for a driver's licence	A permanent residence visa-holder with a current driving licence is able to drive for the first three months after arrival in all states and territories, except for Tasmania where the 3 months commences after the grant of visa. Thereafter, one may have to pass a knowledge test, a driving test and an eyesight test.

Personal finance

Newly arrived migrants would need to organise their personal finance, monitor their living expenses and make prudent financial decisions in purchasing major items like car, house and household items.

There should be provision for living costs prior to receiving an Australian income. It will be two years before an eligible permanent resident is entitled to unemployment benefits. Perhaps, one should consider using this as the benchmark in setting aside reserves for living costs.

Finding a job

For many migrants, finding work means gaining local experience, not having to deplete their financial resources and ease their transition into Australian work culture. Perhaps, one might want to adopt the attitude in the famous Chinese saying *Ride a buffalo while looking for a horse*, i.e. get into the first job first.

For some, there are real challenges in finding work. Often, the lack of Australian experience is mentioned as the main obstacle in not gaining employment. Then, there is also the challenge for professional and skilled workers who had previously held senior positions in their home countries seeking entry level or junior positions in Australia.

It is therefore imperative that a lot of effort be put in to understand the employment market, explore the hidden market, 'Australianise' one's curriculum vitae, understand the job and selection criteria requirements and prepare for the interview.

One should not overlook job opportunities in the governments and the Not-for-Profit organisations. In some rural and regional centres and capital cities (e.g. Canberra, Darwin), they are very significant employers. Permanent residents are accepted for most public service jobs except those in some sensitive sectors where Australian citizenship is required. The Not-for-Profit sector is a reasonably large employing sector.

Perhaps, it is also an opportunity for individuals to think of some personal 'rewiring' initiatives, e.g. pursue a course relevant to the current employment market or starting a business based on their qualification, skills and experience. Many have done just that.

Starting a business

Business migrants would have done a fair amount of background work before submitting their visa applications. They would also have decided on starting business from scratch or purchasing an existing business. In addition to the normal due diligence and business judgement required in starting or buying an existing business, business migrants have to ensure the business they intend to go into is able to meet the turnover, employment and other requirements stipulated in the grant of visa.

Let's Not Forget

Compliance issues

Visa holders have to comply with the visa conditions and obligations listed in their grant notifications. Each visa subclass has its distinct complying requirements.

Permanent residency may be revoked at the discretion of the Minister for Immigration and Citizenship. However, this does not normally happen except in cases of criminal misconduct.

Hence, it is crucial for individuals to ensure that they do not breach Australian laws, including social security laws, tax laws among many others. Any criminal breaches of Australian laws might have unexpected consequences on an individual's subsequent visa renewal or citizenship application.

Fact Sheet 20.1 Inbound Passengers: List of Restricted Items

Restricted Items	Examples
Firearms, weapons and ammunition	Real and replica firearms, Air soft pistols, paintball markers, blowpipes, all knives, nunchukas, slingshots, crossbows, electric shock devices, laser pointers, body armour, batons, pepper sprays, knuckle dusters and parts and accessories for use with firearms and weapons
Illegal pornography	Publications and any media depicting child pornography, bestiality and explicit sexual violence
Performance and image enhancing drugs	Human growth hormone, DHEA and all anabolic and androgenic steroids.
Currency A$10,000 or over	There is no limit to the amount of currency to bring in though one must declare amounts of $10,000 or more in Australian currency or foreign equivalent.
Food, plants animals and biological goods	All food, plant and animal goods, equipment used with animals, biological materials, soils and sand.
Medicines and substances which may be subject to misuse, abuse or dependence	These include steroids, opioid analgesics, cannabis or narcotic based medications, traditional medicines containing endangered plant or animal products.
Protected wildlife and wildlife products	These include traditional medicinal products and regulated products, e.g. coral, orchids, caviar, ivory products and hunting trophies.
Heritage listed goods	Heritage assets including works of arts, stamps, coins, archaeological objects, minerals and specimens.
Veterinary products	All veterinary drugs and medicines.
Defence and strategy goods	Permits are required for importation.

Source: Australian Customs and Border Protection Services

Useful Web Addresses

Australian Curriculum	hhtp://www.australiancurriculum.edu.au/
Australian Curriculum Assessment and Reporting Service	hhtp;//www.acara.edu.au/default.asp
State/Territory Government - Education	hhtp://www.schools/nsw.edu.au hhtp://www.education.vic.gov.au hhtp://www.education.qld.gov.au hhtp://www.det.wa.edu.au hhtp://www.decd.sa.gov.au hhtp://www.det.act.gov.au hhtp://www.education.tas.gov.au hhtp://www.deucation.nt.gov.au
School Profile	hhtp://www.myschool.edu.au
School Leavers	hhtp://www.myfuture.edu.au
Technical and Further Education (TAFE)	hhtp://www.tafensw.edu.au hhtp://www.vic.gov.au/education/tafe-training hhtp://www.tafe.qld.gov.au hhtp://www.central.wa.edu.au hhtp://www.tafesa.edu.au hhtp://www.cit.edu.au hhtp://www.tastafe.tas.edu.au hhtp://www.cdu.edu.au
University Admissions Centre	hhtp://www.uac.edu.au
Going to University	hhtp//www.goingtouni.gov.au
Higher Education Loan Program (HELP)	hhtp://studyassist.gov.au
Housing	hhtp://www.realestate.com.au hhtp://www.domain.com.au hhtp://www.houmebound.com.au
Cars	hhtp://www.carguide.com.au hhtp://www.carsales.com.au
Supermarket Shopping	hhtp://www.aldi.com.au hhtp://www.coles.com.au hhtp://www.foodworks.com.au hhtp://www.iga.com.au hhtp://www.woolworths.com.au
Departmental Stores	hhtp://www.davidjones.com.au hhtp://www.myer.com.au hhtp://www.BigW.com.au hhtp://www.Kmart.com.au hhtp://www.Target.com.au

Electrical, Furniture and Others	hhtp://www.goodguys.com.au
	hhtp://www.harveynorman.com.au
	hhtp://www.ikea.com.au
	hhtp://www.officeworks.com.au
Employment in All Sectors	hhtp://www.alljobs.com.au
	hhtp://www.careerone.com.au
	hhtp://www.jobs.com.au
	hhtp://www.jobsearch.gov.au
	hhtp://www.jobseeker.com.au
	hhtp://www.mycareer.com.au
	hhtp://www.seek.com.au
Employment in Governments	hhtp://www.apsjobs.gov.au
	hhtp://www.jobs.nsw.gov.au
	hhtp://www.careers.vic.gov.au
	hhtp://www.qld.gov.au/jobs
	hhtp://www.jobs.wa.gov.au
	hhtp://www.vacancies.sa.gov.au
	hhtp://www.tas.gov.au
	hhtp://www.careernt.gov.au
	hhtp://www.lgjobs.com.au
	hhtp://www.counciljobs.com
Business and Investment	hhtp://www.trade.nsw.gov.au
	hhtp://www.busines.vic.gov.au
	hhtp://www.invest.vic.gov.au
	hhtp://www.business.qld.gov.au
	hhtp://www.wa.gov.au/information-about/business/investing-wa
	hhtp://www.business.act.gov.au
	hhtp://www.business.tas.gov.au
Department of Immigration and Citizenship	http://www.immi.gov.au/
	http://www.immi.gov.au/skills/skillselect/
Migration Agents Registration Authority	https://www.mara.gov.au/
State and Territory Government Migration Sites	http://www.business.nsw.gov.au/live-and-work-in-nsw
	http://www.liveinvictoria.vic.gov.au/
	http://migration.qld.gov.au/
	http://www.migration.wa.gov.au
	https://www.migration.sa.gov.au/
	http://www.canberrayourfuture.com.au/
	http://www.migration.tas.gov.au/
	http://www.migration.nt.gov.au/

TAFE Colleges (state-run only)

New South Wales

Illawarra Institute	http://www.hunter.tafensw.edu.au/
New England Institute	http://www.newengland.tafensw.edu.au/
North Coast Institute	http://www.northcoast.tafensw.edu.au/
Northern Sydney Institute	http://www.nsi.tafensw.edu.au/
Riverina Institute	http://www.rit.tafensw.edu.au/
South Western Sydney Institute	http://www.swsi.tafensw.edu.au/
Sydney Institute of TAFE	http://www.sydneytafe.edu.au/
Hunter Institute	http://www.hunter.tafensw.edu.au/
Riverina Institute	http://www.rit.tafensw.edu.au/
Western Institute	http://www.wit.tafensw.edu.au/
Western Sydney Institute	http://www.wsi.tafensw.edu.au/

Victoria

Bendigo Regional Institute of TAFE	http://www.bendigotafe.edu.au/
Box Hill Institute of TAFE	http://www.bhtafe.edu.au/
Chisholm Institute of TAFE	http://www.chisholm.edu.au/
Gippsland Institute of TAFE	http://www.gippstafe.vic.edu.au/
Gordon Institute of TAFE	http://www.thegordon.edu.au/
Goulburn Ovens Institute of TAFE	http://www.gotafe.vic.edu.au/
Holmesglen Institute of TAFE	http://www.holmesglen.edu.au/
Kangan Batman TAFE	http://www.kangan.edu.au/
Northern Melbourne Institute of TAFE	http://www.nmit.edu.au/
Royal Melbourne Institute of Technology TAFE	http://www.rmit.edu.au/
South West Institute of TAFE	http://www.swtafe.vic.edu.au/
Sunraysia Institute of TAFE	http://www.sunitafe.edu.au/
Swinburne University of Technology TAFE	http://www.tafe.swinburne.edu.au/
University of Ballarat TAFE	http://www.ballarat.edu.au/
Victoria University TAFE	http://www.vu.edu.au/
William Angliss Institute of TAFE	http://www.angliss.edu.au/
Wodonga TAFE	http://www.wodongatafe.edu.au/

Queensland

The Bremer Institute of TAFE	http://www.bremer.tafe.qld.gov.au/
Brisbane North Institute of TAFE	http://www.bn.tafe.qld.gov.au/
Central Queensland Institute of TAFE	http://www.cq.tafe.qld.gov.au/
Gold Coast Institute of TAFE	http://www.goldcoast.tafe.qld.gov.au/
Metropolitan South Institute of TAFE	http://www.msit.tafe.qld.gov.au/
Mount Isa Institute of TAFE	http://www.mtisa.tafe.qld.gov.au/
SkillsTech Australia	http://www.skillstech.tafe.qld.gov.au/
Southbank Institute of Technology	http://www.southbank.edu.au/
Southern Queensland Institute of TAFE	http://www.sqit.tafe.qld.gov.au/
Sunshine Coast Institute of TAFE	http://www.sunshinecoast.tafe.qld.gov.au/

Wide Bay TAFE	http://www.widebay.tafe.qld.gov.au/

Western Australia

C.Y. O'Connor College of TAFE	http://www.cyoc.wa.edu.au/
Durack TAFE	http://www.durack. edu.au/
Great Southern TAFE	http://www.gsinstitute.wa.edu.au/
Kimberley TAFE	http://www.kti.wa.edu.au/
Pilbara Institute	http://www.pilbara.wa.edu.au/
South West Regional College of TAFE	http://www.swrc.wa.edu.au/
SWAN TAFE	http://www.tafe-wa.com/swan-tafe/

South Australia

TAFE South Australia	http://www.tafesa.edu.au/

Tasmania

TAFE Tasmania	http://www.tastafe.tas.edu.au/

Index

About the Author

Chee Min Ng has lived in Australia for the past 26 years. He has an economics degree and a Master degree in Business. He is also a professional accountant, having qualified as a member of the Chartered Institute of Management Accountants, the Association of Chartered Certified Accountants, the Institute of Public Accountants and remains as a member of the Australian Society of Certified Practising Accountants.

His professional career in Malaysia and Australia over four decades includes CFO and CEO roles in private enterprises and advisory roles in Australian government departments and public institutions. He has taught at university and presented at numerous international seminars and conferences.

Through this book, he hopes to share with readers an objective view and detailed information of what Australia has to offer.